Law & Crime

Key Approaches to Criminology

The *Key Approaches to Criminology* series aims to take advantage of the disappearance of traditional barriers between disciplines and to reflect criminology's interdisciplinary nature and focus. Books in the series offer undergraduate and postgraduate students introductions to the subject, but the aim is also to advance discussion, move debates forward, and set new agendas in the field.

Law and Crime is one of the few books in the *Key Approaches* series not authored by scholars who are based in a Criminology department, group or research institute. This comment is not meant disingenuously. Far from it; I am inordinately proud that the series has attracted two such eminent and respected academics from Law to write for it. In any case, as Gerry Johnstone and Tony Ward acknowledge, they benefit from working in a stimulating interdisciplinary environment and both have made an outstanding contribution to the field of Criminology. Tony's work in areas as diverse as psychiatry and criminal responsibility, crimes of governments, environmental harms, terrorism, and historical perspectives on crime and punishment, has had a significant influence on the development of Criminology over the last decade or more – and all this achieved after qualifying as a Barrister and then working for the voluntary organizations Radical Alternatives to Prison and INQUEST. Gerry, meanwhile, has published widely in the areas of therapeutic interventions into criminal justice, participatory justice and critical legal education but, most notably from a criminologist's viewpoint, he has made the academic study of restorative justice virtually his own!

There can, then, be no two individuals better placed to write a book on *Law and Crime* for this series. They have succeeded in producing a book that covers all the 'basics' in terms of the birth of criminal justice, the development of criminal liability, the tenets of criminal law, and the historico-legal contours that have shaped modern punishment. Theoretically robust and avowedly interdisciplinary, they then apply the insights gained from this broad analysis to the specifics of cases, many of which have reached the criminal courts; some of which typically evade criminalization. Their critique is thoroughly researched, thought-provoking and immensely readable. *Law and Crime* will be greatly appreciated by all scholars working at the interface of criminology, criminal justice and law, and is a very welcome addition to *Key Approaches to Criminology* series.

Yvonne Jewkes
Series Editor

Law & Crime

Gerry Johnstone & Tony Ward

Los Angeles | London | New Delhi
Singapore | Washington DC

First published 2010

SAGE Publications Ltd
1 Oliver's Yard
55 City Road
London EC1Y 1SP

SAGE Publications Inc.
2455 Teller Road
Thousand Oaks, California 91320

SAGE Publications India Pvt Ltd
B 1/I 1 Mohan Cooperative Industrial Area
Mathura Road
New Delhi 110 044

SAGE Publications Asia-Pacific Pte Ltd
33 Pekin Street #02-01
Far East Square
Singapore 048763

Library of Congress Control Number Available

British Library Cataloguing in Publication data

A catalogue record for this book is available
from the British Library

ISBN 978-1-4129-1123-8
ISBN 978-1-4129-1124-5

Typeset by C&M Digitals (P) Ltd, Chennai, India
Printed by CPI Antony Rowe, Chippenham, Wiltshire
Printed on paper from sustainable resources

Mixed Sources
Product group from well-managed
forests and other controlled sources
www.fsc.org Cert no. SGS-COC-2953
© 1996 Forest Stewardship Council
FSC

Contents

Acknowledgements

We would like to thank Yvonne Jewkes, the series editor, for inviting us to write the book and for providing useful feedback on the plan. Peter Young provided useful feedback at an early stage (as did a second, anonymous, referee) and was a constant source of intellectual stimulation while we were writing the book. Peter is one of many colleagues in the Law School, the Centre for Criminology and the Institute of Applied Ethics at Hull who have contributed to making this an ideal environment in which to carry out interdisciplinary work. It is a particular pleasure to acknowledge the stimulating comments of some of our undergraduate students of criminal law, especially in relation to the issues discussed in Chapter 5. Penny Green, Matthew Happold and Kirsten McConnachie all provided helpful and encouraging comments on Chapter 9.

We thank Caroline Porter and Sarah-Jayne Boyd at Sage for their advice, support and, above all, patience. On a more personal note, thanks to Brigid, Eleanor and Pierce Johnstone and Joy Gledhill for their constant support and encouragement.

1

Criminal Law and its Critics

Chapter Contents

OVERVIEW

Chapter 1:

- Explains the purpose of this book.
- Outlines some prominent features of the institution of criminal law.
- Introduces a number of important critical perspectives on criminal law.

KEY TERMS

criminal law the libertarian critique the 'scientific' critique the socio-political critique the restorative justice critique

Introduction

This book is an introductory account of the institution of criminal law, written for students and scholars of criminology and related social sciences. To be clear, it is not a book on 'law for criminologists'. Rather, we seek to provide an inter-disciplinary analysis of key elements of the institution of criminal law. The disciplines we draw upon include not only criminology and law, but also history, philosophy, politics and sociology. Drawing upon works from these disciplines, we explore the creation, development and key features of criminal law, along with some of the ideas, values and projects that have shaped the institution and our expectations of it.

Our account of criminal law is a critical one. We do not start out by making the assumption that criminal law is a necessary social institution – necessary to restrain the tendency which many people have to behave in ways that are seriously wrongful and harmful. Nor do we assume that the criminal law of today is a distinct improvement over what went before. Rather, we want to provide a fair hearing to the viewpoint that criminal law is a deeply flawed institution, e.g. one which causes more harm than it prevents or which unjustifiably violates the liberties of people in order to provide spurious benefits to society. On the other hand, we will seek to avoid the opposite error of taking it for granted that criminal law is a 'failing' social institution. Hence, we will show that, for all its deficiencies, the criminal law has played a crucial role in articulating and defending very important social values.

In order to chart our course more clearly, we will start by identifying some core features of criminal law. We will then describe, in very general terms, some common critical stances towards this institution.

Some features of criminal law

Rules

Probably the most prominent feature of criminal law is that it contains a body of rules. More specifically, these are rules of conduct which are formulated and enforced by society's rulers through its legislatures, courts and penal apparatus. These rules are addressed to all persons when they are within the jurisdiction of the rulers (Duff, 2002a: 14). They tend to specify types of behaviour that the rulers declare to be public wrongs: conduct which in that society is deemed harmful, unjustifiable and of concern to all righteous members of the society. These types of behaviour are called 'offences'. The rules also stipulate that those found guilty of committing an offence are liable to some punishment such as a fine or period of imprisonment. The rules tend to be prohibitory in character, i.e. they refer to conduct from which people must refrain. Less commonly – and also controversially – some rules make it an offence to omit to do something in certain circumstances (Ormerod, 2005: 75ff; cf. Hughes, 1958).

Moral dimensions

Another important feature of criminal law is that violation of its rules is widely regarded as immoral and/or disreputable. Those who violate the criminal law often attract the disapproval, and sometimes even the hatred, of 'respectable society'. Partly, this is because many of the best known rules of criminal law prohibit conduct – such as murder, theft and rape – that is already, outside of the criminal law, regarded as immoral or disreputable (Duff, 2002a: 3–4, 12). As Sir James Fitzjames Stephen – author of the nineteenth-century classic *History of the Criminal Law of England* – put it:

> The substantive criminal law ... relates to actions which, if there were no criminal law at all, would be judged by the public at large much as they are judged of at present. If murder, theft and rape were not punished by law, the words would still be in use, and would be applied to the same or nearly the same actions. ... In short, there is a moral as well as a legal classification of crimes. (Stephen, 1883: 75)

However, even where the conduct prohibited by criminal law is not obviously immoral or disreputable – is not patently wrong independently of its legal prohibition – those who are found guilty of engaging in such conduct can be morally tainted by their criminal conviction. It is as if the criminal law has its own moral authority so that once it prohibits a type of behaviour, to engage in that behaviour becomes immoral or disreputable even though it would not previously have been so. Hence, along with the formal sanction that is incurred by being found guilty of breaking the criminal law (e.g. the sentence of a fine or imprisonment), criminal conviction – or even suspicion of being involved in a criminal offence – tends to attract a social stigma. To get in trouble with the (criminal) law tends to push one towards or over a line that separates respectable from disreputable elements of society.

This 'moral' dimension of criminal law cannot be ignored if we wish to provide an adequate account of it. However, neither should it be overstated. In modern society there is a strong tendency to use the criminal law to regulate more and more conduct which – although considered injurious or dangerous – is not as obviously immoral or disreputable as Stephen's examples of murder, theft and rape. Being found guilty of breaking one of these rules does not patently reveal some deep flaw in one's moral character (in the way that even a minor conviction for theft is often thought to reveal the character flaw of dishonesty). The more criminal law is used in this way, the harder it is to sustain the notion that breach of the criminal law is inherently immoral or disreputable. Also, many of the sanctions for breaches of criminal law (even where the conduct in question does seem immoral or disreputable) are imposed in such a professionalized, bureaucratic way that they become more like mere 'penalties' than 'punishments'. The latter term carries connotations of moral censure which are not so present in the former: penalties provide people with instrumental reasons to obey the law but do not necessarily construct the penalized behaviour as immoral or opprobrious.[1]

Criminal procedure

Another feature of criminal law is that there is a special procedure for determining whether somebody suspected of committing an offence, and who might wish to dispute the case against them, is guilty of violating one of its rules. The actual nature of this procedure has changed significantly throughout the history of criminal law and it still varies considerably between different countries (Delmas-Marty and Spencer, 2002; Vogler, 2005). However, a persistent underlying premise is that determining the guilt or innocence of a person accused of committing an offence – and certainly a serious offence – is a grave matter and should be done on the basis of a very rigorous testing of the case against the accused.

Such an approach is of course time-consuming, costly and likely to result in at least some people who have in fact broken the law evading conviction. Hence, there tend to be counter pressures and temptations to avoid the most rigorous process for many cases. This tends to result in practices designed to avoid having cases contested by, for instance, informally bargaining with accused persons over the charges to be brought against them or over the sort of sentence that will be demanded. It also leads to the creation of more summary processes for what are deemed to be minor offences attracting relatively light sanctions. It can also result in tendencies to remove the regulation of some conduct from the ambit of criminal law proper, by for example creating new 'quasi-criminal' regimes of regulation which use 'on the spot fines' imposed with little formality by agents such as traffic wardens, ticket inspectors or even machines.

In the popular imagination, the process of determining whether somebody accused of breaking the criminal law is guilty or innocent is a weighty affair involving rigorous testing of the case and lengthy and solemn deliberation by the decision-makers. This certainly captures the reality of some criminal law. However, a large proportion of cases are handled in a much more summary manner. It is not surprising that many of the public controversies surrounding criminal law are to do with whether the procedures for determining guilt or innocence are appropriate.

Principles of liability

Along with substantive rules of conduct, criminal law contains principles of liability which indicate who or what can be held legally responsible for conduct which infringes its substantive rules and how their responsibility is affected by various circumstances. Most basically, it contains principles of capacity. Only certain entities are deemed to be within the ambit of regulation through the criminal law. The entities that are included vary between different historical periods and different countries. So, for instance, inanimate objects which cause death have been put on trial in ancient criminal law systems (Hyde, 1916). And, in medieval Europe, animals were sometimes subjected to criminal prosecution and punishment (Evans, 1987 [1906]). Contemporary English criminal law regards inanimate objects and non-human animals as lacking the capacity required to be subject to regulation through criminal law. This does not mean, of course, that they are not subject to regulation (many animals get trained and controlled and animals that behave badly and cause us harm and trouble are dealt with); rather their conduct is regulated through other mechanisms.

Amongst human beings, young children are generally considered to lack 'criminal capacity'. Again, this does not mean that nothing will happen to a child below the age of criminal capacity who engages in the sorts of behaviour prohibited through criminal law. Rather, it simply means that they will not be subject to intervention through the mechanism of criminal law. Ideas about the precise age at which human beings acquire criminal capacity vary significantly over time and between countries. In England and Wales the official age is currently ten, in Belgium 18 and in Scotland eight.[2] Other human beings who are regarded as lacking criminal capacity include those adjudged to be insane at the time they committed an act which would otherwise be an offence.

The other significant entity which is subject to the regulation of contemporary criminal law (since around the middle of the nineteenth century) is the corporation: a legal person with no physical existence (Ormerod, 2005: 235). The development of the idea that a corporate body has duties to comply with the rules of criminal law and can be prosecuted and punished for failure to comply is bound up with the fact that, in modern society, a great deal of harm and injury results from the actions of corporate bodies. Perhaps less obviously, it seems to be bound up with the notion that these bodies have minds of their own, which are not reducible to the minds of individual human beings who contribute to corporate activity. As such, they are considered to be entities which are capable of being *addressed* by the law (see Chapter 6).

For those entities which have criminal capacity, a further question arises of whether they should be held responsible for engaging in conduct prohibited by criminal law given the circumstances under which they engaged in it. The key issue here tends to be the extent to which the person whose conduct is in question had a reasonable opportunity to do something other than the act which – it is alleged – is a criminal offence. So, for instance, human beings are animals that respond instinctively to physical stimuli. Sometimes, instinctive or almost instinctive bodily movements may result in the sorts of 'conduct' that criminal law prohibits. For example, if a person (D) is walking near the edge of a cliff and slips and is about to fall off the edge, it is virtually instinctive to grab something that will prevent them from falling. If that something is another person (V), and if as a result V is pulled over the cliff edge and dies, but D somehow survives, then the question arises of whether D (presuming their story is believed) should be able to avoid criminal liability for the death of V. D's argument, in essence, would be that because their conduct was instinctive it was involuntary and so without fault and that it should not therefore be condemned as criminal.[3]

The above example is fairly straightforward; although various complexities could be introduced. (For instance, if D had ignored various warnings that walking near the edge of this particular cliff was highly dangerous and not allowed, does D's 'prior fault' affect their criminal liability for V's death? Is D's argument one of necessity rather than involuntariness, and if so can necessity ever be a defence where the charge concerns killing? See Chapter 4.) There are however, much more complex situations encountered by criminal law. A person will often engage in conduct prohibited by criminal law but argue that they had no reasonable opportunity to behave otherwise for a variety of reasons. For example, they might argue that they were acting under superior orders, out of necessity, whilst subject to various forms of coercion and pressure, in self-defence, as a result of some psychological compulsion which they were helpless to control, or due to some profound mistake about the nature of their actions. All of these situations raise complex questions about whether the actor should be held criminally responsible for their actions, i.e. whether their actions should be condemned as criminal and the actor punished as a criminal.

Purposes of criminal law

Criminal law has been shaped by various ideas about its purposes. Some of these ideas are compatible with each other; some are in tension with other influential ideas and these tensions manifest themselves within the criminal law (Duff, 2002a).

One patent purpose of criminal law is to control the conduct of persons. More specifically, criminal law tends to be concerned to prevent conduct which directly or indirectly causes substantial harm, trouble or annoyance to other members of society where such conduct lacks justification. Criminal law might be understood then as one institution which constructs outer limits of permissible behaviour in society – and polices those limits by imposing painful sanctions and social stigma on those who cross them. Provided people stay within certain outer limits, the criminal law is not really interested in how members of society live their everyday lives. That is to say, criminal law is not in general the sort of institution that tends to be concerned to regulate the tiny details of everyday behaviour (e.g. it is not usually concerned to control wrong-doing which does not concern the wider public, nor to punish bad manners or unhygienic habits). Still less is it usually concerned with people's thoughts. People can imagine all sorts of mischievous acts without attracting the attention of criminal law; to attract such attention they must at least attempt to act on these thoughts either directly or by inciting or conspiring with others. As we shall see, however, some critics think that criminal law *does* tend to intrude too deeply into the details of our lives. Also, as Foucault (1977) among others has argued, those who are found guilty of transgressing the limits set by criminal law are sometimes subjected to sanctions which do not simply inflict pain but are designed to reshape the habits, routines and ultimately the personalities of transgressors.

If controlling wrongful conduct is a core purpose of criminal law, important questions arise about the relationship of criminal law to other interventions which have a similar purpose and about the precise role which criminal law does and should play in the regulation of wrongful conduct. Again, there is a variety of ideas about such issues. In some, criminal law is a vital but secondary mechanism of crime control: people learn to behave correctly through other mechanisms, e.g. they absorb ideas about honesty from the wider culture so that, even if they thought themselves extremely unlikely to be subject to criminal sanctions, they would still refrain from dishonest acts such as stealing. In such thinking, these other mechanisms occasionally fail for one reason or another, and criminal law is necessary to deal with the results of these failures. There are other ideas in which the criminal law plays a more basic role in shaping human conduct. For example, the regular punishment of offences and the discussion this provokes might be thought to play a vital role in implanting in people a deep sense of the wrongfulness of certain types of behaviour (Braithwaite, 1989).

There are other ideas about the purpose of criminal law which do not see controlling conduct as its sole or even central purpose. For instance, the purpose of criminal law is sometimes explained as being to ensure that those who act wrongly receive the pain which is their just desert. This may incidentally prevent them and others with similar motives and opportunities from committing further offences. But, some suggest, these control effects are useful by-products and not the main purpose of punishing criminal law-breakers. Rather, having some mechanism to ensure that people get what they deserve (be it punishment or reward) might be regarded as an end in itself in a society committed to the value of justice.

Another increasingly prevalent way of thinking about the purpose of criminal law is to regard its main function as being to communicate censure of wrongdoing (see Chapter 4). Criminal law has also been thought of as a means of providing redress for those harmed by wrongful conduct of others. On one view, those injured or threatened by wrongful acts have a natural entitlement to take retaliatory or defensive action. However, to have an orderly society, it is necessary that they forgo self-help and delegate this entitlement to some central authority which then incurs an obligation to inflict retributive suffering on those who commit criminal wrongs.

There are various other views about the purpose of criminal law which are more counter-intuitive than those outlined above. Jareborg (1995), for example, argues that an important purpose of criminal law is to cool down conflicts by providing a formal alternative to spontaneous public reactions to criminal behaviour, thereby protecting suspected offenders (and others) from violence. Also, many sociologists argue that the criminal law has real purposes which are somehow hidden from those who operate and observe it. The most famous example of this is Durkheim's (1960) suggestion that crime and the social reaction to it can help to strengthen social bonds within a community by providing a focus for group moral feelings (cf. Garland, 1990: chs. 2 and 3). In a somewhat similar vein is Foucault's suggestion that criminal law performs the important function of creating a steady supply of criminals who are useful to society in various ways (Foucault, 1977; cf. Garland, 1990, chs. 6–7).

Critiques of criminal law

Given the range of purposes and expectations that criminal law is expected to fulfil and meet, and that many of these are in tension with others, it is hardly surprising that criminal law is often subjected to criticism. Much of this criticism does not call into question the necessity or ultimate value of the institution, but rather points to certain shortcomings that need to be corrected. However, there are some critical themes which appear in discussions of criminal law – especially in criminology and the social sciences – which do raise more fundamental questions about the institution's inevitability or worth. In this section we describe some of these themes. Whilst they overlap a great deal, we will somewhat artificially describe them as distinct themes.

What we aim to depict are broad critical attitudes rather than specific criticisms published by particular authors. That is to say, to a large extent what we are describing are caricatures, but caricatures which we find prevalent within criminology and social science (i.e. although in print they are often expressed in a more guarded form, the caricatures are closer to the spontaneous reactions of many academics and students). With regard to these critical themes, we have two aims which pull in opposite directions. On the one hand, we find these critical themes very useful for sensitizing us to certain dangers and limitations of the institution of criminal law. On the other hand, we think there are valuable aspects of criminal law that are sometimes overlooked, under-appreciated or misunderstood by critics of the institution.

The libertarian critique

This critique accepts that people need to be protected by some entity from injurious and wrongful behaviour of others. Hence, it accepts that an institution bearing some resemblance to criminal law is a social necessity. It suggests, however, that the actual institutions of criminal law that we have, tend significantly to exceed these minimal protective functions. Criminal law tends to interfere without warrant in people's freedom to decide how to conduct their lives.

Criminal law is often criticized, for instance, for interfering with matters of 'private morality'. It prohibits behaviour which does not patently cause harm – or at least harm to non-consenting others – but is simply regarded by a majority (or perhaps even an influential minority) of members of society as distasteful, offensive or morally lax. (The now classic debate on the role of criminal law in enforcing morality is between the positions represented by Hart, 1963 and Devlin, 1965.) The criminalization of some consensual sado-masochistic activities as a result of the House of Lords' decision in *R v Brown* [1993] 1 AC 212 is one example (Beckmann, 2001).[4] Another criticism is that criminal law is frequently used paternalistically: to coerce people into behaving in ways that others think are in their own best interest or for their own protection. Using criminal law to require people to wear crash helmets whilst riding motorbikes is a key example. Such laws, the critique suggests, deprive people of the freedom to decide for themselves what is in their own best interests or to behave in ways that endanger themselves if they so fancy.

This libertarian critical perspective has also been applied to the sanctions that are imposed upon criminal law-breakers. It suggests that criminal law frequently goes beyond what it is entitled to do: imposing penalties on those who break the law. In addition, it uses its coercive powers to subject law-breakers to interventions designed to re-educate them and to render them able and willing to lead useful and law-abiding lives. Offenders are subjected not just to moral lectures but to therapeutic interventions designed to improve their attitudes, behaviour and personalities. For some critics, such use of coercive power is an unwarranted intrusion into the right to be different (Kittrie, 1971).

Libertarian criticism of criminal law often focuses upon particular laws or penal practices which, it is suggested, depart from libertarian standards that are themselves part of the criminal law tradition. According to these standards, criminal law should be based upon certain ideas about the proper relationship between individuals and the wider society of which they are a part. Individuals should be regarded as sovereign beings who are entitled to think and act as they please (e.g. in accordance with their own conceptions of morality and the good life) provided only that they do not interfere with the sovereign rights of other individuals. The criminal law's function is to prohibit and sanction behaviour if, and only if, it does constitute such interference with the rights of others. It is not to be used to coerce individuals into refraining from behaviour which other members of society regard simply as immoral or distasteful. Nor should it be used to coerce people into refraining from behaviour which might harm themselves but is no threat to others. Still less should the coercive power of criminal law be used to compel people to behave or think in ways considered moral or beneficial. Moreover, in sanctioning criminal law-breaking, the concern should be only to provide a disincentive to law-breaking. The coercive power of law should not be used in efforts to mould the thoughts, personality or habits of sovereign individuals.

As indicated, criminal law is to some extent founded upon such libertarian ideas. However, some fear that it is in danger of being shaped by quite contrary – illiberal – understandings of the relationship between individuals and other members of society. In some cases, the source of danger is identified as religious fundamentalism which insists on using coercive powers, such as those of criminal law, to punish breaches of religious rules. In other cases, the danger is seen as coming from those who favour the use of criminal law to repress behaviour that is not patently harmful but which they regard as immoral, be they 'moral conservatives' (e.g. supporters of the criminalization of homosexual behaviour) or 'moral progressives' (e.g. supporters of the criminalization of making hateful remarks about homosexuals).

The 'scientific' critique

The next critical perspective that we will describe will be examined at greater length, since it is crucial to thinking about the implications of criminology for criminal law. Its central themes are: the institution of criminal law is founded upon a pre-scientific understanding of criminal behaviour; as a result, many of its practices are futile and cruel; we need a radically different approach to dealing with crime based upon a more scientifically valid understanding of offending behaviour. This critical perspective is of particular interest for this book as it tends to pitch a scientific understanding of offending behaviour – of the sort that criminology and other social sciences aim and purport to provide – against popular myths about offending behaviour, which it is sometimes claimed underpin much of criminal law. To explain this critique, we need first to say something about the understanding of criminal behaviour that does underlie the practice of criminal law.

Criminal law is founded upon the notion that criminal behaviour is almost invariably the result of a freely made choice to do the deed that is proscribed by criminal law. According to this notion, all human beings above a certain age have the capacity to understand the nature of their behaviour and to control it through an act of will. So, if they do what is prohibited, this is the effect of a conscious choice, unless it can be shown that they were affected by some exceptional condition or circumstance that impaired their understanding or will and hence their capacity to choose how to behave.

Such a notion concerning criminal behaviour is implicit in various rationales proposed for the practice of punishing criminal law-breakers. One rationale for this practice points to the deterrent effects of punishment. By punishing those who break the law, the institution seeks to influence the offender's future conduct along with that of other persons who have similar motives and opportunities. The idea is that, if people form the impression that if they commit a crime they will likely suffer the pain of punishment, they will be more likely to refrain from committing crime in order to avoid the unpleasant consequence. But punishment could only have these effects if people who engage in criminal behaviour have a significant degree of control over their behaviour. To the extent that they lack such control – whatever the reason – the deterrent effect of punishment will be undermined.

Another rationale for the practice of punishing law-breakers is that it is a fair 'reward' (a negative reward) for behaving badly, i.e. punishment is the just desert of those who do wrong. Again, if those who do behave badly do not have the capacity to behave otherwise, it is difficult to sustain the notion that they merit punishment.

A frequently used analogy here is with illness (see Johnstone, 1996). By becoming ill, people can sometimes cause us trouble (they may miss work, become a burden on us, infect us, etc). Yet, we do not punish people for becoming ill. This is not simply because, as people who are already suffering, they deserve our sympathy. Rather, it is because it would strike us as completely pointless and inappropriate because people do not choose to become ill (although they may often be negligent in allowing themselves to become ill). Illness is something that happens to people rather than something they choose.[5] Accordingly, we cannot influence whether people become ill or not through the practice of punishing the ill, and nor does it seem appropriate to say that they deserve to be punished for being ill. It is because we make different assumptions about criminal law-breaking (erroneously according to the 'scientific' critique) – *viz.* that people do have a choice about whether or not to commit it – that we imagine punishment to be an appropriate way of dealing with it.

As well as underpinning the practice of punishment, the notion that criminal activity is almost invariably freely chosen also explains a great deal of judicial doctrine concerning liability for crime. When some unusual condition or circumstance clearly interferes with the person's normal capacity to choose how to behave, we tend to think there may be a case for excluding them from liability for what would otherwise be deemed a criminal deed.

It is this notion that virtually all of those who commit offences have normal capacities to control their behaviour that is criticized by the 'scientific' critique. The argument tends to be that the human and social sciences that have emerged and developed since the nineteenth century (such as biology, psychology, psychoanalysis, sociology and criminology) demonstrate that 'free will' is a myth (this is why we refer to this as the 'scientific' critique: to denote its source, not because we think it is in fact scientific). Although many of those working in the human and social sciences strongly distance themselves from such claims, there is a tendency to suggest that these disciplines – by showing human conduct to be 'determined' or moulded by some factor outside of the conscious control of the person (such as their biological inheritance, the way they were reared in early childhood, the way the society in which they live is structured) – reveal that the notion that humans have unconstrained choice over how to behave is false. In its strongest form the claim is that, whilst we tend to be under the illusion that we control our behaviour, in fact all we do is act out biological, psychological or sociological scripts written elsewhere. Our belief in the idea that we choose our behaviour has about the same status as the idea that the world is populated by invisible ghosts, spirits or angels who sometimes intervene in human affairs. Practices based on these beliefs have the same status as practices such as exorcism, which seeks to deal with certain pathological human behaviour by evicting from the person the demons or evil spirits which are responsible for it.[6]

Criminal law, of course, falls into the category of institutions which are based on the belief in free will – not necessarily in any metaphysical sense,[6] but in the sense that it focuses on individual choice as a real and morally crucial feature of human action. Indeed, it is the institution *par excellence* which takes the notion of free will very seriously. The whole enterprise of governing behaviour through issuing rules and enforcing them by sanctioning violators assumes human control over their conduct. The heavy moral censure which we attach to those who violate criminal law only makes sense if we assume they could have done otherwise. The painstaking efforts to which the law goes to ascertain whether, in any particular case, a claim that one's choice was severely restricted by some exceptional condition or circumstance would be nonsensical if it were not assumed that the norm is that people have such choice. The relatively rare cases in which those conditions or circumstances are investigated reinforce the idea that free choice is the norm.

The 'scientific' critique of criminal law goes further, though, than simply claiming that criminal law is based upon a misunderstanding of offending behaviour. It suggests that, because of this, the interventions of criminal law tend to be both cruel and ineffective in controlling crime. Adherence to the belief in free will leads us to inflict pain and moral stigma on people who actually have little or no control over their conduct. It also leads us to rely on such punishment as a means of control, when in reality punishment can have little influence on the conduct of people who lack control over their conduct.

According to the 'scientific' critique, criminal law should therefore be replaced by an entirely different approach to crime. The factors which cause crime need to be identified – on the basis of scientific research – and eliminated if possible. The logic of crime policy should be modelled on that of medicine and public health (Farrington and Welsh, 2007: 3). As Enrico Ferri, one of the 'founding fathers' of 'scientific criminology' put it in a lecture delivered in 1901:

> The 19th century has won a great victory over mortality and infectious diseases by means of the masterful progress of physiology and natural science. But while contagious diseases have gradually diminished, we see on the other hand that moral diseases are growing more numerous in our so-called civilisation. While typhoid fever, smallpox, cholera and diphtheria retreated before the remedies which enlightened science applied ... we

see on the other hand that insanity, suicide and crime, that painful trinity, are growing apace. (Ferri, 1913: 7–8)

Early texts such as Ferri's are of interest because they pursue the logic of the scientific critique to an extent rarely found in the work of present-day heirs to the same tradition (e.g. Farrington and Welsh, 2007). Here is another example, from an article with the telling title 'Science Approaches the Lawbreaker':

> ... the methods employed by the Man of Science should be extended from the care and treatment of the body to the care and treatment of the soul ... Science has already rescued the body of man from the unscientific hands of the medieval practitioner who, ignorant of the true causes of the maladies he has sought to cure, had recourse to remedies which we now see were not calculated to produce the desired results. ... All that now remains is to allow the Men of Science in a similar manner to rescue the soul of man out of the hands of the medieval psychologist – whose way of thinking underlies and is exemplified by our present penal methods. (Gardner, 1928: 205)[8]

This still leaves the question, of course, of what to do about those who are already predisposed to crime (the equivalent, to stay with the logic, of those who have already been infected with what it is that causes diseases such as typhoid fever). This is an important question because defenders of criminal law could say that it is in fact quite compatible with efforts scientifically to identify and eliminate the causes of crime. Unless and until those efforts are completely successful, we still have the problem of dealing with those who are disposed to commit crime, and criminal law is perhaps an appropriate way of doing this job. Again, however, the scientific critique suggests a different approach. One suggestion is that those who are predisposed to commit crime (because, for instance, they have the gene that makes people dishonest, or their upbringing left them with deeply ingrained violent tendencies) can be identified through some scientific procedure. This has a crucial implication.

Currently, the way we tend to distinguish between offenders and non-offenders is by reference to whether they have been convicted of a criminal offence (there are other methods, such as self-report studies, but they are of far less social importance). Those who have been convicted are offenders and we need to make a decision about how to deal with them. Those who have not been convicted are non-offenders and are of no concern. The scientific critique suggests a different approach. We can distinguish by quite different means (e.g. some sort of a scientific screening programme) between those predisposed to commit crime and those not so predisposed. Many of the former will not actually have committed a criminal offence but, in a sense, they are 'offenders'. They are, so to say, offenders by nature even though they are not yet offenders by deed; they have high 'antisocial potential' (Farrington, 2007: 621). We should not wait until they actually commit a criminal offence before intervening into their lives. Likewise, although this tends to be less stressed, some of those who have committed a criminal offence may not be natural offenders. They are 'accidental criminals': people with no predisposition to commit crime but who happen to have offended on what is likely to be a one-off occasion.

What the scientific critique tends to focus upon is the former group. It suggests, basically, that the way we handle them should be based upon a scientific analysis of their condition and prognosis. For the early positivists, this implied radical changes in the way the courts dealt with offenders. 'Sentencing' should be based upon scientific criteria and not traditional criminal law criteria. Positivist criminologists today rarely take such radical positions. Farrington and Welsh (2007: 3) for example, proclaim that their 'immodest aim is to change national policies to focus on early childhood prevention rather than on locking up offenders' but beyond that they have almost nothing to say about how the courts should respond to crime. We find it regrettable that positivist criminology has lost its critical bite. Ferri, Gardner and their ilk were naïve in thinking that 'science' could of itself provide answers to fundamental questions of justice. But if many offenders' behaviour is the product, for example, of a disastrous early childhood, this does have implications for a system that aims to do justice to them as adults, which criminologists ought to address (see Chapter 4).

The socio-political critique

This critical perspective overlaps with others that we describe. However, it is sufficiently distinctive and important to warrant its own section. There are two strands. The first concerns the range of behaviour that is prohibited by criminal law; the second concerns the way criminal law assigns blame for criminal events.

Punishing trivial misdeeds, ignoring serious harm: The first strand of criticism argues that much of the behaviour prohibited by criminal law causes trivial harm – or may be harmless or even beneficial to society – whilst there is much behaviour that causes great social harm that is either not prohibited by criminal law or, if formally prohibited, is rarely met with significant criminal sanctions (Hillyard and Tombs, 2007, especially pp. 11–13). The implication is that, if one of the major purposes of criminal law is to protect citizens from the harmful behaviour of others in our midst, the criminal law does not in fact serve its purpose well. It fails to protect citizens from behaviour that causes widespread and serious harm, whilst diverting social attention and resources towards the punishment and control of people who cause relatively little harm.

If we agreed with this critical claim we would, of course, want to know why this is the case. Various explanations can be suggested. It may simply be that the institution of criminal law reflects a broader tendency towards irrationality in thinking about the risks surrounding us: we tend to worry a great deal about threats that are actually small, whilst being complacent about things that regularly cause serious social harm. As the authors of *Panicology* put it, we are anxious about the threat of terrorism even though:

> In England and Wales the threat to our lives from terrorism has been much lower than deaths from transport accidents (3000), falls (3000), drowning (200), poisoning (900) and suicide (over 3000) ... It is pretty clear that, so long as you stay away from the world's insurgent hotspots, the chances of being caught up in a terrorist event are minuscule (Briscoe and Aldersey-Williams, 2007, quoted in O'Hagan, 2007).

Some criminologists, however, tell a more politicized story. They suggest that the criminal law – either straightforwardly or in complex ways – serves the interests of powerful groups within society. For instance, it is suggested that it is the minor illegalities of powerless people that tend to be punished and controlled through criminal law, whilst the 'crimes of the powerful' – which cause much greater harm – tend to escape criminalization (e.g. Pearce, 1976; Hillyard and Tombs, 2007; Reiman, 2007). This, some suggest, is because powerful groups within society have control over the social and political processes through which it is determined whether behaviour is to be prohibited by criminal law or, if it is prohibited, through which it is determined how vigorously it is policed, prosecuted or sanctioned. A related theme is that the huge devotion of resources to the punishment and control of conduct that is of relatively little harm occurs because it functions to divert social attention towards that behaviour – as the cause of our misery and suffering – whilst diverting it away from actions and policies of powerful people and organizations, including government, which are in fact a cause of much greater misery and suffering.

This critique might be identified as being about the *substantive content* of criminal law. The suggestion is that, for whatever reason, the criminal law targets the wrong sorts of behaviour and people. What is required, it is implied, is a massive decriminalization of conduct (abolition of many of the prohibitions enforced though our criminal law, most importantly drugs offences) and a corresponding criminalization of seriously harmful conduct currently ignored by criminal law.

The individualization of blame: Whereas the previous strand of criticism goes to the substantive content of criminal law, this one goes more to its structure. It argues that criminal law adheres to and propagates 'a narrow individualistic notion of responsibility' for acts of social harm, which ignores and deflects attention from social or structural factors that cause criminal behaviour (Hillyard and Tombs, 2007: 19).[9] The gist of this critique is that criminal law channels all the blame, condemnation and punishment for criminal actions towards the immediate perpetrators – who may be relatively lacking in power – and that this also has the effect of diverting attention and condemnation away from others (perhaps more powerful) whose actions were, albeit indirectly, a contributing cause to the crime that occurred. The following conveys the flavour of this critique well:

> Behind the man with the knife is the man who sold him the knife, the man who did not give him a job, the man who decided that his school did not need funding, the man who closed down the branch plant where he could have worked, the man who decided to reduce benefit levels so that a black economy grew, all the way back to the woman who only noticed 'those inner cities' some six years after the summer of 1981, and the people who voted to keep her in office. The harm done to one generation has repercussions long after that harm is first acted out. Those who perpetrated the social violence that was done to the lives of young men starting some 20 years ago are the prime suspects for most of the murders in Britain. (Dorling, 2004: 191)

The moral intent of this passage is fairly obvious, as are some of its implications for policy. If we recognize that a great many people (perhaps even ourselves, although that is rarely acknowledged) have some responsibility for the crime that occurs in our society, we might adopt a less condemnatory and less punitive stance towards the actual perpetrators. We might also divert some of the resources that we currently devote to running a hugely expensive criminal justice system towards correcting some of the structural factors that lead many people – who in different circumstances would have been law-abiding – to commit crime. As Dorling (2004) and Pemberton (2007) suggest, in the aftermath of a knife crime, instead of calling for tougher sentencing, we might instead advocate policies that address the social contexts which inexorably lead to knife crime.

What is less clear is the precise implication of this stance for our thinking about criminal law (cf. Reiman, 2006). Despite the rhetorical excess at the end of the quote from Dorling, it is presumably not meant to imply that people who indirectly contribute to crime (e.g. somebody who interviewed 'the man with the knife' for a job but decided not to employ him or somebody who voted for a political party whose social policies have clearly resulted in a rise of crime) should be subjected to criminal conviction and sanctions; we must find other ways of bringing home to them the fact that they share some responsibility for crimes that occur. But what are less apparent are the implications for the way criminal law should treat 'the man with the knife'. How does the fact that others are also partly responsible for his actions, and especially the fact that as well as being an offender he is also, in a sense, a victim of earlier harmful acts, affect our judgement of his culpability or our decision on what should be done to or with him? This, of course, is a very difficult question. Our criminal law provides a fairly clear answer to it.[10] Some criminologists, among others, have rightly questioned the criminal law's 'individualistic notion of responsibility'; but without thinking rigorously about what the proposed alternative might be.

The restorative justice critique

Since the 1970s, a new social movement, *viz.* the restorative justice movement, has emerged and gained significant influence in the fields of criminal policy and criminology. This movement has been the source of a profound critique of criminal law and of proposals for alternative ways of thinking about and handling the sorts of events that criminal law deals with.[11] Advocates of restorative justice take seriously the idea that it is necessary to provide a response to criminal wrong-doing that is effective in controlling crime and delivering justice. However, as Pavlich (2005) puts it, restorative justice attempts to approach these issues with a different moral compass than that used by the institution of criminal law.

Central to the moral compass of criminal law is the distinction between crimes and 'mere' private wrongs (Duff, 2002a: 4; e.g. Ormerod, 2005: 11; Zedner, 2005: 58). Private (or 'civil') wrongs are acts of wrong-doing which interfere with the rights of other individuals (such as failing to comply with contractual duties owed to another). They give rise to liability in private (or civil) law. It is the injured party's decision whether or not to bring the matter to court, and if they decide to do so they bear the responsibility and cost of presenting the case. The most common legal remedy for a private wrong is an order that the wrong-doer compensate the injured party – putting the injured party in a position comparable to that they were in before the wrongful act occurred.

A crime, on the other hand, is a 'public wrong': a wrongful act which has a harmful effect on the public, or which 'threatens the security or well-being of society' (C.K. Allen, quoted in Ormerod, 2005: 11), or which should be the concern of all citizens.[12] It is a commonplace of legal discourse that a crime cannot be remedied only by compensation to the injured party. Something else must be done to vindicate the public interest which has been damaged by a criminal act. It tends to be taken for granted that that 'something' is punishment of the offender. It also tends to be taken for granted that state officials should investigate and prosecute crimes as well as administering the punishment of those convicted. Indeed, the direct victims (where there are direct victims) are generally regarded as having no formal stake in the case; the matter is officially between the state (or 'the crown' or 'the people') and the accused. So, for instance, the victim's wishes – on whether the case should proceed, what charges should be brought, and so on – can be ignored by the prosecutor, whose official responsibility is to the public rather than to the direct victims.

The restorative justice critique attacks the contemporary conception of criminal justice at its heart. It argues that crimes always harm actual people and that by constructing crime as a wrong against an impersonal entity (such as 'the public', society, or 'the state'), criminal law obscures the fact that this interpersonal harm occurs, downplays its significance and fails to provide an adequate remedy for it. As Howard Zehr, a leading advocate of restorative justice, puts it:

> Crime then is at its core a violation of a person by another person, a person who himself or herself may be wounded. It is a violation of the just relationship that should exist between individuals. There is also a larger social dimension of crime. Indeed, the effects of crime ripple out, touching many others. Society too has a stake in the outcome and a role to play. Still, these public dimensions should not be the starting point. Crime is not first an offense against society, much less against the state. Crime is first an offense against people, and it is here that we should start. (Zehr, 1990: 182)

One implication of this is that, in the aftermath of crime, providing a remedy for the person(s) who have actually been harmed should take precedence over providing a remedy for the public interest that might also have been harmed as the effects of crime 'ripple out'. A restorative criminal justice system, then, would be a system in which the priority is to provide a remedy for the direct victims of crime, with taking action on behalf of the wider public very much a secondary goal.

Crucially, according to proponents of restorative justice, we cannot assume that what the victim requires, in order to experience justice, is punishment of the offender. Indeed, it is argued, for various reasons, punishment of the offender is unlikely to be in the interests of the victims. Their interests may be much better served through something like the compensatory approach used in private law. However, in the field of private wrongs, court-ordered compensation is not in fact the norm. Rather, the normal way of settling conflicts arising from private wrongs is negotiated settlements between wrong-doers and injured parties; courtroom settlement is a last resort when attempts to negotiate a private settlement fail. Accordingly, proponents of restorative justice argue, when a crime occurs the wrong-doer and the injured people should be encouraged and facilitated to reach a negotiated settlement, ideally involving restitution or reparation. The state's role should be to facilitate this process of negotiated reparative justice. It is the parties involved – the offender(s), the victim(s) and others with a direct stake in the outcome – who should decide what needs to be done to remedy the harm that has occurred and to oversee acts of reparation. The state should only step in and start making and imposing decisions if all reasonable efforts to bring about a negotiated reparative settlement fail. If the parties involved do arrive at a negotiated solution, then – but only then – should the question of whether anything *further* needs to be done to protect the public interest be addressed. Proponents of restorative justice suggest that that question is also better addressed – initially at least – by local community forums rather than by centralized state officials.

This critique suggests the need for a fundamental realignment of the assumptions and priorities of the institution of criminal law. Just as importantly, a significant shift away from the sort of criminal justice system we have now in most contemporary societies towards a restorative criminal justice system would result in significant blurring of the boundaries separating the institution of criminal law from other institutions and social practices such as private law and community-based conflict resolution practices. The restorative justice critique, if followed through logically, points towards the partial dissolution of criminal law as a discrete social institution.

An open attitude

There are further critical perspectives (partially overlapping with some of those above) that we have not described at length. These include a justice critique, which suggests that criminal law ought primarily to be an institution which seeks to correct injustices, but has become an institution which seeks primarily to control crime. We might also have included an anarchist critique, which suggests that people can govern themselves effectively without coercive laws (Tifft and Sullivan, 1980). However, the critical perspectives we have described are perhaps the most important in the context of this book, and are sufficient to show that criminal law is often regarded – within criminology and the social sciences – as a fundamentally flawed institution which has little call on our allegiance and is in need of fundamental reform.

As indicated at the outset, our position is somewhat different. We regard these critical perspectives as having great value and we are very sympathetic towards many of the values and ideas which inform them. These critiques point towards important shortcomings and dangers of the institution of criminal law and suggest that these could only be remedied through, at the very least, a fundamental redesign of the institution; mere tinkering is not enough.

However, we think there is also a tendency – amongst those who think about criminal law from within these critical perspectives – to fail to see or to misunderstand elements of the institution of criminal law that are of value and worth preserving, even if in modified form. For example, we suggest that holding individuals responsible for their actions, as a general principle, is practically and ethically defensible. Or, to provide just one more example, we suggest that the conception of crime as a distinctive type of wrong – *viz.* a public wrong as opposed to a mere private wrong – is worth retaining, even though many of the assumptions and practices based on this conception could be transformed.

This 'open' attitude towards the institution of criminal law will underlie our account of the institution. That account begins in the next chapter with an attempt to describe the origins and development of criminal law from ancient times up to the end of the eighteenth century, when the institution underwent a fundamental transformation. That transformation and its aftermath are described in Chapter 3, where we show how criminal law became a central institution of social governance from the nineteenth century onwards, with profound implications for the nature of the institution. In Chapter 4, we return to the issue of free choice and the way the law constructs criminal responsibility, which are discussed further in Chapter 5 with reference to murder and manslaughter. Chapter 6 looks at attempts to use criminal law to control corporate wrong-doing and crimes of the powerful and at the strains and tensions that surface when criminal law is extended beyond its traditional concerns with predatory crimes against persons and property. Chapter 7 deals, again in a long-term historical perspective, with issues of criminal procedure and evidence. Chapter 8 discusses criminal law's distinctive mode of sanctioning – the punishment of offenders – and in Chapter 9 we consider the growing fields of international criminal justice and transitional justice (where a state's former officials are on trial for crimes committed under a previous regime). We then end with some concluding reflections.

Summary

The purpose of this book is to provide an introductory account of criminal law for criminologists, social scientists and others interested in criminal law as a social institution. At the outset, the main features of criminal law are introduced: enforceable rules of conduct, the moral dimensions of criminal law, criminal procedure, criminal liability and different views about the purposes of criminal law. The institution of criminal law is often viewed as a deeply flawed institution. This chapter introduces some important critical perspectives on criminal law. We call these: the libertarian critique, the 'scientific' critique, the socio-political critique and the restorative justice critique. These critical perspectives sensitize us to important limits and dangers of the institution of criminal law. However, there is also a tendency to fail to recognize or to misunderstand elements of criminal law that are of significant value and worth preserving. The account of criminal law provided in this book attempts to steer a course between a complacent acceptance of the obviousness and rightness of criminal law and ultra-critical perspectives.

STUDY QUESTIONS

1. Why is an analysis of the institution of criminal law important for criminology?

2. What are the purposes of criminal law? Is its function solely to control crime?

3. What are the implications of the discoveries of the human and social sciences about the determinants of criminal behaviour for the institution of criminal law?

4. Does the institution of criminal law criminalize the most harmful behaviour in society? What implications do criminological studies of white-collar crime have here?

5. Is the law's model of individual responsibility for one's wrongful actions defensible? Are there any viable alternatives?

6. What is the basis for the distinction between private wrongs and public wrongs? How fruitful is it to make such a distinction?

FURTHER READING

Anthony Duff's contribution to the *Stanford Encyclopedia of Philosophy*, titled 'Theories of Criminal Law' (2002a) is an excellent introduction to thinking about the purposes of criminal law, its proper scope, and whether the institution should be preserved; it is available online at http://plato.stanford.edu/entries/criminal-law/. Nicola Lacey's chapter 'Legal Constructions of Crime' (2007, in the *Oxford Handbook of Criminology*) provides a useful examination of the relationship between legal and social constructions of crime. Of the many short introductory books on criminal law aimed at law students, Christopher Clarkson's *Understanding Criminal Law*, 4th ed. (2005) is recommended as most accessible to non-law students. Three very different critical studies of criminal law that we recommend for criminologists are: Alan Norrie's *Crime, Reason and History*, 2nd ed. (2001), Laceys et al.'s *Reconstructing Criminal Law*, 3rd ed. (2003), and Andrew Ashworth's *Principles of Criminal Law*, 5th ed. (2006).

Notes

1 See Feinberg (1994 [1970]). On the 'rationalization' of criminal law, justice and punishment in modern society, see Garland (1990: ch. 8). For many, this distancing of criminal law from moralistic conceptions of crime constitutes progress; others think it has gone way too far (see, for instance, Braithwaite, 1989).

2 Such comparisons need to be supplemented by other material to become meaningful. In many countries, such as England, children above the age of criminal capacity but below a higher age

(usually in the range 16–21) are not subject to the adult system of prosecution and punishment. We discuss age and criminal responsibility in more detail in Chapter 4.

3 In this example D denotes defendant, V denotes victim.

4 For an explanation of case citations such as this, see p. 199.

5 This 'passive' conception of the process of becoming ill is challenged by some sociologists of illness and medicine. For an excellent introduction to this field see Turner (1995).

6 Although exorcism itself is of course based on deterministic beliefs about some human conduct – in this case the determining entity is a demon or evil spirit.

7 For example, the view of free will advocated by Kant; for discussion of Kant's ideas in a criminological context, see Beyleveld and Wiles (1979).

8 For discussion of these ideas and their influence see Johnstone (1996). It is very important to recognize that the claim was that the approach to criminal law-breaking should be modelled upon the *logic* of the scientific approach to controlling disease. It is not necessarily implied that crime – like disease – has biological determinants (although many developed such ideas in this direction). This logic is equally compatible with the idea that crime is caused by social factors such as social deprivation or particular patterns of child-rearing. The logic is that the causes of crime should be ascertained through some scientific process and then rectified, as a way of preventing crime.

9 Hillyard and Tombs' critical target is the discipline of criminology, which they argue has uncritically adopted legal conceptions of crime. But they clearly have a critical attitude towards legal constructions of crime.

10 But that answer is nowhere near as clear as Reiman (2006) seems to suppose; cf. Norrie (2001).

11 The nature and scope of this critique of criminal law is not always clear. The literature of restorative justice contains within it the outlines of an extremely radical and challenging critique which, if followed to its logical conclusion, would result in a call for the abolition of the entire institution and its replacement by a wholly new approach to crime. In practice, restorative processes have tended to be developed and employed within the institution of criminal law, functioning more as alternative processes for dealing with some aspects of some cases (Johnstone, 2002).

12 The same act can constitute both a private wrong and a crime. A famous example is the O.J. Simpson affair of the mid-1990s. Simpson was prosecuted for murder and acquitted. The families of the two murder victims subsequently successfully sued Simpson in a civil trial for private wrongs: causing the wrongful death of one victim and committing battery against the other.

2

The Formation
of Criminal
Justice

Chapter Contents

OVERVIEW

Chapter 2:

- Explains the importance of understanding how criminal law began and developed.
- Introduces two influential theories about origins of criminal law: social contract theory and self-help theory.
- Looks at how troublesome conduct and conflict were handled before the emergence of criminal law.
- Traces the emergence of criminal law in medieval Europe.
- Describes important developments in criminal law, such as how crime came to be shaped by notions of sin and how liability became increasingly individualized.

KEY TERMS

social contract theory self-help theory communal punishment private vengeance compensation crime and sin *mens rea*

Introduction

Criminal law is such a familiar aspect of contemporary societies that it can appear to be a natural phenomenon or at least 'an inescapable feature of the developed societies in which we live' (Duff, 2002a: 6). As Simpson puts it:

> Even quite young children, long before they take up shop-lifting, or driving uninsured mopeds, or scrumping apples, are at least familiar with the criminal law, with its court dramas of wickedness and tragedy, its parables of right and wrong, its fearsome denunciations of cruelty and greed. They know only too well what becomes of the likes of Mr Toad and others who violate the more serious rules of social behaviour, once they fall into the hands of the stern and brutal minions of the law. The tales they read, the movies they see, the television they watch, familiarize them with a whole range of conceptions intimately related to the existence of law. (Simpson, 1988: 1)

Even if it is realized that societies have existed in the past (and that some societies may still exist today) in which there was no criminal law, it is difficult to avoid presuming that such societies must have been extremely simple or primitive.

A problem with this way of thinking is that it limits our imagination. Because we regard the institution of criminal law as natural, the question of whether we ought to maintain the institution – although it has certainly been asked – is seldom taken seriously. To open up the question of whether we should maintain an institution such as criminal law, it is necessary first to disturb the air of naturalness and inevitability that it has acquired over the centuries. One way of doing this is to look with an open mind at how historical societies which did not have criminal law viewed and handled troublesome conduct (that we might today call 'crime') and at how and why our distant ancestors developed institutions of criminal law. (In Chapter 7, we look at long-term historical developments in criminal procedure and evidence.)

Theories about the creation of criminal justice

In the history of western political and legal thought, there have been some highly influential theories about the origins of criminal law. We will start by briefly describing two of the most influential theories: the social contract theory and the self-help theory.

Social contract theory

Social contract theory is a general theory about the nature of political and legal obligation. Since the eighteenth century, its ideas have had a profound influence on thinking about criminal law. There are numerous versions of the theory. However, the basic idea is that people are obliged to obey the state and its laws because they have agreed, at least tacitly, to obey them. This invites the question: why would people agree to such a restriction of their liberty? In answering this, social contract theory imagines what life would be like in a 'state of nature', i.e. before a regular system of government, law-making and law-enforcement existed.

One of the most memorable depictions of life in a state of nature is that of Thomas Hobbes.[1] According to Hobbes, in a state of nature every man is roughly equal in physical strength and cunning. No man is sufficiently stronger than others that he can avoid being killed by them. This makes men wary of each other. Each man dreams of having dominion over others, but no man can achieve such dominion. Realization that others have the same dreams of dominion increases each person's feeling of insecurity. In this situation, each man will do whatever he can to preserve his life. This makes his behaviour unpredictable. None of the goods that are possible only as a result of human co-operation exist. In Hobbes' famous phrase, the life of man in a state of nature is 'solitary, poore, nasty, brutish, and short' (1914: 65).

In such a state of nature people have liberty, but it is useless to them. Accordingly, it is rational to give up some liberty to gain security. The rational man will agree to obey laws and give up his right to defend himself, if he can be sure that every other person will do the same. In Hobbes' scheme this is achieved by men coming together to create a sovereign with power to make and enforce laws.[2]

So, in the Hobbesian state of nature people live in fear of each other. What they fear above all is predatory behaviour: killing, violent attacks, plunder of possessions, rape, and so on. Crucially, in the absence of criminal law, such predatory acts are not properly speaking 'crimes'. In the absence of some sovereign with the authority and power to define certain acts as wrongs, punishable by the sovereign, 'crimes' do not really exist. Such predatory acts are more like acts of war.

Through the social contract crime itself comes into being. The people create a sovereign with the authority and power to define some actions as crimes punishable by the sovereign. People will tend to refrain from conduct which the sovereign prohibits because they fear the sanctions which the sovereign may impose. Because other people know this, they become less wary and fearful of others. People can begin to accumulate property, build permanent dwellings, trade with others and join in other co-operative ventures.

If we think about the institution of criminal law in the terms suggested by Hobbes' version of social contract theory, abolition of criminal law becomes virtually unthinkable. To abolish criminal law would be to return to a state of nature. Society would simply crumble.

Self-help theory

The self-help theory of the origins of law and the state was developed by scholars in reaction to social contract theory.[3] Like social contract theory, self-help theory assumes that, prior to the emergence of the state, there was a state of nature which was characterized by high levels of inter-personal and inter-group violence. But, in the self-help theory, far from being chaotic and unpredictable, this violence was organized around fairly sophisticated principles of vengeance. Acts which were perceived as injurious were met with 'private vengeance'. Custom dictated the situations in which vengeance was permissible (and, as we shall see, mandatory) and the sorts of things that could be done in the name of vengeance. Moreover, rather than eliminating private vengeance, early states tended to supervise and institutionalize it. It was only later that states began to take over the administration of 'punishment' and later still that they reserved a monopoly of the legitimate use of punitive violence. In place of the simple dichotomy – state of nature/governed society – posited by social contract theory, the self-help theory suggests that the early development of law and the state took place through four stages (Whitman, 1995: 42).

1 There is a state of nature, in which individuals or clans exact vengeance for wrongs done to them in accordance with social customs which regulate – albeit roughly – the circumstances in which an individual or clan will seek vengeance and the nature of vengeful acts.
2 The early state emerges and supervises the system of private vengeance, requiring wronged parties to seek state approval for customary vengeful action.
3 The state begins to take vengeance against wrong-doers on behalf of injured parties.
4 The state moves to outlaw private vengeance, reserving for itself the legitimate use of penal violence. It also institutes a system of composition substituting monetary compensation for penal violence for some wrongs.

Shortly, we will point to certain revisions of this theory which have been suggested. First, though, we will briefly look at some implications of the self-help theory, as described by Whitman, for our understanding of criminal law.

One implication is that criminal law has its roots in the ancient practice of private vengeance (cf. Saleilles, 1911: ch. 2). The state tames private vengeance. It formalizes the customary norms which determine the actions for which vengeance is permitted and the severity of vengeful actions, makes rules about who is a legitimate target for vengeance, and gradually replaces violent killings and mutilations with gentler forms of punishment such as fines or imprisonment. The state transforms the wild justice of private vengeance into the domesticated justice of state retribution. But, the urge to exact vengeance from those who wrong us lies at the root of criminal law. Whilst contemporary criminal law is often discussed as if it were simply about identifying and repressing socially harmful behaviour, it is moulded by a quite different social practice: taking vengeance on those who wrong us (some of the implications of this view are explored by Gardner, 2007: ch. 10).

Crucially, the self-help theory can lead us to a different way of thinking about the social necessity of criminal law than that encouraged by social contract theory. The self-help theory suggests that criminal law did not arise from people agreeing to set up a sovereign with the power to punish in order get out of a chaotic and inconvenient state of nature. In the self-help theory, the state of nature is violent but its violence is by no means unpredictable. There are customs governing private vengeance which make it predictable and so not an automatic obstacle to social co-operation. Indeed, the knowledge that certain injuries are likely to give rise to vengeful attacks may provide a significant degree of security. It is not quite so obvious then why people in such a state of nature would be willing to transfer their right to take vengeance to a central state. It therefore becomes important to understand the state's motives for gradually taking over the power to punish and the consequences of this takeover. There is no reason to suppose that the motive was purely disinterested or that the effects of this development were wholly beneficial. Rather these become matters to be investigated, and the results of such investigation have implications of our assessment of the desirability of maintaining an institution such as criminal law.

Revisions to the self-help theory

Before leaving the self-help theory, it is important to note some important modifications that have been proposed.

The first concerns composition. As we have seen, self-help theory suggests that composition emerges at the final stage of the transition. The state introduces a system of buying off penal violence by paying monetary compensation. However, there are good reasons for thinking that compensation was always a possibility in a system of private vengeance (Whitman, 1995: 70ff). Miller (2006), for instance, suggests that retaliation is inherently governed by principles of reciprocal payment for injuries done. The *talionic* principle – eye for an eye, tooth for a tooth, etc. – suggests as much. In systems of private vengeance there is almost always an option to substitute that which is to be lost as the result of wronging another by something of commensurate value (e.g. 50 cattle in exchange for a life instead of a life for a life). Some, such as restorative justice advocate Howard Zehr (1990: ch. 7) suggest that (in what he calls community justice) there was a presumption that injuries would be compensated by things other than lives and body parts, and that killing and mutilation were resorted to only when an agreement on appropriate compensation could not be reached.

We will return to this idea, but for the moment we should note that, if Zehr's claim is plausible, an implication is that to characterize what existed before criminal law as a system of private vengeance is itself highly misleading. Rather, what existed was a hybrid system of negotiated settlement of conflicts through compensatory payments, with the threat of private vengeance in the background as a possibility should a wrong-doer refuse (or be unable) to pay whatever compensation was customary. Although such a system would have all sorts of problems, and may be less desirable than a system of criminal law, simple assumptions about the superiority of criminal law over whatever existed before its creation become even more tenuous.

A second modification to self-help theory, proposed by Whitman (1995), concerns the notion that state criminal law is simply an institutionalized form of private vengeance. State punishment of offenders, it is suggested, has independent origins in social practices that have little to do with vengeance. What Whitman points to in particular are ritualistic practices of sacrifice-based religions. Ancient religious systems often featured human, animal and food sacrifices as ways of appeasing or invoking interventionist gods. The sacrificial use of money is also quite continuous with these practices. The mutilation of bodies, too, was an act carried out not only as vengeance but as a religious practice. From this perspective, the emergence of state punishment must be understood as a continuation and extension of these religious practices, as well as an attempt to institutionalize customs of private vengeance.

To these, we would add a third modification, which is related to that of Zehr (1990: ch. 7) mentioned above. Arguably, both social contract and self-help theory focus upon conflict between strangers. This is most explicit in Hobbes' version of social contract theory which takes as its starting point a society of isolated individuals (who in a state of nature remain solitary). However, before the emergence of the state people did not live in isolation from each other. Rather, most lived in communities. This raises the question of how wrongs were dealt with when they were committed between people who had a strong communal relationship with each other. It may be that wrongs committed within such a setting were dealt with differently to wrongs committed between 'strangers'. This opens the possibility that criminal law may have been modelled as much upon these intra-community practices as it was upon the practice of private vengeance.

Punishment, vengeance and compensation

We will now turn from these general theories about the emergence of criminal law to look a little closer at how criminal law might have emerged in Europe. In most of western Europe prior to the eleventh century, and in many regions for several more centuries, the largest units in which the vast majority of people lived were very small, economically self-sufficient villages. Central imperial and religious authorities existed, but exercised very little control over day-to-day life of people in these villages (Berman, 1983: 85–6). These villages were relatively self-governing, yet they lacked specialized laws and law enforcement agencies. What we want to look at here is how, in such a context, incidents that we would today call crimes (homicides, assaults, thefts, etc.) were normally handled. To start, we need to distinguish two quite different situations: (i) wrongs committed within the village or communal circle and (ii) wrongs committed by (or against) 'strangers' (Moberly, 1968: 97).

Punishment within the communal circle

In the former, it is likely that wrong-doers were frequently admonished and/or chastised by fellow villagers without much formality. Given that the offender would not be a stranger but an intimate member of the community, it is also likely that the 'punishment' meted out would be shaped by much wider considerations than the nature and gravity of the particular wrongful act. The close relationship between those punishing and those being punished, and the probability of that relationship continuing, would play a major role in shaping the likelihood of punishment and its severity and nature when it did occur. Often, we can guess, the fact that 'there is a background of kinship or sympathy between judge and culprit' (and we might add economic interdependence) would result in a punishment being strongly influenced by compassion and considerations of the offender's welfare (quote from Moberly, 1968: 97). However, the nature and severity of 'intra-village punishment' no doubt varied enormously from village to village and would have been shaped by a wide range of economic and cultural factors. It is also possible that certain wrongs breached taboos and aroused strong emotional reactions and were met with particularly harsh punishments (ibid.). We can also assume that a small proportion of wrong-doers – such as habitual wrong-doers or perpetrators of particularly atrocious wrongs – were banished from their communities, and that this almost invariably resulted in their death.

Vengeance amongst 'strangers'

Let us turn now to the second situation, where an offence is committed against a 'stranger'. One widespread way of responding to such events was private vengeance. Those who suffered by a misdeed – or more often the kin or companions of the injured party – retaliated against the perpetrator of the injury and that person's kin or companions. Such retaliation often took a violent form: the perpetrator might be killed or mutilated, property might be seized or destroyed, and so on.

As we have seen, there are important questions about how we characterize such 'private vengeance'. It is tempting to characterize it as a primitive form of punishment (cf. Saleilles, 1911: ch. 2). However, punishment implies some pre-existing relationship of authority between the punisher and person or group punished: punishment is inflicted by a superior authority upon an (at least formally) inferior subject. Private vengeance might be better characterized, then, as an act of warfare. In the absence of a central authority able and willing to impose order from above, a state of war and pillage prevailed. In this context, attacks upon others and retaliatory violence were common occurrences and every individual and group assumed 'the right to defend himself and to take vengeance when attacked' (ibid.: 21).

An important question is why people would undertake acts of vengeance. After all, this is a very risky activity: it commits one to what may become a drawn-out violent feud. Acts of vengeance were always likely to be perceived by those on the receiving end as wrongs done to them, which in turn needed to be avenged. So, far from vengeance putting an end to conflict, the outcome could be to instigate or continue a cycle of tit-for-tat violence. There must have been a temptation, then, for those wronged to simply endure the wrong done to them rather than risk becoming embroiled in blood-feud.

What seems clear is that there was in fact significant social pressure to avenge an attack on oneself or one's kin, despite the risks involved in doing so. In Anglo-Saxon Britain, for instance, the kinship group of a person killed felt a strong *obligation* to take vengeance against the killer and their kin (Whitelock, 1952: 29ff; Harding, 1966: 14). To fail to avenge the killing of a kinsman was regarded as dishonourable at a time when a person's or group's honour was amongst their most prized possessions (Berman, 1983: 55–6; Miller, 2006). Similar duties were entailed in the close bond that existed, in this period, between a lord and his followers (Whitelock, 1952: 29). One aspect of the relationship between a man and his lord was a duty to avenge the homicide of either by killing the slayer or, as we shall see, obtaining compensation which was high enough to do honour to the man killed.

The motive behind acts of vengeance, then, was usually provided by the dynamics of shame and honour. No doubt, another important concern was to deter attacks upon the group, by establishing a reputation as a group which would not hesitate to exact vengeance upon any who attacked one of its members (Berman, 1983: 55). Indeed, the practice of vengeance probably contributed to the control of wanton violence in a society in which there was no central authority.

Compensation: buying off vengeance

We have suggested that a consequence of private vengeance is that it tends to produce chains of tit-for-tat violence that can go on for years and even generations. These 'blood-feuds' create insecurity, offsetting the degree of social control provided by the fear of vengeance. They also act as an obstacle to the co-operation necessary for economic advancement. Hence, even where a people lacked a strong central authority, there was often significant incentive to settle disputes peacefully by negotiating mutually acceptable compensation (Berman, 1983: 49ff). The strength of this pull towards settlement was influenced by a range of factors. For instance, in Anglo-Saxon Britain, settlement was less common in areas inhabited by the Danes – who had a tendency to regard acceptance of compensation in place of vengeance as unmanly – than it was in other areas (Whitelock, 1952: 44). On the other hand, the Christian Church encouraged settlement as it regarded vengeance (other than divine vengeance) as conflicting with Christian ethics. This became an important factor from the end of the sixth century when the English largely converted to Christianity (ibid.: 42).

Even those not directly caught up in a feud had an interest in peaceful settlement, since the security and well-being of an entire people was to some degree threatened when some of them engaged in a prolonged blood-feud. Hence, members of the surrounding 'society' often brought pressure to bear upon parties with a dispute to settle it peacefully.

The question was how to do this whilst preserving honour (Miller, 2006). One way to avoid vengeance was to settle disputes by payments of compensation to the injured party by those responsible for the injury. But this simply pushes the question back, i.e. the question now becomes: how could compensatory payments ever satisfy honour? If one of your kin is killed, and honour demands that you avenge the killing by taking the life of the killer (or one of the killer's kin) would it not be dishonourable to settle for a payment, e.g. to accept a number of cattle as settlement for the injury? In order to understand how one *might* be able to accept a payment, whilst preserving one's honour, it is crucial to grasp that vengeance itself, far from being a wild and unregulated practice, was itself governed by customary principles of exchange (Miller, 2006).

Pre-state societies had complex systems for valuing lives and body parts (ibid; Whitman, 1995). For example, they might measure the value of a person's life in terms of how many lives of a certain sort would make up for it. A lord might be equal to ten freemen; if the lord was killed, it would be necessary to take the lives of ten freemen to avenge the lord. Or, if one person maimed another by cutting off the person's arm, custom would dictate how much the arm was worth (with the price depending on the status and possibly other characteristics of the maimed person). Because vengeance was governed by a complex exchange system, it already had some of the features of compensation. The rules governing vengeance were like rules specifying how much compensation the injured party could help themselves to (in terms of lives or body parts) for the injury suffered. This made it relatively easy to conceive of offering and accepting something of equal value to what the injured party was entitled to as a way of satisfying the demands of vengeance.

However, as Miller (2006) makes clear, negotiating compensation was an extremely precarious business. To accept too small a payment could lead one to be judged as a person with little or no honour. Those who allowed their right to vengeance to be bought off too cheaply could appear avaricious and/or cowardly. On the other hand, refusing to accept a reasonable offer of compensation, and insisting on exacting vengeance, would make one appear unreasonable and raise questions about one's motives. Then again, some injuries were seen as non-compensable and vengeance was mandatory. Moreover, the rules governing all of this varied from people to people, and would be influenced by the wider values and beliefs of a people.

All of this suggests that, although we tend to talk of 'private vengeance', vengeance and compensation were far from being purely private matters. The practices were governed by customary expectations. Also, members of the society often helped disputing parties to reach an agreement. They could do this in a number of ways. They might, for instance, guarantee the safety of disputing parties whilst they undertook negotiations (Bianchi, 1994). They might also help the parties reach an agreement by reminding parties of the customary amount of compensation for a particular injury. Or they might suggest outcomes which would preserve the honour of both sides of a dispute – enabling each side to go away feeling that they had won (Roberts, 1979: 20–1; Baker, 2002: 4–5).

Some legal historians suggest that, in some societies, such communal intervention became so habitual that parties with a dispute began routinely to take their 'case' to a communal forum (Berman, 1983: 56). As this happened, vengeance came to be seen more and more as an exceptional rather than primary response to injury, to be resorted to only when the process of settlement through negotiated compensation broke down or where the injury is considered so serious as to be redressable only by violent retaliation. This seems to have happened, for instance, in Anglo-Saxon Britain where, according to Pollock and Maitland (1898: 46–7), as settlement through negotiated compensation became more and more usual, and customary scales of compensation became established, the kindred of an injured party became expected first by public opinion and then by public authority not to pursue a feud if proper compensation was forthcoming.

Some general features of pre-criminal law handling of wrong-doing

As we have seen, in the absence of a central authority, a range of models of handling wrong-doing are likely to exist. Which model guides the response to wrong-doing will depend on the context. Wrongs committed within a village circle are likely to be met with what we might call 'community punishment', provided we bear in mind that the term 'punishment' can cover reactions ranging from the mildest rebuke to harsh sanctions such as banishment and death. When it comes to wrongs committed by (or against) strangers, a different model is likely to come into play: vengeance and compensation. It is tempting to see these as forerunners of the institution of criminal law; to see the emergence of criminal law as involving the formalization and institutionalization of these ancient practices. However, it is also important to recognize the differences between these practices and also that the institution of criminal law may have its own independent origins.

The birth of criminal justice

We have suggested, in line with self-help theory (at least in a modified form), that prior to the emergence of criminal law there existed reasonably sophisticated and practical ways of dealing with injurious behaviour. This being so, the emergence of criminal law requires more explanation than we might suppose. We cannot assume that life without criminal law was simply so chaotic and unpredictable that the need for such an institution would be obvious, with the only problem being how to create it. We cannot assume that people would willingly give up their traditional practices in preference for state punishment of what the state defined as criminal conduct. Rather, the historical emergence of criminal law becomes more of a puzzle.

In what follows, we will look a little more closely at this development, focusing upon two broad themes developed by legal historians in accounting for the birth of criminal law. Both see a crucial shift occurring in the eleventh/twelfth centuries. One concerns the fiscal and political needs of the emergent (secular) state. The other focuses upon a quite different set of changes: changes within the social mission of the Christian Church.

Secular criminal justice

If we focus on England for the moment, one impetus for the creation of criminal law was the movement to strengthen royal power following the Norman conquest (Stenton, 1964; McAuley and McCutcheon, 2000: 3). The precise course of increasing Royal involvement in the handling of incidents of wrongful injury seems unclear, as does the precise nature of the complex of motives behind this development. However, the development pattern can be roughly reconstructed with sufficient accuracy for our purpose.

In the Anglo-Saxon era, kings undertook some responsibility for maintaining the peace in their territories, and sometimes sent officials to supervise local assemblies which mediated in cases of conflict (ibid.: 86). This corresponds to the second phase of self-help theory. After the Norman invasion, however, central authorities sought to exercise control on a more regular basis throughout society through delegated officials (ibid.: 86). The Crown's officials increasingly took over the role, previously played by community representatives, of mediating between conflicting parties (Weitekamp, 2003). In the process, the Crown started retaining a portion of the compensation paid by the perpetrator to the injured party, as a payment for helping to bring about a settlement. Driven by its fiscal needs, the Crown gradually increased the proportion of the compensation that it retained, whilst the proportion that went to the injured party correspondingly declined. Eventually the 'penalty' for 'criminal' wrong-doing effectively became a 'fine' payable to the Crown (ibid.).

The representatives of royal authority were, however, in a very different position vis-à-vis the conflicting parties than were community representatives who had previously played this mediating role. Royal authorities had greater power with which to compel conflicting parties to comply with a decision reached in a negotiation session. We can surmise that the Crown's role gradually shifted from helping parties negotiate an agreement amongst themselves to imposing a solution upon the parties, with the threat of force should they refuse to co-operate. Hence, there was a shift from the second to the third phase postulated by self-help theory. It is also likely that, over time, the solution imposed at first was one which took into account the interests of the Crown (e.g. in social peace) – and the wider society whose interests the Crown claimed to protect – as well as the interests of the conflicting parties. Eventually, it seems, the interests of the Crown and society came to dominate over those of the parties to the conflict.

A growing central power clearly gained much – in terms of revenue, capacity to govern, and perceived authority – by taking control of criminal conflicts. It is likely that, recognizing this, it started to insist that criminal cases come before it, and that resort to self-help and private bargaining was increasingly suppressed, i.e. there was a move to the fourth phase stipulated by self-help theory.

The Church

If we focus not just upon Britain but look at developments in Europe more generally, another important development becomes visible. Starting in the eleventh century, a momentous transformation occurred in the position of the Christian Church vis-à-vis society and in the Church's conception of sin.[4] The hub of this transition was the Gregorian Reformation – or, as Berman describes it, the papal revolution – of the eleventh/twelfth centuries. Before this, there was no clear separation of Church and society. Secular rulers were the religious heads of their peoples (Berman, 1983: 63). They appointed bishops and dictated liturgical matters (ibid.):

> The church as an organization was almost wholly integrated with the social, political and economic life of society. It did not stand opposite the political order but within it. Religion was united with politics and economics and law, just as they were united with one another. Ecclesiastical and secular jurisdictions were intermingled (Berman, 1983: 64–5).

As a result of the papal revolution, the Church became a distinct, independent body. It became detached from 'secular' government and claimed superiority over it (ibid.: 83). The Church also became a hierarchical institution. Crucially, it sought with considerable success to exert authority throughout society. According to Berman, it became the first modern state.

The Church regarded itself as having a special mission: the care of souls. In order to fulfil this mission, it regarded it as necessary to reform and regulate social life. The Church therefore claimed the right to make new laws as required by the times. This entailed a radical break with prevailing understandings of law as codified custom. Whereas law had previously been virtually synonymous with custom – and even when written was usually no more than an attempt to record custom – it was now becoming something deliberately created by a professionally staffed, hierarchical bureaucracy for the purpose of reforming society. Concomitantly, the law was increasingly systematized. Within the Church, for the first time, canons – i.e. laws of the Church – were clearly demarcated from theological doctrines, moral exhortations and so on. They were also sorted and arranged in a hierarchy. The product was a new type of law, disembedded from the society in which it was to operate as a regulatory force.

Deeds which contravened these laws had a different meaning to deeds which simply caused injury to others. From the Church's perspective, they were not interpersonal injuries which required vengeance – or extraction of compensation – in order to vindicate the injured party's honour. Rather, they were sins, i.e. conscious disobedience of God's commands (McAuley and McCutcheon, 2000: 4–8). Viewing crime as sin had a number of inter-related, crucial, long-term effects.

First, it pointed towards a restriction of criminal liability to those who deliberately did something wrong, excluding those who caused harm to others through their actions but clearly acted without malevolence or mischievous intent. The principle developed that those who caused harm without any moral fault would be liable to make amends for the harm they caused, but they would not be regarded and handled as criminals.

Second, the concept of crime became imbued with a new moral significance and danger. To commit a crime was not simply to injure another person; it was consciously to disobey divine authority. To commit a crime therefore marked the offender as somebody lacking virtue or at least moral fibre. It was also something dangerous since it invited God's wrath and vengeance; a community which failed to distance itself from the criminal risked being tainted and subject to God's wrath and vengeance.

If we look at these two effects together, we can see that whilst viewing crime from the perspective of sin may have narrowed the scope of 'criminality' (the label of criminality and the consequences of this label now attached only to those who caused injury through some culpable action) it also deepened the significance of that label. Criminality now implied something about the moral and spiritual state of the offender, and the authorities regarded this moral and spiritual state as a matter of their concern. As Raymond Saleilles wrote:

> While previously the law recognized only the injury to the individual or society – that is, the material crime in its direct relation – the ecclesiastical law looked to the soul of the man who had committed the crime. In its own language, its concern was the soul that had sinned, that was to be healed, purified, and regenerated through expiation and punishment. (Saleilles, 1911: 37)

A third effect of viewing crime as sin was that it shifted thinking about the appropriate response to the criminal. Crimes required a response designed to reclaim the malefactor spiritually, to reassert the authority of the sacred law that had been violated, and to demonstrate clearly that the community did not endorse the offender's behaviour but regarded it as odious. Eventually, this new set of objectives of intervention came to predominate over the traditional idea of satisfying the honour of the injured party.

This insistence that crime should be regarded from the viewpoint of sin occurred at a time when the Church's conception of sin was also undergoing a transformation. In this period, the conception of sin itself became increasingly 'legalistic', in the sense that sin became identified more with specific sinful acts rather than with more amorphous states of mind. Sinful conduct thus became more clearly defined and at the same time a new doctrine of penance emerged, specifying precise amounts of penance required to atone and earn forgiveness (it is worth noting that prior to the twelfth century, penance could consist not only of undergoing something painful and purifying – such as fasting – but also of compensating those injured by one's sinful actions and assisting their relatives – see Berman, 1983: 68ff). In this context it became important to assess the precise gravity of each sin, so that the appropriate amount of penance could be determined (Cayley, 1998: 128–9). Moreover, what made sin problematic was not only its effects in the world, but also, and more so, its alienating affect upon the soul of the sinner. Accordingly, in assessing the gravity of a sin, more attention was paid to the desire behind the act (i.e. the crucial question was whether it was inspired by a sinful state of mind) than to its consequences for the victim.

The very 'legality' of this new conception of sin eased the process by which 'crimes' became conceived as sins. Hence, crime became increasingly conceived as problematic, less because of the actual injury caused to others, more because it violated divine law and the Church's authority and damaged the spiritual welfare of the offender. Eventually, the harm actually incurred by the victim would become of secondary concern (though never irrelevant) and the spiritual state of the offender of primary concern. Hence, in assessing the gravity of an offence, less and less attention was paid to the harm emanating from it (e.g. the dishonour it brought to the injured party), while more and more attention was paid to what the offender's mental state was at the time of committing the breach of law. And in order to make amends for crime, it was not sufficient to satisfy the injured party – to do something to restore their sense of injured honour. Rather, it was necessary for the offender to undergo penance. Crime, eventually, became something to be purged by undergoing pain. The Church, as responsible for the care of souls, had a duty to inflict this pain.

Corresponding with these changes, the Church assumed the right to seek out and prosecute crime on its own initiative. As an institution responsible for enforcing God's law and caring for souls, it could not be satisfied with intervening only when complaints were made by those injured though criminal acts. A crime violated the law and damaged the welfare of the offender, and required atonement, regardless of whether the injured party sought intervention. Even if the injured party received compensation, and had its honour satisfied, the deeper damage caused by crime – to the authority of the Church, the well-being of society and the spiritual well-being of the offender – had to be atoned for.

Subsequently, the Church separated itself from secular justice and the secular courts emerged as the predominant institutions for the dispensation of criminal justice in society. However, within the secular courts, the understanding of crime and of what constituted an appropriate response were profoundly shaped by the Church's canon law. The Church's conception of crime as a sinful act to be sought out and atoned for through suffering of the offender constituted one of the most important cultural forms that would shape the secular criminal law (cf. Garland 1990: 193ff; Gorringe, 1996). This was probably the case even in Britain, where ecclesiastical courts were less central to the administration of early criminal justice, although they certainly played a role (Baker, 2002: ch. 8).

Of course, in the hands of secular authorities, this conception of crime and the appropriate response to it became intertwined with more obviously secular concerns such as maintaining peace and protecting society from mischievous or dangerous individuals. But in some ways, the social authority of secular courts was bolstered by their inheritance of functions once dominated by the Christian Church. For instance, secular courts became perceived as neutral bodies standing above society, enforcing a law which itself came from above and had a higher (virtually sacred) status than mere codified convention. The notion that secular justice agencies were the instruments of some earthly and personal force *within* society, and operated to protect material and often partial interests, was veiled by the religious conception of crime and justice bequeathed to secular authorities by the Church.

The development of criminal liability

By the thirteenth century, the institution of criminal law was becoming established and gaining familiarity. It would take many centuries, however, for something reasonably resembling contemporary criminal law to emerge. One of the most important developments was the doctrine of *mens rea* (a guilty mind). As we have seen, the notion that crime was akin to sin created the 'cultural space' within which the notion that crime existed only where injurious behaviour was accompanied by some degree of moral fault could develop. However, it took several centuries for this idea to become embedded in secular criminal law, and the doctrine of *mens rea* was central to this development.

In contemporary criminal law, the meaning of *mens rea* is quite complex (see Chapter 4). Here, a brief and simplified explanation may suffice. A common way of analysing the legal concept of crime is to say that crime has at least two necessary ingredients: *actus reus* (a guilty act) and *mens rea* (a guilty mind). The former concept refers to 'outward' conduct (or conduct accompanied by certain consequences). For example, 'appropriating property belonging to another' is the *actus reus* ingredient of the offence of theft. The latter concept refers to the mental state accompanying the *actus reus*. For example, in order to have the *mens rea* ingredient for theft, the person who appropriates property belonging to another must (i) do so dishonestly and (ii) intend to deprive the other of it permanently. If either of these *mens rea* ingredients is absent, the person is not liable at criminal law (although they still might be liable to return the property or compensate those harmed by their actions at private law).

It is generally assumed that early criminal law did not formally require proof of *mens rea*. If somebody committed what we would now call the *actus reus* of an offence (e.g. took somebody's property) they could be convicted of a crime without any need to prove that they acted dishonestly, or intended to take somebody else's property, or were even being careless when they took somebody else's property. It was only around the sixteenth century that a concept of *mens rea* began to emerge firmly in criminal law. This is generally understood as a sign of moral progress, since it meant that those who did something that outwardly infringed the criminal law, but did so without mischievousness or fault, would no longer be convicted and punished for criminal behaviour. However, the assumption that the emergence of the doctrine of *mens rea* constituted unambiguous moral progress is not accepted by all criminal law scholars.

In some historical accounts of criminal law, the emergence of the concept of *mens rea* is attributed, not to some straightforward awakening of awareness of the injustice of punishing those who outwardly broke the criminal law but lacked fault, but to attempts to address more specific problems encountered as criminal law developed. One was the problem of distinguishing felonies from trespasses. The former were regarded as heinous crimes punishable by forfeiture of property and life or limb; the latter resulted in lesser penalties, such as a fine or corporal punishment (Baker, 2002: 523–5). Increasingly, the presence or absence of fault became one of the main bases for making this distinction. Another concern was to provide a basis for pardoning certain groups of people, such as lunatics and young children, who – as we might now put it – lacked some minimal capacity requirements (McAuley and McCutcheon, 2000: 14–17).

One of the most significant contexts for the emergence of *mens rea* was the attempt to restrict benefit of clergy. Clergymen were historically exempt from worldly punishment and would be handed over to ecclesiastical authorities to be dealt with according to Canon law, where the penalties were generally less severe. But, by the fourteenth and fifteenth centuries, 'benefit of clergy' was regularly being granted to laymen who could read and write, which enabled judges at their discretion to avoid imposing the death penalty on literate men – i.e. men (but not women) who somehow could display some degree of literacy – who had committed what would otherwise be a felony (Baker, 2002: 513–5). In the sixteenth and seventeenth centuries, the secular law was 'reformed' with a view to preventing what was depicted as abuse of benefit of clergy. Distinctions began to appear between crimes committed with and without malice aforethought, with the former becoming 'non-clergyable' (McAuley and McCutcheon, 2000: 18–19). For instance, 'murder' (homicide committed with prior malice) began to be distinguished from 'manslaughter' (homicide without prior malice). According to McAuley and McCutcheon, this constituted a 'mutation of malice aforethought': the emphasis on moral fault as a criterion of criminal responsibility, which previously 'had been used to soften the impact of the regime of absolute liability inherited from the Anglo-Saxon codes', was now re-deployed to ensure that offenders regarded as morally culpable received the secular penalty for their crimes rather than receive benefit of clergy (ibid.).

It was around this period (sixteenth to early seventeenth centuries) that the term *mens rea* began to appear in treatises explaining the criminal law. The concept was used to refer to the 'mental element' that had to accompany the 'material component' for a particular felony to have been committed. The idea that *mens rea* was an essential ingredient of felony served to exclude from felonious liability those who 'outwardly' did something prohibited by criminal law but acted without mischievousness. But, it did not entail the restriction of felonious liability to those who intended to bring about the precise harm with which they were charged. *Mens rea* was often defined quite loosely, to refer to any maliciousness or mischievousness behind the act which resulted in criminal harm. For instance, a person who without lawful justification struck another person intending to hurt but not kill them, but in the process caused their death, was deemed to have the *mens rea* necessary for murder.[5]

Indeed, it should not be assumed that the overall result of the incorporation of the concept of *mens rea* into criminal law was to restrict the scope of criminal liability. In many ways, the function of the concept of *mens rea* was to produce the opposite effect. For instance, in the law of larceny, at the same time as the concept of *mens rea* emerged, the 'conduct element' of the offence started to be interpreted more and more loosely (McAuley and McCutcheon, 2000: 21–6).

Whereas larceny had previously required 'forcible taking' of the goods belong to another, increasingly cases where somebody had acquired goods lawfully and then kept them or even simply interfered with them in an unauthorized way, began to be interpreted as falling within the conduct element of larceny.[6] The concept of *mens rea* then began to be used to distinguish between those who committed 'larcenous conduct' (now widely construed) and were 'as bad as thieves' and those who committed larcenous conduct and were not as bad as thieves. The whole focus of the criminal process shifted significantly away from the outward observable conduct of the person and the consequences of that conduct, towards the mental state of that person and whether their general purpose was mischievous.

Conclusion: gains and losses

Estimating what was gained and lost as a result of the creation and early development of criminal law – in anything other than the most general of terms – is extremely difficult. Perhaps the most we can do is indicate a few pertinent questions and explain why they are so hard to answer.

An obvious question is whether the creation of criminal law resulted in the security which social contract theory suggests was the chief purpose of its creation and, if so, how high a price was paid for this in terms of liberty. Answering such questions is particularly difficult. Just how insecure European or British societies were prior to the emergence of the state and criminal law is a moot point. They were probably much more secure than the Hobbesian state of nature, but how much? And, to the extent that society did become more secure in the period following the emergence of the state and criminal law, how much of this can be attributed to the creation of criminal law would be very hard to ascertain. A useful starting-point for such a historical inquiry might be Elias's (2000 [1939]) *The Civilizing Process,* which argues that the state monopoly of violence was an essential element in a complex and very long-term process of cultural and psychological change that brought about the low levels of interpersonal violence (by historical and comparative standards) experienced in contemporary Europe.[7] Even if Elias's analysis is (very approximately) correct,[8] it must be emphasized that when the power to resolve conflicts by inflicting violence on perpetrators of injury was transferred from private bodies to public authorities, and regulated by law, what occurred was not the elimination of 'penal violence' but its (gradual) monopolization by the state. The state's use of such violence is itself in many societies a source of insecurity. Poorly regulated state violence often coexists with high levels of 'private' violence, as in much of Latin America and Africa (see Green and Ward, 2009). So, even if the institution of criminal law has contributed to long-term processes of pacification in European and some other societies, we cannot assume that such benefits exist wherever the institution has been exported. The kind of comparative and historical research needed even to begin to address such questions is all too rare in the criminological literature (but see Archer and Gartner, 1984).

The question of how much liberty was lost as a result of this process is also difficult to answer. Even if we could assess whether and to what extent people in any particular society were more dominated – less free – following the creation of criminal law, the extent to which the creation of criminal law contributed to this would be hard to establish.

Perhaps we might gain a better impression of what was gained and lost by focusing on the logical implications of the creation of criminal law for individuals affected by the sorts of conduct that would come to be called 'crime'. In theory, victims of crime (and their kin) should have gained a great deal. Those who did not have the power to exact vengeance or obtain compensation from those who injured them would now be able to get some redress. Even those who did have such power would gain, since they would now be relieved of the responsibility of taking vengeance and negotiating compensation – which, as we have seen, is a risky business. However, as we shall see in the next chapter, such benefits did not automatically flow from the creation of criminal law. Rather, victims retained much of the responsibility for bringing cases to criminal justice well into the nineteenth century.

There were also losses for victims. With the creation of state criminal law, victims eventually lost the right to resort to self-help in dealing with those who injured them. With this, at least in Britain (developments in continental Europe were somewhat different), their ability to gain compensation for injuries was eroded. Victims could still seek compensation through action at private law, but the state's punishment of offenders tended to take priority over such private law actions.

For offenders and their kin, the suppression of private vengeance is beneficial in important respects. It protects them from the unpredictable and possible excessive reactions of those they injure. Crucially, it saves them from being economically ruined by having to meet demands for compensation. On the other hand, with the emergence of criminal law, offenders – at least in theory – lost the right to negotiate with those they injured, avoiding penal violence by paying compensation.

Summary

Whilst criminal law might appear to be an inevitable feature of society, it is a human invention. The question of whether we should maintain such an institution is an important one, and one way of addressing it is to look afresh at how and why criminal law was created. Social contract theory is one of the most influential attempts to explain the origins of criminal law. Self-help theory modifies social contract theory in significant respects.

In Europe, prior to the creation of criminal law, what we today call crime was dealt with in various ways. Some 'offences' were met with communal punishments. Others could result in private vengeance, although there was probably always the possibility of 'buying off' vengeance by compensating those injured. Pre-state societies, then, probably functioned tolerably well without criminal law. Criminal law was not therefore an obvious institution, but was the result of specific initiatives by the emergent state and the Christian Church.

One of the most important developments in the early centuries of criminal law was the emergence of the doctrine of *mens rea* – the term itself first began to appear in treatises about criminal law in the sixteenth century. For many, this development constitutes unambiguous moral progress as it ensures that only those at fault for breaking the criminal law receive its condemnation and punishment. Other scholars see this development as arising from efforts to solve particular problems confronting the developing institution, such as the need to eliminate 'abuse' of benefit of clergy. They suggest that the impact of the doctrine of *mens rea* was to expand the scope of criminal law in some ways, rather than being simply to restrict its scope.

The actual impact of the rise of criminal law – on levels of security and liberty and on the plight of victims and offenders – is difficult to estimate. This chapter simply points to some pertinent ways of thinking about this impact.

STUDY QUESTIONS

1. Is the institution of criminal law best understood as something created by the people who are subject to it or as something imposed upon people by external institutions?

2. What implications does social contract theory have for the way criminologists think about 'crime' and 'punishment'?

3. What are the implications of the idea that a significant impetus for the development of criminal law was the state's need to consolidate its power?

4. What role has the Christian Church played in the creation and development of 'crime' and criminal law?

5. How might we account for the emergence of *mens rea* as a vital ingredient of criminal liability?

FURTHER READING

McAuley and McCutcheon's *Criminal Liability* (2000) is one of the few contemporary criminal law textbooks to adopt a significantly historical approach to the subject. The first chapter, a long chapter entitled 'Origins and Development', is a useful starting point. Part IV of J.S. McClelland's *A History of Western Political Thought* (1996) is a good introduction to social contract theory (but it does not deal directly with its implications for understanding criminal law). James Q. Whitman's 'At the Origins of Law and the State: Supervision of Violence, Mutilation of Bodies, or Setting of Prices?' (1995) provides a useful explanation and critique of self-help theory. William Ian Miller's *Eye for an Eye* (2006) is a fascinating account of revenge and justice. Chapter 7 of Howard Zehr's *Changing Lenses* (1990) (entitled 'Community Justice: The Historical Alternative') provides his critical account of the origins of state criminal justice. Harold J. Berman's *Law and Revolution* (1983) contains his theory of the role of the Church in the creation of western legal institutions including criminal law. A useful general introduction to legal history is J.H. Baker's *An Introduction to English Legal History*, 4th ed. (2002). James Fitzjames Stephen's *History of the Criminal Law of England* (1883) is the classic treatment of the history of the institution.

Notes

1   Hobbes' account is contained in his book, *Leviathan*, published in 1651 (page references here are to the 1914 *Everyman* edition). In describing ideas such as Hobbes', it is awkward to try to avoid using the gendered nouns of the original (Part 1 of *Leviathan* is titled 'Of Man'); in what follows we will therefore suspend our usual gender neutrality. McClelland (1996: ch. 11) provides an excellent account of Hobbes' theory. Hobbes was in fact untypical of social contract theorists in that he used the idea to support 'absolute' government, whereas the idea was more commonly used to undermine absolutism.

2   Other social contract theorists differed from Hobbes in their depiction of the state of nature. John Locke, for instance, did not see the pre-contractual state as being quite so bleak and chaotic (McClelland, 1996: ch. 12). Nevertheless, for Locke too, the predictability and security that would arise from a mutual contract to obey laws made by a central authority is advantageous.

3   Our main guide for this section is James Q. Whitman's paper 'At the Origins of Law and the State' (1995). In this paper Whitman provides a brief account of the self-help theory as a prelude to making some important criticisms of it. See also Miller (2006).

4   What follows is drawn mainly from Harold Berman's (1983) study of the formation of the western legal tradition and Cayley's (1998: 123–36) useful summary and drawing together of the ideas of Berman (1983), Bianchi (1994) and Gorringe (1996).

5   This position continues, more or less, to the present day. The *mens rea* of murder in contemporary English law is either an intention to kill a person *or* an intention to cause grievous bodily harm to a person (Ormerod, 2005: 437).

6   This occurred at a time when expanding trade increasingly required that goods be transported or processed by third parties.

7   For historical evidence see Eisner (2001). For comparative statistics see WHO (2002).

8   An important limitation of Elias's work is that he begins the story several centuries too late (see Gillingham, 2002).

3

The Modernization of Criminal Justice

Chapter Contents

OVERVIEW

Chapter 3:

- Describes some features of pre-modern criminal law.

- Outlines different accounts of the modernization of criminal justice.

- Looks at the professionalization of policing and its significance for the scope of criminal law.

- Discusses the expanding scope of criminal law and some key developments in legal doctrine in the nineteenth century.

- Traces the emergence of a concern about habitual offenders in the nineteenth century and the impact of this concern on strategies of legal reform.

KEY TERMS

pre-modern criminal law modernization of criminal law policing public order habitual offenders

Introduction

From its formation until the early nineteenth century, the criminal law was very different from the institution of today. Moreover, by today's standards, pre-nineteenth century criminal law seems backward. At first glance, it looks barbaric, capricious and irrational (Smith, 1998: 2). Accordingly, the transition from 'pre-modern' criminal law (which existed until sometime in the nineteenth century) to 'modern' criminal law (of the sort we have today) was once (and occasionally still is) commonly characterized as 'reform' or 'progress' (ibid.). Since the 1970s – as a result of a lot of historical work focusing on criminal justice administration since 1650 – it has become clear that the transition from pre-modern to modern criminal law was much more complex than can be captured by such notions (Dubber and Farmer, 2007; for a useful review, see B.P. Smith, 2007a). Pre-nineteenth century criminal law was less bloody and more principled and rational than had been supposed. Moreover, the 'reform' of criminal law in the nineteenth century was motivated by complex political and cultural concerns which arose in the context of a rapidly changing society, and is not reducible to some simple awakening of humanitarianism and rationality.

At the same time, it is worth highlighting those aspects of pre-nineteenth century criminal law which still strike us as dreadful and unjust and which make notions of 'progress' seem apt, at least to those not steeped in the historical detail. In what we might call its 'pre-modern' phase, many of those who broke the criminal law were subjected to appalling physical violence. Offenders were regularly killed, often in public and indeed in a carnival atmosphere. Death was the penalty for a wide range of crimes including many that people today regard as fairly trivial. Many of those put to death were children. The methods were sometimes brutal and involved torture, dismemberment and disembowelling. Bodies and parts of bodies were exhibited in public.

It may well be that the use of the death penalty in pre-modern criminal law has been exaggerated, and that many offenders suffered more modest penalties. However, even then, the penalties tended to be based upon the principles of physical violence and public degradation. Whipping, flogging, mutilation and subjection to degrading public exposure were common penalties. Also, from the middle of the seventeenth century, many offenders were transported; a penalty that was preferable to death but often extremely harsh.

Almost as notorious is the seeming arbitrariness of the decision-making process which determined who would suffer such fates. In the absence of regular enforcement of criminal law, many crimes were dealt with informally outside of the legal institution. In some cases, this meant criminal wrong-doers avoiding judicial punishment by compensating those they wronged. In others, it meant deviants from community norms being subjected to humiliating rituals – referred to by historians as 'rough music' – which could be as terrifying and damaging as anything inflicted by the formal system (Thompson, 1991). In the case of the latter, the likelihood of suffering such informal sanctions could depend as much upon one's standing and popularity within the community as upon what one had done.

Those cases which did reach something resembling a formal courtroom were often processed with what seems, by today's standards, to be excessive haste. However, criminal conviction did not automatically result in punishment. Through various devices, such as being granted benefit of clergy, many offenders avoided being sentenced to the law's prescribed punishment for their offence. Also, many of those sentenced to death were pardoned and reprieved. This discretionary use of mercy alleviated the impact of a brutal justice system. However, it may also have resulted in that system being riddled with what, by today's standards, seems to be glaring unfairness. A cynical view of the use of discretion might lead us to conclude that those who were relatively well-regarded or valued within their community often avoided punishment for their misdeeds, whilst unpopular people or strangers tended to suffer the law's full severity. Historical work over the last few decades has qualified such a view considerably, suggesting that the use of pardons was more principled and based upon genuine efforts to reprieve those deemed less blameworthy (see B.P. Smith, 2007a). However, there is still the possibility that those making such judgements were influenced by factors that, from today's perspective, seem extraneous.

From the perspective of the present, some of the 'crimes' targeted by criminal law prior to its modernization also seem strange. Whilst pre-nineteenth century criminal law targeted much that is familiar today (murder, robbery, rape, theft and so on) it also intervened against 'offences' such as witchcraft, fornication and profanation of the Sabbath. It seems as if the criminal law failed to distinguish between reality and fantasy and between behaviour which was a threat to the peace and order of society (which today is regarded as the proper target of penal sanctions) and that which is merely offensive according to conventional morality (cf. Erikson, 1966).

It is hardly surprising, in the light of this, that the emergence of 'modern' criminal law was traditionally characterized as a great humanitarian reform. The story of this reform usually begins in the eighteenth century. Penal reformers – applying the humanitarian and rationalistic principles of the enlightenment to thinking about crime and justice – condemned the barbarity of the penal system and sought to replace it with a system of humane penal sanctions imposed in accordance with rational laws (see Heath, 1963). A central theme in the traditional story of criminal law since the second half of the eighteenth century is that of how the institution has been humanized and rationalized – albeit in fits and starts – in line with the reformers' ideals. For many this process of reform is still far from complete (and, indeed, in many parts of the world is barely underway) and the appropriate stance to adopt towards criminal law today is to celebrate the reforms that have been achieved but to continue to push for further refinement of the ideas of classic reformers and further reform of criminal law in line with these ideas.

This characterization of the modernization of criminal law as a straightforward reform has of course been challenged. In the 1970s, Marxian social historians produced a more complex story in which the 'reform' of criminal law is characterized, less as simple moral progress, more as a changing style of social control which was necessitated by changes in the socio-economic structure and also motivated by changes in the outlook of the dominant social class. On this view, beneath its impulsive cruelty, pre-modern criminal law had a 'hidden' political rationality (see Hay, 1975; cf. Garland, 1990: Chs. 4–5; B. Smith, 2007a). For instance, dramatic displays of the state's power to punish, combined with discretionary granting of mercy to those with a record of showing deference to powerful persons (who could influence such decisions) could be construed as a cunning strategy for controlling the lower orders of a society that lacked the huge bureaucratic apparatus of regulation we have today. As the massive social changes of industrialization and urbanization made this strategy less workable, and also brought new socio-economic classes with different interests and outlooks to the fore, a new strategy of control was designed: one based on regular professionalized surveillance of the lower orders of urban and industrial society and routine sanctioning of deviations from the standards of disciplined behaviour required of these people.

Another renowned challenge to the tendency to characterize the emergence of modern criminal law as a straightforward 'reform' is that of Foucault (1977). In some ways, Foucault's analysis supplements that of Marxian scholars. What it adds is a more detailed and nuanced account of the new 'technologies' through which social power was exercised over the lower classes of urbanized, industrialized society (Garland, 1990: 6–7). Foucault's analysis is of particular interest here in that it suggests that the strategy of eighteenth-century penal reformers – of a new mode of control operating through regular (but relatively gentle) enforcement of clear and published criminal laws – was not the only or even most dominant strategy of control to be instituted in the nineteenth century. Rather, other strategies emerged which did operate partially through the criminal law, but in which the criminal law played a quite different function. Criminal law became a site at which deviants from social norms were subjected to an array of disciplinary techniques – operated by new type of social expert (doctors, psychiatrists, psychologists etc.) – which went against the grain of the juridicalized style of control imagined by many classic penal reformers.

Since the 1970s, a new school of legal historians has in turn challenged many of the shibboleths of the critical social history of criminal law (B. Smith, 2007a). A whole host of densely researched and nuanced studies have suggested that the story of transition from pre-modern to modern criminal law cannot be reduced to any single theme. However, one clear message that can be drawn from this work is that criminal law, whilst it was certainly shaped by and in turn helped to sustain broader power relationships, was also often shaped by a genuine concern to protect otherwise weak victims of predatory behaviour.

This is familiar to criminologists and we do not intend to summarize the full story of the modernization of criminal justice or give a detailed account of the different schools of thought concerning this phenomenon. Rather, our aim is to focus on significant changes that occurred in the scope and operation of criminal law in this transitional period that are crucial to the understanding of the contemporary institution. We start with a short account of some further distinctive features of eighteenth-century criminal law. Then, we look briefly at the movement for reform that emerged in the eighteenth century, i.e. at what is sometimes referred to – after one of its most renowned proponents – as 'the Beccarian strategy' (Cornish and Clark, 1989: 568). We then turn to some important developments in nineteenth-century criminal law. These include: the emergence of professional policing; the expanding scope of criminal law in the nineteenth century as a result of increased criminalization of disorderly and unrespectable behaviour and lifestyles and reduced tolerance of impulsive wrongdoing; and the emergence of a concern with and strategy for controlling a 'criminal class'. We suggest that, overall, what occurred in this period was an expansion of the scope of criminal law, in which the project of repressing malicious conduct was joined by a new project of policing disorderly, impulsive and non-respectable conduct and lifestyles. We conclude by mentioning some of the more important developments that have taken place within the institutional framework of modern criminal law.

Some features of eighteenth-century criminal justice

The first important point to make about criminal law prior to its modernization is that it was not such a central institution within overall patterns of crime control as it is today. By the eighteenth century, the institution had achieved considerable social presence, especially in large towns. However, within what was still a largely rural and agrarian society, it was by no means regarded as the only or even routine way of responding to deviant conduct. Community punishment, in the shape of informal and relatively spontaneous shaming rituals – of the sort depicted and analysed by E. P. Thompson in his classic essay 'Rough Music' (in Thompson, 1991) – continued to occupy a significant place in the overall repertoire of social responses to deviance (see also Braithwaite, 1989). Other forms of 'self-help', such as duelling – which became popular among the upper classes from the late sixteenth century – were also frequently preferred to the state's criminal justice as a way of settling scores (Sharpe, 1984: 96–7).

One of the main reasons for the relatively marginal importance of criminal law in this period was the dearth of public enforcement and prosecution agencies. Prior to 1830 there was little professionalization of policing; as we shall see, policing in England was largely the responsibility of parish constables. Similarly, right up to the last quarter of the nineteenth century, criminal prosecution was largely private in character (but see B. Smith, 2007b). For most crimes, the actual victims had to initiate and manage the prosecution process – either individually or though membership of prosecution societies – in order to obtain criminal justice from the state. Overall, the criminal law depended a lot more upon private initiative than it does today. The chances of an offender being brought to state criminal justice still depended significantly on the willingness and capacity of the victim to pursue the matter at considerable personal cost through the criminal justice system. No doubt, many victims opted simply to 'lump it' while others came to some form of private negotiated settlement with the offender (probably, on occasion, using the threat of prosecution as leverage to obtain a favourable deal). Resort to criminal law was a relatively unusual step:

> Taking a criminal grievance to court was often the ultimate step in a quarrel which had become either too important or too difficult for the parties to settle in any other way ...
>
> Only those who were desperate or determined – and solvent – could face the uncertain outcome and certain expense which a court action entailed. (Lenman and Parker, 1980: 19)

For those who were prosecuted, the trial process tended to be quite swift. In the eighteenth century, there was relatively little lawyerly involvement in criminal trials and many courts got through 10–15 cases a day (Cornish and Clark, 1989: 562). Conviction was frequently achieved through the evidence of accomplices who were granted immunity from prosecution in return (ibid.: 561–5).

The range of punishments that could be imposed on those convicted was quite limited (see Sharpe, 1990: Ch. 2). In addition to the death penalty, transportation to colonies was a major punishment for much of the eighteenth century (as well as the first half of the nineteenth century) and many minor offences were met with corporal punishment (ibid.: Chs. 2–3). There was also increasing use of imprisonment as a punishment – in prisons and hulks – which grew in significance in the period between the cessation of transportation to America (1776) and the start of transportation to Australia (1787).

The movement for reform

Following a period of population growth, European and North American society was transformed in the nineteenth century by the processes of rapid industrialization and urbanization (Perkin, 1969 is a classic account). These processes gave rise to intense concerns about criminal, unruly and 'sinful' behaviour. As a result of these developments, the influence of traditional agents of social control – the family, the church and the community – had declined. At the same time, the boundaries of acceptable conduct were changing. In particular, more disciplined behaviour and lifestyles were required of industrial workers and dwellers in large towns and cities. So, at a time when stronger mechanisms for controlling conduct were deemed necessary, the existing mechanisms were destabilized.

In this context, those concerned with social control looked towards the state and its criminal justice system to provide it directly. As a result, criminal justice became increasingly regarded as a key mechanism of social control (Rothman, 1971: 57–62). In order to perform this function, it had to be radically transformed. The brutal and spectacular but sporadic interventions of pre-nineteenth-century criminal justice had to be replaced with more gentle and mundane, but more regular, interventions into anti-social behaviour (Foucault, 1977). This entailed the creation of professional police forces (Reiner, 2000) and fundamental reforms in the nature of criminal law.

The case for reform, and the principles which should underlie a reformed criminal law, had in fact been pushed in the eighteenth century by countless reformers (Heath, 1963). Traditional criminal justice was criticized for its inhumanity, heavy-handedness and capriciousness. Major concerns of this classic critique of traditional criminal justice were to reduce unnecessary human suffering and to liberate individuals by reforming an institution which not only subjected those suspected of crime to torture and excessive and barbarous punishments, but did so in such an arbitrary way that many law-abiding individuals lived in fear of it. But, as Foucault (1977: 78–82) among others has pointed out, this concern meshed well with the concern to make criminal law less costly and more effective as a form of crime control. The arbitrariness and cruelty of traditional criminal justice were not only inhumane and an impediment to individual liberty, they were also inconsistent with effective crime prevention and efficient use of the 'human resources' required to produce goods.

Practices which classic reformers found particularly repugnant were the torture of those suspected of crime and the subjection of convicted criminals to public mutilation and killing. Part of the intention of these practices was to strike fear into the hearts of those contemplating crime. Reformers argued, however, that these practices were not only cruel but also ineffective because the law was so vague, its procedures so fickle and its working so mysterious that the link between crime and punishment was too uncertain. Accordingly, they argued for a system of criminal justice which was much more transparent, systematic and regular and at the same time more humane. Their underlying idea was that if people contemplating crime knew that there was a strong likelihood that they would be apprehended and punished they would be deterred from committing it. Criminal justice did not need to be terrifying in order to prevent crime; consistency and certainty of punishment were far more effective.

This had profound implications for the criminal law. According to the reformers, the behaviour that constituted a crime should be described in ordinary and perfectly clear language, as must the precise penalty for each crime. These criminal laws then needed to be published so that every member of society knew exactly what the criminal law prohibited them from doing and what the penalties were for doing what was prohibited. These published laws needed to be enforced systematically by a professional police force. The criminal procedure needed to be strict and focussed only on the question of whether an accused person committed a specific crime. Those who committed crime should not be given reasons for hoping that they might avoid being punished because of some extraneous factor.

Efforts to reform criminal law in line with these ideas were not completely successful. Partly, this was because old traditions died hard and could not be completely eradicated. But in addition, as we shall see, the criminal justice system was influenced, from the second half of the nineteenth century onwards, by quite different strategies of control. Nevertheless, the principles of classic penal reformers had a huge impact on the development of criminal law from the early nineteenth century onwards. Their effects are felt throughout every aspect of criminal justice. Crucially, they became one of the main foundations for critical engagement with the actual law and they continue to be so today.

The professionalization of policing

Probably the most significant development affecting nineteenth-century criminal law was the emergence of a new style of policing (Godfrey and Lawrence, 2005: Ch. 2). The parish constable system – in which policing was a non-specialist task undertaken by ordinary citizens sometimes supported by paid watchmen and deputies – gave way throughout the nineteenth century to policing by specialized, publicly-funded professional police forces. These police forces were organized and featured 'uniformed officers, a hierarchy of ranks, and a pattern of operation based on patrol and prevention' (ibid.: 9).

In their accounts of these changes, traditional 'police historians' such as Charles Reith suggested that the parish constable system, which had been fairly effective until the end of the seventeenth century, was unable to cope with the rising rates of crime and mob disorder that followed urbanization and industrialization (Reith, 1948; see also Critchley, 1967). These social changes created novel and complex problems of crime and disorder which had not previously existed. They created poverty and poor living conditions, which led directly to an increase in crime as people who might previously have been honest turned to crime in order to live. Urbanization also created conditions in which committing crime was easier and catching criminals more difficult. The dark streets, with their hidden corners and alleyways, were ideal places for robbery, rape and murder. Industrialization also resulted in an increase in disorder and riot, as people began to express grievances about conditions in factories, food prices and so on.

Efforts to deal with these new problems through a system of severe punishment, in which people could be put to death for committing even relatively minor thefts, were unsuccessful and resulted in injustice, according to traditional police historians. Prosperous professional criminals tended to be successful in their efforts to avoid conviction and punishment, whilst every week wagon loads of young and poorer offenders were executed for petty thefts which were often first offences (Reith, 1948). Accordingly, from the late eighteenth century onwards, reformers attempted to shift the emphasis of crime control from fearsome punishment to systematic policing. To this end, they aimed at and eventually succeeded in establishing new professional police forces, first in London and then throughout the country.

According to police historians, this change in policing style succeeded in controlling crime and disorder, turning Britain into a relatively law-abiding and orderly society. A large part of this success is attributed to the fact that, although they abandoned the parish constable system, the reformers did not create a 'continental' style of policing, in which the state used agents recruited from outside of communities to enforce laws within communities, often in a cruel and tyrannical manner. Rather, in Britain, police reformers maintained continuity with the long tradition of communal self-policing or 'policing by the people' that the parish constable system represented. For instance, the 'new police' were recruited from people of the same class and background as those they would police. They were also not direct agents of the central government, but were answerable to local authorities. A policy of minimal force, with the police armed only with wooden truncheons and relying heavily upon the co-operation of the people who were policed, was also adopted.

The professionalization of policing was of huge significance for the development of public consciousness of criminal law. Prior to professionalization, the criminal law was a generally distant (but occasionally spectacularly present) and inaccessible institution. With the birth of the 'new police', criminal law was brought into people's neighbourhoods. It became, at least potentially, accessible and applicable to all regardless of wealth or status. At the same time, if the new system was indeed continuous with the tradition of communal self-policing, the new police would have helped in constructing the criminal law as something which belonged to the mass of people and was theirs to enforce, rather than as something which was imposed upon the people from outside, over which they had little control and in which they had little stake.

In the 1970s, 'revisionist historians' began to challenge conventional accounts of the nineteenth-century transition in policing (Newburn, 2007: 28–9; Reiner, 2000). They contested a whole range of assumptions and claims found in more conventional police histories, especially concerning the assumption that the new police continued a long tradition of communal policing or policing by consent. Of particular importance here is that they sought to show that the 'new police' did not simply carry out the task of crime control more efficiently; they also performed other functions which had little to do with the control of criminality as traditionally conceived. Storch (1976), for instance, argued that the new police were preoccupied with the task of disciplining the working class and other lower orders of industrial-urban society (cf. Philips, 1983). They sought to purge society of behaviour that was considered unrespectable, such as drunkenness, vagrancy, prostitution, begging, disorderly behaviour by juveniles and Sunday trading. And, they sought to monitor and control behaviour that was not deviant but actually customary – such as gambling, drinking, unlicensed street trading and the holding of popular fetes – but considered problematic from the perspective of the new standards of discipline required of the urban working class.

It would be a mistake, however, to characterize this by saying that the new police went beyond enforcing the criminal law by carrying out such disciplinary work. Rather, as we shall see, in performing these disciplinary tasks, the new police were acting consistently with the new direction which criminal law itself was taking in the nineteenth century.

The expanding scope of criminal law

Relatively little has been written about the general development of substantive criminal law in the nineteenth century – although there are signs of this changing (Smith, 1998; B. Smith, 2007a). The repeal of the 'bloody penal code' of the eighteenth century has been the subject of much discussion, but we know less about positive developments in the substantive law of crime (even accepting that the distinction between procedure and substance is problematic in this context – Stuntz, 1997). Writing in 1997, Farmer went so far as to state:

> We know very little about the history of criminal law in the nineteenth century. … the substantive law has only a shadowy presence in the histories of the nineteenth century. (Farmer, 1997: 102)

Focusing on Scots law, Farmer made some efforts to redress this, but it is still difficult to put together a general account of how the substantive law changed in this period.

This is the case even though there was a huge growth in the use of criminal law in the first half of the nineteenth century. For instance, Wiener (1990: 50) points out that 'numbers prosecuted in assizes and quarter sessions rose from 4,605 in 1805 to 31,309 by 1842'. This expansion would accelerate in the second half of the nineteenth century. What is of fundamental importance is that such expansion does not seem to have been due mainly to more effective police interventions into 'traditional' crimes such as homicide, rape, theft and arson. Numbers convicted of such crimes grew but not dramatically. Rather, the expansion of criminal law seems to be due more to the bringing of new types of behaviour within the ambit of criminal regulation. Specifically, what the law began to target in this period were things like minor assaults, disorderly conduct, breaches of the peace, being drunk and incapable, prostitution, begging and palmistry. What tied all of these together was that they involved ways of life that were perceived as bothersome from the perspective of Victorian visions of discipline and respectability (Farmer, 1997: Ch. 4).

To some extent these offences were created by statutes such as the Vagrancy Act 1824. The sorts of offences created by this legislation included becoming chargeable to the parish as a result of wilful neglect to work, wandering to hawk goods without a pedlar's licence, begging in a public place or encouraging a child to do so, prostitution, refusing to work when in receipt of poor relief, running away and leaving one's spouse chargeable to the parish, trying to procure alms by exposing wounds or deformities, gaming in an open and public place, and telling fortunes (Turner, 1962: 433–7). The offences created by this legislation were often defined very loosely. For instance, under the Vagrancy Act a suspected person or reputed thief who was found loitering in a street or public place with intent to commit a felony was guilty of an offence; but it was not necessary to prove any particular acts showing the person had such intent – rather it could be inferred from the circumstances or the character of the suspect (ibid.: 435). Such provisions led the Vagrancy Act to be denounced by some nineteenth-century commentators as 'the most unconstitutional law yet lingering on the statute book' (see ibid.: 433). However, a large part of the expansion of the scope of criminal law was due, not to such legislation, but to increasing and increasingly flexible use of the old common law charge of 'breach of the peace'. Whilst this charge was previously of little significance, in the nineteenth century it was exploited to prosecute and convict people for all sorts of conduct and lifestyles that constituted an affront to Victorian norms of order, decorum and respectability (Farmer, 1997: Ch. 4).

The definition of such crimes in practice, as well as the process for trying them, departed significantly from that for 'traditional' crimes. In order to process large numbers of cases – of public drunkenness, begging, disorderly conduct and the like – without creating expensive new courts, a speedier and smoother way of trying offenders was needed. The process was therefore a 'stripped-down' summary one in which important attributes of the adversarial trial were absent. There was little lawyerly involvement, little concern for evidential rules and so on. Also, there was little concern with whether offenders had *mens rea*. Rather, it was usually sufficient to prove conduct, perhaps with some evidence of dissolute character. Indeed, as we have seen in the case of 'loitering with intent to commit a felony', in many cases the offence was expressed in 'passive' terms, so that it was not even necessary to prove any particular conduct. For many offences it was sufficient to record that the offenders were found in a particular state such as 'drunk and incapable' or 'in suspicious circumstances and unable to prove that they were earning an honest living' (ibid.).

This expansion of the scope of criminal law was therefore not only a quantitative one; it marked a qualitative shift in the 'targets' of criminal law. In the nineteenth century, criminal law became more than an instrument for dealing with predatory behaviour that threatened fundamental social values such as human life and property (Farmer, 1997: 200). It also became one mechanism for dealing with what was considered to be a major social problem in the nineteenth century: the conduct and lifestyles of those in the lower orders of society who had not been integrated in the disciplined, respectable and orderly working class. Their conduct and way of living, whilst it did not directly threaten life and property, was regarded as a grave danger to public order and respectability. In dealing with this social problem, the criminal law departed significantly from the principles of 'classical jurisprudence' that emerged from the eighteenth-century movement for reform. However, even more radical departures would follow once it became clear that tackling this social problem meant dealing not with occasional offenders but with those whose whole way of life was at odds with the social norms which criminal law was now charged with upholding.

Expanding liability for 'traditional' offences

We have suggested that the expansion of criminal law in the nineteenth century was due mainly to the increasing use of the machinery of criminal law to deal with conduct which threatened the ideal of an ordered and respectable society. However, the reach of criminal law was also expanded as a result of people being prosecuted and convicted of 'traditional' offences, where their conduct – although 'shady' – would previously have been regarded as beyond the reach of criminal law. There were various aspects to this, of which we will briefly mention three.

First, legislation increasingly defined, and judges increasingly interpreted, serious crimes such as larceny and murder in broader terms, so that conduct which would previously have fallen outside the definitions of such offences now fell within them. For instance, keeping lost property that one had found without making a reasonable effort to find the owner and making no effort to return an overpayment became defined as larcenous in the nineteenth century (Wiener, 1990: 67–8). Also, as we shall see in Chapter 5, practices such as survival cannibalism – which were common at sea and in frontier territory – which many people regarded as lawful provided they were carried out in accordance with long-settled customs, were increasingly deemed to amount to murder (Simpson, 1984).

Second, the nineteenth century witnessed the emergence of criminal liability for attempting to commit a crime (Fletcher, 1998: 171). As Fletcher points out, this was highly significant in that it created a whole new target for criminal law. Previously, the law intervened only once an offence was committed; securing oneself from crime was a person's own responsibility. The emergence of a concern to deal with attempted crime signified a growing concern to prevent harmful conduct before it occurred. And, crucially, the logic of policing now changed. Instead of reacting to crimes that had been committed, the criminalization of attempts required – or at least encouraged – proactive surveillance of those with anti-social tendencies. As Fletcher suggests, this shifts the whole focus of criminal law: from a concern mainly with criminal *acts* (events which have taken place), it now became concerned with 'criminal' *characters*, i.e. people with a propensity to commit crime.

Third, the courts became increasingly reluctant to recognize various 'excuses' which might previously have been regarded as rendering people non-liable for criminal acts they had committed or as mitigating their guilt. One example of this is drunkenness, which previously had often been regarded as a factor which excused or mitigated some criminal deeds. In the nineteenth century, such tolerance for drunkenness greatly diminished (Wiener, 1990: 78–9). With the rise of a temperance movement and the increasing tendency to regard drunkenness as a major cause of crime, drunkenness increasingly became seen as an aggravating rather than a mitigating factor – something that should result in a more severe punishment rather than being deemed an excuse (cf. Norrie, 2001: Ch. 6).

The problem of habitual offenders and the repositioning of criminal justice

From the middle of the nineteenth century a new problem surfaced in the discourse of crime and criminal justice: the problem of habitual criminals. These were people who were repeatedly convicted of criminal offences and who seemed, to those who discussed them, to 'pursue crime as a calling' rather than simply being 'led astray by casual temptation, or by temporary indulgence of the passions' (Matthew Davenport Hill, uttered in 1839, quoted in Radzinowicz and Hood: 1990: 74). Proposals to tackle this problem emerged which had a profound impact on thinking about criminal law, its underlying assumptions, and its place in broader strategies of crime control (Radzinowicz and Hood, 1990: 73–84 and Ch. 8).

The problem of habitual criminals was, in itself, as much a product of various changes that had taken place in the scope and administration of criminal law as it was of changing social conditions which made a 'criminal calling' a reasonable one for many people. A society which killed or transported a large proportion of its offenders was less likely to suffer from problems of repeat offending than one which only temporarily excluded offenders from society by means of imprisonment, especially short-term imprisonment. A society which used criminal law to repress all sorts of 'minor illegalities' – many involving behaviour that was customary rather than deviant within certain 'communities' – would be particularly prone to suffering the problem of recidivism. However, even if repeat offending existed, other conditions were necessary before it could be *recognized* as a social problem. It required efficient ways of recording arrests and criminal convictions, organizing this information and making it available to various agencies so that a person could be firmly identified as a repeat offender (Radzinowicz and Hood,

1990: 261ff). Hence, the category of habitual offenders is also, in part, a product of bureaucratic and technical developments within criminal justice.

Estimates of the number of habitual offenders in the population, and of the proportion of the crimes committed that were attributable to them, varied significantly and were hotly debated. What does seem to have been widely accepted was that a significant proportion of crimes (estimates were usually between 50 and 80 per cent) were committed by habitual criminals. This had a profound impact upon thinking about the problem of controlling crime. Whereas previously the problem had been conceived as one of deterring 'normal' people who might occasionally be tempted to commit crime, it now became conceived as requiring the control of a much smaller (but still sizeable) group of people who were abnormal in that for them crime was a way of life. The methods of deterring the population more generally, *viz.* consistent punishment of offences with punishment proportionate to the gravity of the offence, did not seem to influence the conduct of these habitual offenders. The very fact that they repeatedly committed crime, despite being subjected again and again to judicial punishment, was interpreted as evidence that they were beyond the influence of such measures. New methods of control were increasingly deemed necessary for this group. A great deal of penal policy debate from the middle of the nineteenth century was concerned with the best approach to take.

An assumption which many participants in the debate found hard to resist was that habitual criminals must be, in some sense other than the mere fact of their habitual offending, different from other people – 'a separate and foreign social species' (Radzinowicz and Hood, 1990: 231). The fact that repeated punishment did not seem to discourage them from committing crime suggested to some that habitual offenders must lack the mental capacity to control their behaviour. Some toyed with ideas, popular on the continent but less influential in England, that habitual offenders might suffer from some inborn moral idiocy (ibid.: 5–6). Others laid more stress on the fact that habitual offenders were products of immoral environments which – whilst they remained within them – exerted a force over their will much stronger than that of the threat of punishment (Johnstone, 1996). But whatever the explanation, the notion that the habitual offender had a weak or damaged *will*, which rendered him or her beyond the influence of ordinary judicial punishment, became an underlying assumption in debates about how to deal with them.

The conclusion invariably drawn from this was that, for the control of habitual offenders, ordinary judicial punishment was not enough. Something else had to be done to restore their damaged will and/or to make society safe from them whilst they remained unreformed. Various solutions to the problem of incapacitating the habitual criminal were proposed (Radzinowicz and Hood, 1990: Ch. 8).

One set of proposals, advocated for habitual drunken offenders but representative of a wider way of thinking, drew upon environmentalist explanations but gave these an individualist twist (Johnstone, 1996). It tended to be suggested that living in an immoral environment damaged the will of people, making them unable to control their behaviour and live honest and respectable lives. In the long term, these immoral environments might be eradicated. In the meantime, the proposed solution to habitual offending was to remove individuals who had demonstrated a potential for habitual offending from these environments.

Those who were reformable (and some were very optimistic about the possibility of reform, even of fairly hardened adult habitual offenders) needed to be sent to a reformatory institution. There they would live in a moral environment for a period long enough to restore their powers of will or control. These institutions should be far away from the normal dwelling place of the habitual offender. They were to be light and clean – in contrast to the usual dark and squalid dwellings of habitual offenders. In these institutions, habitual offenders would live, eat and work according to a regular timetable and hence learn the value of routine, order and industriousness. They might also be subjected to the good moral influence of carefully chosen visitors, moral lectures and so on. They needed to stay in these institutions for long enough to break up their old habits and to instil and cultivate a capacity for self-control. Most agreed that reform would take a lot longer than the length of the standard prison sentence for the types of nuisance crime which many habitual offenders committed, which tended to be between two weeks and three months.

What is important to note about proposals such as this is that they tended to be attached to the criminal law. In particular, although many proponents of these schemes likened habitual offenders to lunatics and referred to them using medical terms such as 'moral imbecile' (or, in the case of habitual drunken offenders, 'inebriates') the proposed process for classifying somebody as an habitual offender was not usually one of medical diagnosis and civil commitment. Rather, in most proposals it was the number or rate of criminal convictions that mattered. So, for instance, somebody convicted of three offences of public drunkenness or related offences within a 12 month period would be classified as an 'habitual drunken offender' (see Johnstone, 1996). Then, instead of simply being given the normal sentence for their third offence (which might a five shilling fine or a week in prison), they would be sentenced, in the criminal court, to detention in a reformatory for a period of six to 12 months. This sentence was not decided or justified by the classical principle of punishment proportionate to the crime. Rather, it was to be determined by reference to a different criterion: their 'treatment' needs, i.e. what it would take to repair the mental damage (such as a disordered will) that led to them behaving as they did.

Actual experiments with reformatory treatment were fairly short-lived. By the end of the nineteenth century, with the exception of those aimed at young offenders, most had ended. Yet, despite its failure as a social policy, the reformatory experiment had an important impact upon the development of criminal law. In particular, it disturbed the assumption that sentencing was to be based upon an assessment of the seriousness of the crime for which the person had been convicted. It introduced the idea that sentencing might be forward-looking and 'individualized'.[1] Within the criminal court, an assessment might be made of what the individual offenders needed to have done to them in order to change their habits and attitudes and to protect society from them. This assessment was to be based, not simply upon their specific offence, but upon a wider assessment which would take into account factors such as the environment they came from, the extent to which they had been damaged by that environment, the chances of their developing new habits and attitudes if subjected to the right influences, the sorts of treatment they might respond to, and so on. The judge or magistrate would make the decision. But, it reflected not a narrow legal judgement but also a broader social and psychological assessment. In making the decisions, the court's frame of reference would not be the narrow legal ones of what crime they had committed, whether there were any aggravating or mitigating circumstances, and the range of penalties available for that offence. Rather, the court would be advised by various experts drawing upon clinical expertise obtained in various fields and on related knowledge produced by the human and social sciences. The criminal law, accordingly, became infiltrated with new experts, new types of knowledge, new ways of assessing offenders. Criminal conviction itself took on a new significance as one indication of the nature of and prognosis for the person before the court.

In order to grasp the significance of this, it is useful to think of criminal law in the context of wider strategies for controlling troublesome conduct. We suggested earlier that, prior to the nineteenth century, criminal law was fairly marginal within the overall field of practices employed within society to deal with troublesome conduct. In the eighteenth century, a reform movement emerged which proposed that a reformed criminal law play a much more central role in the control of crime. It would do this by adopting a particular style of control: clear rules prohibiting well-defined types of unwanted behaviour and specifying penalties for those convicted of doing what was prohibited were to be published and regularly and consistently enforced by a professionalized justice machine. In the nineteenth century, criminal law started to play a central role in the society's overall set of processes for controlling crime. However, at the same time, other modes of control emerged. These targeted specific lifestyles rather than isolated deviant acts, and proposed intensive forms of institutional treatment to alter the habits, attitudes and even personalities of those who adhered to such lifestyles. Importantly, though, rather than displacing criminal law, these new forms of control operated through the criminal law. In the process, they transformed the nature of the institution turning it into something very different from what had been imagined by the classic movement for reform.

Developments within modern criminal law

There were many other important developments in the nineteenth century and since that would need to be dealt with at length in a more comprehensive treatment of the actual development of modern criminal law. Here, there is space merely to mention some of the most important of these.

The ending of public execution, the restriction of the death penalty in practice to murder (although 'in the books' it was retained for some other offences) and its eventual abolition, as well as the restriction and eventual abolition of corporal punishment in criminal law, were extremely important and did much to alter the meaning of criminal legal sanctions. The emergence of fines and imprisonment as the main punishments for most criminal offences and the ongoing search for alternatives to imprisonment have set the context for penal policy and debate since the nineteenth century. The creation of public prosecutors, the introduction of limited rights of appeal and the transformation of criminal procedure in the nineteenth century were amongst the most important developments (Chapter 7 focuses on developments in criminal procedure and evidence).

The nineteenth century also saw a huge growth in criminal legislation – legislation which differed fundamentally in style and sophistication from that of the bloody penal code of the eighteenth century. Also important was the creation of masses of 'minor offences' by local by-laws. There were a number of attempts to create a codified criminal law in the nineteenth century, which did not succeed in England. However, efforts to consolidate the law in particular areas were more successful. The nineteenth century saw the creation of the huge Offences Against the Person Act, 1861 – which is still a major source of law in this area. The consolidation of the law of theft would have to wait another century; the Theft Act 1968 laid down the structure for the contemporary law of theft.

There were also significant developments within legal doctrine concerning responsibility. Indeed, a distinctive feature of the criminal law which emerged in the nineteenth century and developed significantly only in the twentieth century is the attempt to develop and elaborate general principles of criminal liability, i.e. principles which address the questions of when it is appropriate or fair in general to hold an individual responsible for criminal conduct. The so-called 'general part of the criminal law' is concerned with matters such as what constitutes voluntary conduct for the purpose of criminal law, what sorts of mental states must be proved in order for there to be criminal liability, what sort of excuses and justifications should the law recognize as undermining the case for criminal liability and how should the scope of general defences (such as self-defence, duress, mistake and above all insanity) be defined, and what degree of participation in a criminal event is sufficient to hold one responsible for an offence relating to it.

Such questions were virtually absent from William Blackstone's *Commentaries on the Laws of England*, which was published in the 1760s and contained perhaps the first sustained attempt to present the criminal law as a rational and systematic entity (Lacey, 2001). They were present, but not central, in James Fitzjames Stephens' *History of Criminal Law*, published in 1883 – which contained a significant discussion of the implications of insanity for criminal responsibility (ibid.). By the time of Glanville Williams' hugely influential *Criminal Law: the General Part*, published in 1953, such questions were centre stage in criminal law texts (although it is important to note that this was intended originally as one part of a four-volume work rather than the self-standing text it became). This hugely important development was no doubt bound up with the development of sophisticated reporting of judicial opinions in criminal law appeal cases and with emergence of criminal law as an academic subject taught at universities; as Lacey points out, the development was more evident in legal treatises than in the actual criminal law (Lacey, 2001: 358). In Chapters 4 and 5 we address the issue of criminal responsibility in some detail.

A rather different development – the significance of which has been much less registered in contemporary criminal law texts – is the huge growth of offences of strict and vicarious liability since the nineteenth century (Leigh, 1982). The emergence of this form of liability was closely connected to the growing use of criminal law to enforce 'government-imposed standards relating to food and drugs, factories legislation and traffic offences' (ibid.). We look at this development in more detail in the context of our discussion of white-collar and corporate crime in Chapter 6.

Conclusion

At the beginning of the twentieth century, the institution of criminal law was firmly established as a central and familiar landmark on the social and cultural landscape of English society. It was regarded as the obvious centre of society's response to and attempts to control 'traditional' criminal behaviour. Moreover, it was a major instrument of governmental efforts to control a whole range of conducts and lifestyle that were deemed inconsistent with prevailing notions of public order, and indeed an instrument for protection of public welfare from the danger represented by food and drug production and sale, industrial processes, and new mechanical modes of transport.

Criminal law would certainly be developed and refined throughout the twentieth century. But, for the most part, these developments took place within the institutional framework which had been established by the start of that century. So, somebody at the end of the nineteenth century looking back at the criminal law at the beginning of that century, would have seen much that was strange and – to their eyes – barbaric and irrational. As one commentator put it in a lecture, delivered in 1900, discussing 'changes in criminal law and procedure since 1800':

> To go back to the beginning of the century is to go back, so far as the Criminal Law is concerned, to an age of barbarism. (Sir Harry Bodkin Poland, 1901: 43)

However, somebody at the end of the twentieth century, carrying out a similar exercise, would have seen much that was familiar. They would certainly have lots of changes to note – but changes that took place largely within the same institutional framework.

Some contemporary commentators suggest that that institutional framework may now be in crisis (cf. Garland, 1990: Ch. 1). Developments such as restorative justice and the rise of 'penal populism' are sometimes interpreted as signs of a desire to step outside the institutional framework of criminal law – to address the problem of crime from within a radically different political and moral paradigm. The emergence of the 'new penology' is also seen as a trigger for the emergence of 'a new criminal law' (Feeley and Simon, 1994). Whether this is the case, and if so what its implications are, requires a firm understanding of the historical development and character of the institution of criminal law.

Summary

By today's standards, pre-nineteenth century criminal law seems barbaric and irrational. Many of those who broke the criminal law were subjected to appalling physical violence and degradation.

As European and North American society was transformed in the nineteenth century, a new strategy of control emerged. It involved clear criminal laws, systematically enforced by professionalized police, prosecution agencies and judges.

The actual development of criminal law was not, however, a simple realization of this 'Beccarian strategy'. In the nineteenth century the scope of criminal law expanded vastly as it was used to repress a variety of disorderly and unrespectable behaviour. 'Traditional' offences such as larceny were interpreted more broadly, attempts were criminalized and there was less tolerance of excuses such as drunkenness. Those who frequently broke the criminal law were assessed by experts who prescribed new forms of penal intervention which were conceived as therapeutic rather than merely punitive and which were not constrained by principles of proportionate punishment. Rather than de-centring the criminal law, these new forms of intervention tended to operate through it – in the process transforming its nature.

STUDY QUESTIONS

- To what extent is it appropriate to describe the modernization of criminal law as a 'great humanitarian reform'?

- How did the social functions of criminal law change in the nineteenth century? What sorts of values does the criminal law now protect?

- What role does criminal law play in the penal-disciplinary complex assembled since the nineteenth century?

- How does an historical understanding of criminal law help us think about key issues in contemporary criminology, such as the rise of restorative justice, 'penal populism' and the 'new penology'?

FURTHER READING

Two landmark works which transformed the history of criminal law are Hay et al.'s *Albion's Fatal Tree* (1975) and Foucault's *Discipline and Punish* (1977). Chapter 8 of Cornish and Clark's *Law and Society in England 1750–1950* (1989) is still a useful place to start reading about the 'great transformation' of criminal law in this period. For something a bit longer and more up-to-date, Godfrey and Lawrence's *Crime and Justice 1750–1950* (2005) is useful and provides good guidance to more specialist literature; V.A.C. Gattrell's *The Hanging Tree: Execution and the English People 1770–1868* (1994) is a superb in-depth study. Smith's *Lawyers, Legislators and Theorists* (1998) is distinctive in focussing upon developments in substantive criminal law between 1800 and 1957. It needs to be supplemented, however, by something more contextual and critical; Norrie's *Crime, Reason and History* (2001) is well worth reading in this context. Although focussing on Scots law, Farmer's *Criminal Law, Tradition and Legal Order* (1997) is an essential study of the development of criminal law since the middle of the eighteenth century. Wiener's *Reconstructing the Criminal: Culture, Law and Policy in England, 1830–1914* (1990) is a fascinating study of the relationship between developments in criminal law and broader intellectual and cultural transformations. Developments in thinking about habitual offenders and the implications of these developments for criminal law are studied in Johnstone's *Medical Concepts and Penal Policy* (1996). Dubber and Farmer's *Modern Histories of Crime and Punishment* (2007) is a recent collection of interesting essays regarding criminal law historically.

Note

1   Deterrent sentencing is also forward-looking, but in a different sense.

4

Law, Criminology and Responsibility

Chapter Contents

OVERVIEW

Chapter 4:

- Discusses the importance attached to free choice in criminal law.

- Explains the most important legal doctrines about responsibility in English law (other than those specific to homicide, which are discussed in Chapter 5).

- Considers a number of criticisms of the way the criminal law assigns blame.

KEY TERMS

responsibility voluntary act *mens rea* excuse justification

Criminal law attaches social censure to individuals or corporations: that is, it communicates, in a formal, bureaucratic way, negative value judgements about their conduct, and often their character (Sumner, 1990). Those who are censured are held *culpably* to have done things that are prohibited (on the ground that they are deemed wrongful and contrary to the public good in some way). When harm is caused by, for example, a young child or a dog, the child or the dog is not censured, or in other words, not *held responsible*, although their parents or owner may be. The question of what sort of person or other entity can properly be held responsible is a central concern of criminal law theory, and the main topic of this chapter.

Crime and free choice

Lord Bingham, the then senior Law Lord, said in a recent judgement that:

> criminal law generally assumes the existence of free will ... generally speaking, informed adults of sound mind are treated as autonomous beings able to make their own decisions how they will act. (*Kennedy (no. 2)* [2007] UKHL 38, para. 14)

Modern criminal legal doctrine claims that, in general, individuals can be held culpable only if they *freely choose* to do the prohibited act. An act will be regarded as freely chosen unless it was done under certain narrowly defined forms of compulsion, for example at gunpoint or as a result of a muscular spasm. In some cases, the defendant will be treated as choosing to do the prohibited act even though he was not aware of the circumstances that made it prohibited. For example, a 15-year-old boy who has what he thinks is consensual sex with a girl he thinks is also 15, but is in fact 12 and so legally incapable of giving consent, can be convicted of rape. Baroness Hale robustly defended such a conviction as consistent with the principle of free choice:

> Every male has a choice about where he puts his penis. It may be difficult for him to restrain himself when aroused but he has a choice. There is nothing unjust or irrational about a law which says that if he chooses to put his penis inside a child who turns out to be under 13 he has committed an offence. (*G* [2008] UKHL 37, para. 46)

An internal (structural) feature of criminal law, then, is that it recognizes a distinction between freely chosen (and hence culpable) behaviour and behaviour which is not freely chosen (and hence not culpable). It is also a structural feature of criminal law (and law in general) that it makes binary divisions: legal/illegal, guilty/not guilty, responsible/not responsible. In everyday moral judgement, by contrast, it is commonly understood that culpability, like freedom, is a matter of degree (the boy in *G* above was culpable, but less so than a typical rapist or child abuser). The law has a number of devices by which it tries to reconcile its need for clear dividing lines with the perception of a continuum of responsibility. One is to employ vague standards such as 'reasonableness', leaving the courts to determine after the event whether those standards have been complied with. Examples include 'reasonable force' in self-defence and manslaughter by 'gross negligence'. Another technique is to formulate a very strict definition of legal responsibility but then allow many of those who are formally convicted to be either exempted from punishment, or punished in a way that reflects their lesser perceived culpability. This is, broadly speaking, the way in which English and US law deals with older children and the mentally ill (Zimring, 2000). A third technique is to create an intermediate verdict between 'guilty as charged' and 'not guilty'. The main example is in the law of murder, where a successful plea of provocation, diminished responsibility or a suicide pact results in a conviction for manslaughter, not in an outright acquittal (see Chapter 5).

Given this range of possibilities, it is by no means inevitable that the division between liability and non-liability should be structured in the particular way that it is in English law. For example, in the famous Victorian case of *Dudley and Stephens* (1884–85) LR 14 Q.B.D. 273, the courts had to decide the fate of two shipwrecked sailors who had killed and eaten one of their shipmates to stay alive. 'Common sense' in such circumstances, as Simpson (1984: 233) argues in his detailed account of the case, 'would perhaps suggest that responsibility can ... be looked on as a matter of degree'. At this time there was no defence of diminished responsibility, which could perhaps have been stretched to cover the facts, and the judges opted for the second of the three solutions discussed above: they refused to admit 'necessity' as a defence, but passed a death sentence which was known to be a formality and was in due course commuted to six months' imprisonment. It would have been possible, however, to create a broadly-defined defence of necessity and leave it to the jury to decide after the event whether the killing was a 'reasonable' response under such desperate circumstances. Or the situation could have been regarded as analogous to provocation, resulting in a conviction for manslaughter.

Although English law draws a distinction between acts which are freely chosen and those which are not, judges and legal scholars are not usually much concerned with metaphysical debates about 'free will'. In simple terms, people act voluntarily when they act for reasons (Hart, 2008 [1968]; Duff, 1990). If there are good reasons against their action which they are capable of understanding and responding to (Fischer and Ravizza, 1998), and they disregard those reasons in favour of morally bad reasons for committing the act, they are properly subject to moral criticism. The degree to which criticism will seem appropriate depends largely on what other options are available and the strength of the reasons against them. Thus, although it is certainly true that Dudley and Stephens killed their shipmate *voluntarily* – they had reasons to kill him and they acted on those reasons, despite a number of contrary reasons of which they were well aware – their choices were severely limited, and the alternative of a slow death from starvation was distinctly unattractive. Hence it was debateable whether their choice was sufficiently free or unconstrained to make it fair to condemn them as murderers. Nevertheless the judges considered that they had *some* choice, and that to the extent that the law was something that sailors and others in similar situations might take into account, it should use its influence to discourage killing. Specifically, as Simpson shows, the judges were anxious to dispel the notion that survival cannibalism was lawful because sanctioned by custom. It does not really make a difference to this argument whether we think that Dudley and Stephens had 'free will' (whatever that means) or whether we think their choice was causally determined by a complex set of physiological, social and psychological factors. The important point is that they were seen to have acted for reasons for which others should be discouraged from acting, and by censuring their actions the judges hoped to give other people in similar circumstances reasons to act differently. What matters, in other words, is not whether an act has causes, but whether its immediate causes include the actor's consciousness of reasons for doing it.

The view sketched in the previous paragraph is known philosophically as 'soft determinism' or 'compatibilism' – the view that even if every event in the world, including human actions, is causally determined, some human actions are still 'free' in the sense which matters for purposes of moral evaluation (Fischer and Ravizza, 1998). This view is, we think, tacitly taken for granted in most English legal discussions over the last 200 years or so (although it would require another book to demonstrate this). It is also implicit, and sometimes explicit, in much criminological work (e.g. Matza, 1964, 1969) which seeks to understand deviants as agents acting for reasons, rather than biological organisms whose behaviour is to be causally explained. If we are right in this, it is a mistake to think that law and social science are divided by a deep philosophical chasm over the 'free will' issue.

Responsibility and the reactive attitudes

Both criminology and law are concerned with the reasons why people do things. Criminology is concerned primarily with understanding the reasons, law with evaluating them. It is often fallaciously assumed that understanding and moral criticism are mutually exclusive ('to understand all is to forgive all'). To understand people's reasons for action is, on the contrary, a precondition for criticising those reasons. A more difficult question is whether understanding people's behaviour makes us less prone to react to that behaviour with emotions such as resentment, indignation or (in the case of our own behaviour) guilt – what Strawson (2001 [1962]) called the 'reactive attitudes'[1] – and if so whether that is a desirable or an undesirable effect. Strawson's view, in his highly influential article, was that such attitudes were an essential part of human social interaction and no amount of knowledge of the causes of human behaviour could or should lead to their being given up. Other philosophers, notably Spinoza, have taken a different view: that emotions of hatred or indignation are intrinsically bad, that punishment is morally acceptable only when it is inflicted purely for the wider social good and without any emotional animus towards the culprit, and that understanding how human conduct is causally determined helps to rid us of negative emotions (see Spinoza, 1997 [1677], Part 4, especially propositions XLV and LI; Goodman, 1987).

Like Spinoza, Henry Maudsley, one of the earliest exponents of a positivist form of criminology (see Davie, 2005), advocated what Strawson would call an 'objective' attitude:

> [W]e should ... get rid of the angry feeling of retaliation that may be at the bottom of any judicial punishment, and of all penal measures that may be inspired by such feeling. Society having manufactured its criminals has scarcely the right, even if it were wise for its own sake, to treat them in an angry spirit of vengeance. (Maudsley, 1874: 28)

More recently, the utilitarian philosopher J.J.C. Smart argued that acceptance of determinism was compatible with holding people responsible by treating them as capable of changing their behaviour and by 'dispraising' them in a 'dispassionate and clear headed way', but that 'the ordinary man' had 'unhealthy' attitudes towards praise and blame which could be dispelled by clearing the metaphysical fog of free will (Smart, 1961: 305).

From a sociological or criminological perspective, views like Spinoza's and Smart's may seem unduly dismissive of the emotional dimension of social norms. There is, we may think, some element of truth in the Durkheimian view that shared sentiments of anger and indignation towards serious crime are important to social cohesion (Garland, 1990). An important point about Durkheim's view is that punishment has a communicative function but the 'message' is primarily directed to (and ostensibly on behalf of) society at large. The community is, as it were, talking to itself, reminding itself what its important values are. The message is one *about* rather than *to* the defendant, and at least in common-law systems the defendant is not expected to communicate anything in return (see Chapter 7).

Many criminologists, criminal law theorists, and especially advocates of restorative justice, consider the lack of meaningful communication with offenders themselves, and with their victims, to be a major failing of existing systems. The lack of social bonds between those inflicting and receiving punishment (and the 'moral spectators' whose emotional demands the punishment is supposed to satisfy) may lead to 'a lack of inhibiting emotions of sympathy and empathy' towards the offender, and the infliction of forms of punishment that tend to induce anger rather than remorse in those punished (Karstedt, 2002: 310). The emotional dimension of social norms might be reinforced much more effectively by a system which allowed those directly or indirectly affected by a crime to express their emotions themselves, in a setting designed to foster reconciliation and 'reintegrative shaming' (Christie, 1982; Braithwaite, 1989).

Whether or not we agree with these criticisms, as long as we think that the reactive attitudes have a part to play in social responses to harmful behaviour, we shall need some way of sorting out those who are appropriate targets for such attitudes, because they wrongfully chose to do harm, from those who are not.

An influential view of moral responsibility equates it with being an appropriate target for the reactive attitudes (Fischer and Ravizza, 1998; Wallace, 1994). If we assume that one function of the criminal law, at least in some cases, is to single out people as appropriate targets for an institutional expression of the reactive attitudes, it seems to follow that criminal responsibility – liability to criminal conviction – at least in those cases, ought to be closely related to moral responsibility. In all legal systems that we know of, criminal liability for what are perceived as serious crimes is, in fact, tied to ostensible moral culpability. What follows is a brief sketch of the doctrinal framework by which English law determines whether individuals are responsible or not.

Aspects of responsibility

Within criminal legal doctrine, the distinction between agents who are responsible and blameworthy for particular acts, and those who are non-responsible or blameless, is marked in a number of ways.

The requirement of a voluntary act

Behaviour which is patently involuntary is deemed not to satisfy one of the essential conditions for criminal liability, that of an *'actus reus'* or guilty act. Where a defendant admits making a bodily movement that caused some prohibited consequence, but denies that it was a voluntary act, this is known as a defence of automatism. Despite the apparently fundamental nature of the voluntary act requirement, automatism has developed as a distinct defence only in the last half-century. The law was able to do without it for so long because, in addition to the *actus reus,* most offences require *mens rea* – a mental state such as an intention to do the prohibited act. To claim that an act was involuntary can be interpreted as a denial of the *mens rea* rather than the *actus reus* (see e.g. Stephen J's remarks on sleepwalking in *Tolson* (1889) 23 Q.B.D. 168: 187). Such an interpretation, however, has two major drawbacks from the defendant's point of view. One is that it will afford no defence to crimes of strict liability, such as most motoring offences, for which no *mens rea* is required. The other is that a denial of *mens rea* on the basis of some kind of mental or physical disorder is difficult to distinguish from an insanity defence. An insanity defence used to result automatically in indeterminate confinement in an institution, and although this is no longer true (except in murder cases), to be labelled insane carries an obvious stigma. Framing a defence of automatism as a denial of the *actus reus* rather than the *mens rea* seems to offer an escape from these drawbacks.

Although the courts have been willing to allow automatism as a defence in strict liability cases (e.g. *Hill v Baxter* [1958] 1 Q.B. 277), they have been very reluctant to allow defendants to escape the consequences of an insanity defence. Cases of automatism which are attributable to some 'internal cause' – including sleepwalking – are classified as insanity (see Mackay, 1995, Ch. 1; Wilson et al., 2005). A further peculiarity of this area of law is that while normally the onus is on the prosecution to prove a voluntary act beyond reasonable doubt, where a defence is classified as insanity it must be proved by the defence on the balance of probabilities (Jones, 1995).

Mens rea

There are three main gradations of fault in English criminal law: intention, recklessness and negligence. In simple terms, I intend to cause harm if I choose to bring that harm about, I am reckless if I know there is a risk of causing harm and unjustifiably choose to take the risk, and I am negligent if I am not aware of the risk but would have been had I taken reasonable care.

Similar distinctions apply where the offence is not one of causing a particular kind of harm, but of committing a certain act in certain circumstances. For example, I intend to commit rape if I know my victim does not consent to penetration; I am reckless if I 'couldn't care less' whether the victim consents or not; and I am negligent if I do not form a reasonable belief that she consents, or (perhaps better) if I do not take reasonable steps to ascertain whether she consents. English law used to require either intention or recklessness; under the Sexual Offences Act 2003, negligence (in the sense of lack of reasonable belief, to be determined in part by the steps the defendant took to ascertain consent) is sufficient.

Some cases, however, do not fit neatly into any of these three categories. In *Hyam* the defendant set fire to a house in order to frighten one of the occupants; two children died in the blaze. If Mrs Hyam had started the fire *despite* the risk to the occupants of the house, she would undoubtedly have been reckless, and so guilty of manslaughter but not murder; but it seemed she had, rather, acted *in order* to put them at risk. The majority of the House of Lords upheld her conviction for murder. Lord Hailsham held that the *mens rea* of murder included not only an intention to cause death or serious physical harm, but an intention to expose someone to the risk of such harm – a decision based partly on the argument that a narrower definition would make it too difficult to convict terrorists of murder (*Hyam v DPP* [1975] A.C. 55: 76). It is not clear, however, that the other Law Lords in the majority accepted this view.

In criminal appeals on points of law, the courts are mainly concerned with the legal accuracy and clarity of the judge's summing-up of the law to the jury. In the later case of *Moloney*, the Law Lords abandoned Lord Hailsham's view on the ground that it made it too difficult to explain to a jury how it should distinguish between murder and reckless manslaughter. To be guilty of murder, the Law Lords now said, the defendant must *intend* death or serious injury, and the jury could *infer* intention if death or serious injury were the 'natural consequences' of the defendant's act, and the defendant foresaw them as such. The word 'natural' was supposed (oddly) to convey to the jury 'the idea that in the ordinary course of events a certain act will lead to a certain consequence unless something unexpected supervenes to prevent it'. Foresight and the inferences to be drawn from it belonged 'not to the substantive law, but to the law of evidence' (*Moloney*, [1985] A.C. 905: 928–9, Lord Bridge).

In *Nedrick* (1986) 83 Cr. App. R. 267, a very similar case to *Hyam*, the Court of Appeal made it clear that only where the defendant appreciated that a consequence 'was a virtual certainty (barring some unforeseen intervention)' could intention be inferred (271). The House of Lords later approved the decision in *Nedrick* with one amendment: the jury should be told it 'may find' rather than 'infer' intention in such circumstances. Lord Steyn said that the effect of that direction 'is that a result foreseen as virtually certain is an intended result' (*Woollin* [1999] A.C. 82: 93). *Woollin* appears to be based on the view that, rather than being a matter of evidence as Lord Bridge indicated in *Moloney,* intended results *by definition* include those foreseen as virtually certain. As Duff (1990) argues, it is reasonable to say that when I choose to do an act which I know will almost certainly have a particular consequence, I cause that consequence *intentionally,* even if I do not *intend* it in the sense that it is a reason for my action (but cf. Hornsby, 1993, Norrie, 1999).

Both *Moloney* and *Woollin* show the difficulty of establishing *mens rea* in cases where the defendant's action does not appear to be instrumentally rational. Mr Moloney engaged in a drunken contest with his 'adored' stepfather to see who could load a gun more quickly; he pulled the trigger because his stepfather dared him to do so. Mr Woollin lost his temper and threw his baby son onto a hard surface. Terms like 'intention' and 'foresight' hardly capture the phenomenology of such actions:

> Our actions tend not to be accompanied by mental thought bubbles by which we self-consciously account to ourselves for our actions before embarking on them. Typically we just 'do'. We swat a fly. We hit a ball. We shoot a person. Whether we intend the results of our actions at the time of acting is something that may never cross our minds. (Wilson, 2002: 137)

When Mr Woollin was asked what was going through his head at the time he threw the baby, he could only reply: 'I just did not want to know him' (*Woollin* [1997] 1 Cr. App. R. 97: 100). As Norrie (1999) argues, concepts like 'foresight' can be used to arrive at what feels like the morally right result in such cases, but they are 'simulacra of morality' which do not engage with the real moral issues (for example, should we see Woollin's act as an isolated loss of temper or a grave abuse of power over a helpless infant?). The law's determination to shoehorn such impulsive actions into categories appropriate to rationally planned behaviour reflects the moral attitudes of the Victorian judges who shaped much of modern criminal law. As Wiener (1990) argues, a pervasive assumption of early Victorian law and morality was that treating people *as if* they had rationally planned their actions would encourage them to act with greater rationality and foresight in fact. In other words, the law did not, and does not, reflect a naïve perception of psychological reality: it is, rather, a tool of social discipline, intended to shape human conduct and psychology in a particular way.

A somewhat similar problem arises on the borderline between recklessness and negligence. Is it negligent or reckless to fail to notice a risk that would be obvious to most people? Until recently such cases were governed by the House of Lords' decision in *Caldwell* [1982] A.C. 341. Lord Diplock, who gave the main judgement, thought that juries should not have to undertake 'meticulous analysis ... of the thoughts that passed through the mind of the accused' to determine whether he foresaw the risk and decided to take it or, in a state of intoxication or rage, was oblivious to the risk (ibid: 351–2). If the risk would be obvious to a reasonable person, the accused was guilty. The injustice of this test when applied to children and the mentally disabled, as well as Lord Diplock's unacceptably blatant disregard of Parliament's intentions in passing the Criminal Damage Act 1971, led the House of Lords to reverse the *Caldwell* decision in *G* [2003] UKHL 50, holding that a defendant is reckless only if he is aware of a risk and unjustifiably decides to take it. Lord Bingham argued that the 'common sense' of the jury could be relied upon to ensure that awareness of the risk would not be too hard for the prosecution to prove. Arguably, however, *G* goes too far towards subjectivism: that is, towards judging behaviour from the accused's point of view (Keating, 2007). It excuses not only those who fail to notice risks because of their youth or limited intelligence, but also those who remain oblivious to risk because they simply do not care about the interests of others (Duff, 1990).

It might seem obvious that, other things being equal, it is worse to harm someone intentionally than to harm them recklessly or negligently. If I am reckless and harm results, then to some extent both my victim and I are unlucky; I am responsible for creating the risk, but not fully responsible for the harm coming to pass (though if the risk is very high, the difference between intention and recklessness may be very slight). Hillyard and Tombs (2004: 14; Tombs, 2007: 540) challenge this moral hierarchy as 'counter common-sensical', drawing on Reiman's (2007) argument that an 'absentee killer', such as an employer who refuses to provide workers with safety equipment, may show a more culpable moral attitude than a murderer who kills in a moment of passion. Reiman plausibly argues that someone who knowingly exposes a large number of people to the risk of death, and actually kills one of them, shows a contempt for human life in general that is worse than that shown in intentionally killing a single individual. It was this sort of worry (albeit in the context of terrorism rather than white collar crime) that tempted the courts to blur the boundary between recklessness and intention. Surely, though, Reiman's absentee killer is less culpable than an employer who *intends* that one of his employees should die (but does not care which). So long as we compare like with like – doing the same act with an intentional, reckless, or negligent attitude towards the same kind and degree of harm – the law seems 'commonsensical' enough. That is a different question from that of whether a more punitive attitude towards some kinds of negligence would serve a disciplinary purpose in encouraging individuals and firms to be more careful (see Chapter 6).

Justifications

A defendant who pleads justification accepts full responsibility for her act but asserts that it was the right thing – or at least a permissible thing – to do in the circumstances. By contrast, a defendant who pleads an excuse accepts that she has done something wrong but denies that she is blameworthy. This distinction is more important in theory than it is in practice. A shop assistant who hands over the contents of the till at gunpoint could say 'I'm sorry, I was terrified' (excuse) or 'of course I handed over the money, I'd be daft to get myself killed trying to save the insurance company a few hundred quid' (justification). Either way, she is raising the defence of duress, although which of these explanations she adopts may make a great deal of difference to her feeling of self-respect.

The main justificatory defences are self-defence, or more accurately *private* defence (defence of oneself or another), and necessity. Self-defence, however, straddles the boundary between justification and excuse, since it covers a person who uses *reasonable* force in response to his *perception* of the threat posed by the victim, whether or not that perception is reasonable. Necessity is a rare defence which the courts only reluctantly countenance. As Lord Denning put it, 'if hunger were once allowed to be an excuse for stealing, it would open a way through which all kinds of disorder and lawlessness would pass' (*London Borough of Southwark v. Williams* [1971] 2 All ER 175: 179). In *Re A (Conjoined Twins)* [2004] 4 All E.R. 961, Lord Justice Brooke held that doctors had a defence of necessity if they separated two conjoined twins to save the life of one of them, even though the death of the other was a virtually certain consequence of the operation and therefore fell within the *Woollin* definition of murder.

Excuses

Excuses are defences which recognize that the defendant has done a wrongful act, but wholly or partially exempt her from blame. The orthodox view (Hart, 2008) is that these defences reflect the defendant's limited opportunity to choose what to do.

(1) *Internal excusing conditions.* Some biological or psychological drive outside the individual's conscious control overcomes his capacity for rational action. In this category are the narrowly defined defence of insanity and the much vaguer defence of diminished responsibility. Diminished responsibility, which applies only in murder cases, is a *partial* defence which reduces the crime from murder to manslaughter (see Chapter 5).

(2) *External excusing conditions.* Some circumstance, or the action of another person, puts such pressure on the accused that her 'will is overborne' or she 'loses her self-control'. One such excuse is duress, where the defendant acted in response to a fear of death or serious injury (either to herself or to a relative or friend). In recent years a defence of 'duress of circumstances' has developed, where the accused acts in order to avert death or injury, but no-one has threatened

him with these consequences for failing to act. In *Abdul-Hussain* [1999] Crim. L.R. 570, this defence was held to be available to a group of men who hijacked an aircraft to escape from Sudan because they were terrified of being deported to Iraq to face torture and summary execution. Provocation (or 'loss of control' as it is soon to be renamed) is a partial defence to murder which arises where the accused experiences a 'sudden and temporary loss of self-control' in response to some provocative act (see Chapter 5).

The crucial difference between these two types of excuse is that the external defences involve an objective test: the pressure on the accused must be such that a reasonable person, or 'person of reasonable firmness' might have reacted as she did. Remarkably, the House of Lords held in *Howe* [1987] A.C. 417 that the 'person of ordinary fortitude' would *never* kill – even with the intent to cause no more than serious harm – in response to any threat whatever.

Why are the two types of excuse distinguished in this way? The answer seems to be that external factors excuse only in so far as the defendant's response to them is reasonable, whereas the internal conditions impair the defendant's ability to act reasonably at all. As Lord Hoffman put it:

> There is a clear philosophical distinction between a claim that an act was at least partially excused as normal behaviour in response to external circumstances and a claim that the actor had mental characteristics which prevented him from behaving normally. (*Smith (Morgan)* [2001] 1 AC 146: 167)

As Lord Hoffman went on to point out, however, this distinction is not always easy to draw in practice. For example, being a victim of repeated domestic violence (clearly an external factor) may affect both one's 'reasonable' perception of impending violence – victims may become acutely sensitive to cues that another assault is imminent – and one's ability to act 'reasonably' in response to that threat (Downs, 1996; Tadros, 2005).

In the remaining sections of this chapter we want to sketch in general terms the nature of the debate over excuses and responsibility. There are really two different debates, which it is important to distinguish. Again it is convenient to use the labels 'internal' and 'external'.

The internal debate

This often takes place in the context of actual cases, and indeed within the trial process, or in criminal appeals. The question under debate is: how wide should the category of non-responsible, and therefore non-culpable, behaviour be?

The courts often define this category very narrowly. In particular, the defences of automatism, insanity, duress and necessity are very tightly circumscribed. Some legal scholars and practitioners are critical of this practice, and insist that the law should recognize a much wider range of conditions and circumstances as undermining criminal responsibility. Other defences, however, can be criticized as unduly broad. We shall examine some criticisms of the breadth of provocation and diminished responsibility in Chapter 5.

In recent years the internal debate has become highly sophisticated. Philosophical theories of criminal law and criminal justice have been a growth industry in the common-law world since the publication of George Fletcher's seminal *Rethinking Criminal Law* in 1978. As a necessarily simplified way of introducing some of the key issues, we want to suggest that criminal law theories (and theories of criminal procedure and evidence) can be divided into two broad types which we shall call (with apologies to Lea and Young, 1984) liberal idealism and liberal realism. By calling these theories 'liberal' we mean simply that they accord central value to individual freedom and autonomy. Even writers who distance themselves from some aspects of liberalism as a political philosophy (Lacey, 1988, Sanders and Young, 2006) can be considered 'liberal' in this broad sense.

Liberal idealists believe that criminal law and punishment are, or should be, an embodiment of a community's most important moral values. They promote these values through retribution (see Chapter 8) and/or through symbolically communicating to the offender and society at large the seriousness of offences against fundamental values, while also providing a vehicle for the offender to express remorse. Some theorists, particularly Duff (1986, 2001), attach particular importance to the idea of a two-way communication between the offender and the community. The overarching retributive or communicative goal of punishment is taken as the basis for explaining and evaluating the definition of offences and defences. Legal responsibility is seen as inseparable from moral responsibility. Influential exponents of this perspective include Ashworth (2006), Duff (1986, 2001, 2007) Lacey (1988, 2001), Moore (1997) and Tadros (2005).[2] It is the dominant perspective in current theoretical debates.

By liberal realism we mean the position epitomized by the seminal (and recently reissued) work of H.L.A. Hart (2008 [1968]). Hart was sceptical about any attempt to explain criminal law in terms of single overriding value. The general aim of criminal justice was simply 'to encourage certain types of behaviour and discourage others' (Hart, 2008: 6) and it pursued this goal by a variety of means. The behaviour it aimed to discourage did not necessarily offend against important or consensual moral values; many laws served economic goals as to which social morality was silent or divided (ibid: 37). The unbridled use of coercion to influence behaviour could, however, be extremely oppressive and unfair. It had to be constrained by certain principles, one of which was that conduct should not be punished unless it was in some sense 'voluntary'. This would enable people to make choices that would protect them from the law's coercive sanctions.

The main criticism directed at Hart's theory is that it explains criminal law as 'a compromise between partly discrepant principles' (2008: 10) but does not provide a criterion for prioritizing the principles of social protection and fairness to individuals when they conflict (Lacey, 1988; Norrie, 1991). The absence of a single overarching moral goal can, however, be seen as a recognition of the diverse nature of penal practices and of their 'tragic' quality (Garland, 1990) – the impossibility of completely reconciling the competing values they serve. In his Introduction to the new edition of Hart's book, Gardner (2008) argues that the plurality of goals he espouses does not lead to any incoherence or incompleteness in his theory, but it fails as a defence of *punishment* because it does not explain why an offender's guilt should, *in itself*, be a reason for inflicting suffering on her. In other words, Hart provides a rationale for 'penality' (Garland and Young, 1983), an organized coercive response to crime, not specifically for punishment in the strict sense of making the offender suffer for his offence. We are inclined to see this as a strength, rather than a weakness, of Hart's work, because it leaves him largely immune to the restorative justice-based critique of criminal law. A Hartian could accept that the reductionist aims of criminal law would be better served by restorative forms of justice that would not necessarily involve punishment, but still insist that it was important in the interests of freedom to limit interventions to those who chose to break clearly defined rules, and to maintain some proportionality between the intervention and the gravity of the breach. In the terms we use in Chapter 8 below, this is a form of 'weak retributivism': it is *permissible* for the state to punish those who are morally culpable to an extent proportionate to their culpability, but whether they *should* be punished depends on other, instrumental, considerations.

Liberal realism also recognizes the important point that 'when we go beyond traditional crimes such as murder or theft, the actual content of the criminal law is only marginally concerned with upholding community values *per se*' (Wilson, 2002: 36). Idealists can retort that some 'regulatory' offences – including Wilson's example of selling unsafe food (cf. Tombs and Hillyard, 2004: 47–50) – *ought* to be regarded as gravely immoral (Tadros, 2005); but this is surely implausible for many motoring offences, licensing offences etc. Importantly, too, liberal realism – in common with E.P. Thomson's (1977) brand of Marxism – can recognize that key legal principles, such as those of legality (no punishment without the prior promulgation of a law), the restriction of punishment to voluntary acts, and 'limiting retributivism' (punishment must not be grossly disproportionate to the harm done by the offender: Morris, 1982), serve important values even when they are part of an unjust system. This is what leads Duff (1986) to end one of the most impressive liberal idealist manifestos by endorsing a simple realist prescription for deterrent punishment constrained by basic principles of justice as the least of the evils available in societies like our own which fall too far short of being just communities to realize his ideal model.

These two philosophical perspectives do not map neatly onto particular doctrinal positions. It is not the case that idealists necessarily support broader defences than realists do, or vice versa. The main difference between them is in how they see the social function of criminal law. Is it a tool of the state, which can be used for a variety of purposes but needs to be kept in check by rules designed to ensure the fair treatment of individual citizens, or is it the organized moral voice of the community? From a sociological point of view, understanding 'the community' as a homogenous entity united by a common morality raises all the problems associated with Durkheim's 'collective conscience' (see Garland, 1990). The advantage of liberal realism, then, is simply that it is comparatively realistic. We do not, however, want to dismiss the idea that criminal justice can, at its best, provide a public forum in which people suspected of morally wrongful behaviour are called to account (Duff et al., 2008), nor to deny the importance of this role of the law in formulating defences to serious crimes (Gardner, 2007, Ch. 9). We also believe that some 'idealist' perspectives – particularly Duff's work – are valuable both in highlighting the moral shortcomings of the existing law and encouraging us to think how it might be possible to create islands of morally valuable practice even within a deeply flawed system.

The major alternative to these two varieties of liberalism is the critical perspective developed in a series of works by Alan Norrie (1991, 2000, 2001, 2005). Norrie's work contributes to the 'internal' debate in the sense that he takes doctrinal issues of responsibility very seriously, and shares with liberal idealists like Duff the view that a defensible approach to responsibility must reflect a nuanced moral perspective. Unlike Duff, however, he maintains that criminal law can *never* arrive at a morally adequate account of responsibility; as an ideological justification of practices of control in a profoundly unjust society, criminal law is *necessarily* blinkered and contradictory. Norrie also goes beyond the mainstream internal debate in seeking to explain the contradictions within, and disagreements about, legal doctrine in historical and sociological terms.

The external debate

By this we mean a debate in which one side challenges quite fundamentally the premises on which the internal debate is based, and in particular the very idea that there is any meaningful distinction to be drawn between 'responsible' and 'non-responsible' offenders. This position is associated with what we called in Chapter 1 the 'scientific critique' of criminal law and was expounded by many of the 'founding fathers' of criminology. The early criminologists' position can be understood as a reaction to the contradictions generated by the involvement of (purportedly) scientific experts in the internal debate. For example, one of the most important Victorian contributions to the internal debate, Henry Maudsley's *Responsibility in Mental Disease* (1874), criticized the law from a medical perspective for ignoring 'the obvious difference between him who *will* not and him who *cannot* fulfil the claims of the law' (p. 111), while also embracing a deterministic theory of crime (discussed above) which made that difference anything but obvious. Havelock Ellis, in one of the first English books devoted to positivist criminology, saw it as a sign of the 'semi-barbaric' condition of the law that 'the grave interests of society and of the individual are made to hinge on a problem that must often be insoluble. Practically it cannot make the slightest difference whether the criminal is sane or insane' (Ellis, 1890: 291). The important question was not whether the criminal was 'responsible' but how society could best be protected from him.

After Ellis, many criminologists simply opted out of the internal debate over responsibility. The debate over legal tests of responsibility was seen either as misguided (like the search for accurate tests to detect witchcraft), or as one that might be important to lawyers but had no possible 'scientific' basis. There were two variations of this position. One was the simple positivist view that the only important question about crime was what *caused* it; understanding or criticizing the offender's reasons was beside the point. 'Christianity forbids men to "judge", deterministic science equally forbids them to "blame" their fellow men', declared Maurice Hamblin Smith (1922: 172). Probably very few criminologists held this view consistently (it did not stop Hamblin Smith from giving fairly conventional expert testimony in numerous trials where insanity was in issue), and some notable positivists, such as Goring (1918), explicitly rejected it. The other variant of the 'scientific' critique was the psychoanalytic view that offenders did act for reasons, but not primarily for the reasons of which they were conscious, or which courts attributed to them. At best, the legal understanding of responsibility was a socially useful fiction. As Freud put it, 'The physician must leave it to the jurist to construct for social purposes a conception of responsibility that is artificially limited to the metapsychological ego' (1961[1925]: 134).

In the most sustained analysis of criminal responsibility from the perspective of psychoanalytic criminology, Alexander and Staub (1956 [1931]) argued that although responsibility could not be justified on grounds of 'free will', treating people 'as if' the Ego were free had 'a practical, or still better, a tactical justification' (ibid.: 67). Although this looks like an endorsement of the 'useful fiction' view of responsibility (Moore, 1985), it was a fiction they took very seriously. The 'internalization of the feeling of responsibility' was vital to the construction of the individual as a 'social being' within a 'free society' (Alexander and Staub, 1956: 131). Responsibility should be defined in such a way as to promote such

internalization, which might mean that some careless, but probably uncon-
sciously motivated, behaviour should attract criminal liability (ibid.: 130).
Whether people should be held responsible was a different question from
whether they should be punished, which would be psychologically counterproductive in many cases. Responsibility, for Alexander and Staub, was an important and valuable social construct rather than a moral or metaphysical truth.
The question was not 'is this individual responsible?' but 'is it good for the individual and for society to hold her responsible – and if so how?'.

Arguably, such a pragmatic approach to responsibility would take a lot of the
emotional heat out of social reactions to crime. But for social definitions of responsibility to be 'internalized' seems to imply that they must carry an emotional
charge. The ideal, from this psychoanalytic perspective, would appear to be that
judges should understand the unconscious roots of their own and the public's
emotional urge to punish, and seek not to extinguish such emotions but rather to
modify and channel them so as to serve utilitarian social goals. Rather than being
consistent external critics of responsibility, Alexander and Staub offered at least
the beginning of a sophisticated contribution to the internal debate.

A relatively recent example of external critique in a utilitarian, positivist criminological vein is Lady Wootton's *Crime and the Criminal Law* (1963). Hart's
(2008 [1968]) articulation of the liberal realist position was written largely as a
rejoinder to Wootton. Wootton argued that 'If the law says that certain things are
not to be done, it is illogical to confine this prohibition to things that are done
with malice aforethought; for at least the material consequences of an action,
and the reasons for prohibiting it, are the same whether it is the result of sinis-
ter malicious plotting, negligence, or sheer accident' (1963: 51). Whether the act
was malicious or accidental should be taken into account in deciding what
action to take to prevent recurrence, but not in deciding whether an accused had
committed a prohibited act.

It is not the law that is illogical, but Lady Wootton's argument. The point of a
prohibition, as Hart argued, is to guide people's conduct. 'Do not damage other
people's property by sheer accident' does not provide any intelligible guidance.
'Take reasonable precautions against damaging other people's property' (or 'do
not damage property negligently') is a perfectly sensible piece of guidance, but is
not infringed by people who cause accidental damage despite taking reasonable
precautions. Taken to its logical conclusion, Lady Wootton's 'prohibition' of accidental harm would amount to a licence to the state to take discretionary 'preventive' action against anyone who was unfortunate enough to have an accident.

A more sophisticated version of Wootton's argument has recently been defended
by Slobogin (2005). Slobogin accepts that non-negligent or justified actions would
need to be excluded from the scope of any criminal justice system, and thus some
doctrine of *mens rea* would remain. His model would, however, dispense with the
present gradations of responsibility (intention/recklessness/negligence) and would

allocate offenders to penal measures on the basis of an assessment of risk. Communicating moral judgements would still be important, but this would form part of the measures designed to prevent reoffending, such as cognitive-behavioural rehabilitative programmes or forms of restorative justice:

> As modern rehabilitative efforts routinely demonstrate, a regime based on prediction does not have to insult the notion that past choices have consequences and that the offender is responsible and held accountable for them. There is a difference in message, however. The punishment model says to the offender: 'You have done something bad, for which you must pay'. The prevention model says: 'You have done something harmful, which you must not let happen again'. (Slobogin, 2005: 132–3, footnotes omitted)

As with Spinoza's and Smart's views, Slobogin's proposal raises a question about the appropriate emotional content of penal communications. For some offences, such as speeding,[3] Slobogin's message may seem entirely appropriate. But what about torture, murder or rape? Murderers whose crimes have solved their domestic problems, or torturers whose regimes are out of power, may pose little risk of reoffending; should they therefore be exempt from punishment? Do we want to communicate something more to the rapist than 'don't do that again'? On the other hand, as experience of ASBOs shows, measures that are ostensibly preventive rather than punitive can be very harsh on people who commit repetitive minor misdeeds.[4] Risk-based sentencing would almost certainly lead to social injustice, focussing on those groups who are subject to most intense surveillance and are most likely to have 'risk factors', such as previous convictions, recorded against them. Slobogin's model appears to take the 'new penology' (Feeley and Simon, 1992), based on the identification of high-risk groups rather than culpable individuals, to something like its logical conclusion, while at the same time sharing some common ground with abolitionism (Hulsman, 1981–2). Like Alexander and Staub (1956), in restating the external critique in a tenable form, Slobogin reinstates the concept of criminal liability (and extends it to a wider range of negligent conduct), thus bringing us back to the internal debate.

Criminology and the internal debate

More recent criminological theories, at least those within the sociological tradition, have tended to eschew hard determinism and a view of deviance as pathological, which were the premises of the earlier external critiques of crime. There is a good deal of intellectual common ground between some criminological theories, perhaps most notably Matza's in *Delinquency and Drift* (1964) and criminal law theory. Matza explicitly adopted the 'soft determinist' view that 'human actions are not deprived of freedom because they are causally determined' (1964: 9), and his famous 'techniques of neutralization' (first formulated in Sykes and Matza, 1957) are, as he notes, very similar to legal defences, but stretch them farther than the law is willing to contemplate. Sykes and Matza (1957: 666) originally described the techniques of neutralization as 'an unrecognized extension of defenses to crimes', but Matza's (1964) later view is that both reflect common cultural concerns, which the law interprets narrowly and the delinquent expansively. There is a clear implication in his work that an over-broad legal definition of excuses, like the pretence that juvenile courts do not engage in punishment, may encourage further deviance – an argument also developed by Cressey (1971) and Taylor (1976) – yet criminologists of this school were dismayed when their work was interpreted as a justification for tougher punishments (Cohen, 1979: 18). Cohen's (1979) attempt to grapple with this dilemma and to 'balance, guilt, justice and tolerance' raised many of the issues we discuss in this book. A critical response to Matza's (1969) work also inspired Beyleveld and Wiles (1975, 1979) to make a philosophically sophisticated attempt to formulate a conception of the self-determining subject that would be equally relevant to criminological analysis and to the attribution of moral responsibility.

Despite these promising beginnings, criminology since 1980 has not made any very sustained contribution to rethinking legal conceptions of responsibility. Here we briefly consider three interrelated areas in which criminological insights might be thought relevant to debates over responsibility: the age of criminal responsibility; the responsibility of adults who were gravely abused as children; and the wider issue of 'rotten social background'.

Age

Although it is a generally accepted principle of criminal law that some children are too young to be criminally responsible, different systems vary widely in where they fix the age of criminal responsibility, and in how far they differentiate between the treatment of young people who are formally deemed responsible and adults. In England and Wales the age of criminal responsibility is ten and a system of youth courts deals with most defendants aged under 18.

It is not easy to state the principles which determine what the age of criminal responsibility should be. One explanation is that children lack 'moral capacity' (Morse, 1998). Historically this appears to be the basis of the common law rules that developed between the twelfth and seventeenth centuries (Bandalli, 2000). Children under seven were conclusively presumed to be *doli incapax* – unable to discern good from evil – and those aged between seven and 14 could be convicted only if the prosecution proved that they had this capacity. A similar rationale is adopted in the UN Standard Minimum Rules for the Administration of Juvenile Justice:

> The modern approach would be to consider whether a child can live up to the moral and psychological components of criminal responsibility; that is, whether a child, by virtue of his individual discernment and understanding, can be held responsible for essentially anti-social behaviour. (UN, 1985, commentary to Rule 4)

The difficulty with this rationale is brought out in Cynthia Ward's discussion of a case in the US where a six-year-old boy was charged with attempted murder. The boy had at least a basic moral understanding – he knew he was seriously harming a baby in a way adults would see as seriously wrong – and if that level of understanding is not adequate for criminal responsibility, it is not clear that many of the most violent and dangerous adult offenders can be held responsible either. Similarly the ten-year-old boys who killed Jamie Bulger in the UK were held to have the level of moral understanding that the law then required: a knowledge that they were doing something seriously wrong rather than merely naughty. Subsequently the Criminal Justice Act 1998 abolished the *doli incapax* principle for children aged ten to 14: all children over the age of ten in England and Wales (eight in Scotland) are deemed criminally responsible (subject to the extremely remote possibility of an insanity defence).

It is of course true that children of six or ten (and some adults) have a relatively limited capacity to grasp the moral reasons why some actions are wrong and to regulate their behaviour accordingly (Wallace, 1994). What is not so obvious is whether this justifies a complete exemption from responsibility or only a form of 'diminished responsibility' which is implicitly recognized in the separate systems of courts and penalties imposed on children (Zimring, 2000).

Similar arguments apply to younger adolescents, whose brains are not fully developed and who, in particular, 'have not yet attained their adult neurological potential to respond effectively to situations that require careful or reasoned decisions' (Scott and Grisso, 2005: 813). On average, under-14s differ significantly in their psychological development from 16–18 year olds, who are close to an adult level of development (ibid.: 826). Such neurological and psychological evidence supports the view that adolescents have, on average, lesser moral capacities than adults and hence a lesser degree of moral responsibility. That their moral capacities have yet to develop fully is also a strong reason for why young offenders should not suffer long-lasting punishment and stigma.[5] Again, it is less clear that it justifies exempting adolescents entirely from criminal responsibility. If extended to adults, a complete exemption from responsibility on the grounds of impulsiveness or poor planning abilities would have drastic consequences (taking us back to the 'scientific critique' in its strongest form: see Chapter 1).

A second rationale for the age of responsibility is that even if young children have a basic moral understanding, they cannot be expected to understand and participate in the process of criminal justice (Duff, 2002b). The six-year-old discussed by Cynthia Ward (2006) was eventually found incompetent to stand trial, and the European Court of Human Rights held that the boys who killed Jamie Bulger had not had a fair trial as they could not understand or participate in the proceedings (*T v UK* (1999) 7 BHRC 659). A US study found that over a third of 11–13 year olds, and a significant number of 14–16 year olds 'may have significant impairments' in their ability to understand a trial and make legal decisions (Scott and Grisso, 2005: 829). Much clearly depends on the way the trial is conducted (Weijers, 2002) and the ECHR accepted that, in principle, children of 11 (as the Bulger defendants were at the time of trial) could receive a fair trial. It is difficult to quarrel with the proposition that either a criminal trial or something with equivalent procedural safeguards is necessary before the fate of a child, however young, is determined by the belief that he has done a particular act.

A third rationale relates to the division of labour between parents and the state. It is parents and teachers who are generally expected to call children to account for bad behaviour, and if they are unable to do so the state has a duty to intervene in the interests of the child's welfare. Serious harm-doing by young children may therefore be seen as a failure of parenting and welfare services, rather than something for which the individual child can fairly be punished. As Cynthia Ward (2006) argues, if the state gives children no means of escape from a criminogenic situation, it cannot fairly punish them for the consequences.

It is very difficult, and inevitably somewhat arbitrary, to identify an age at which such considerations cease to apply. Although a few countries have even lower ages of responsibility, the English one is lower than those of most Western countries, which generally plump for somewhere between 12 (as in Canada and The Netherlands) and 18 (as in Belgium and Luxembourg: Goldson and Muncie, 2006). Raising the age to 14 could be said to bring the law 'into line with international norms' (Allen, 2007: 29)[6] but as Goldson and Muncie (2007: 61) observe, there is no clear 'criminological rationale' for this particular age.

Rather than making a case for one age limit or another, let us pose two questions that deserve more discussion. First, assuming that we see moral education or communication as an important goal in the regulation of youthful misbehaviour, is there any reason to think that criminal justice is a more effective means of communicating moral ideas to children than purely educational or therapeutic measures? In other words, even if we think children should be held responsible, is there any good reason why this should entail holding them *criminally* responsible? Is there, for example, anything more than populist 'common-sense' to the Government's claim that a system that too readily 'makes excuses' for young people's behaviour impedes the development of personal responsibility (Home Office, 1997)? Would it be more effective to switch resources to schools, youth services, training, employment etc., and would raising the age or responsibility to 16 or 18 support such a shift of priorities? (See Goldson and Muncie, 2006, for a well-argued case on these lines.)

Secondly, to what extent and over what age range are practices of holding children responsible characterized by an 'as if' quality (Weijers, 2002)? Do parents, teachers, etc. treat children *as if* they had a greater degree of moral understanding than they actually perceive the children to have, in the hope that this will encourage them to develop such qualities (and does it really have this effect)? If, as Strawson (2001: 324) argued, the 'reactive attitudes' adults display towards children are at first in the nature of 'rehearsals' for their role as responsible subjects, which 'insensibly modulate towards true performances', then a criminal court is hardly the place for rehearsals. At what age do, or should, children and adults understand the performance to be entirely real? To turn the Government's 'culture of excuses' argument around: does a system that refuses to admit childhood as an 'excuse' encourage inappropriate and harmful reactive attitudes among the adult population?

Adult offenders abused as children

The idea that the state should not punish children for the consequences of being brought up in a criminogenic environment from which they cannot escape (C. Ward, 2006) raises a wider and more troubling question: can we hold *adults* responsible for those consequences either? In his defence of a preventive model, Slobogin (2005: 160) cites evidence 'that most character formation occurs in the developmental years leading up to age fourteen, when the person can hardly be held responsible for how he or she turns out' as presenting a problem for any desert-based account of punishment.

The philosopher Gary Watson illustrates this problem in his discussion of an American murderer called Robert Harris, described by a fellow death row inmate as 'a total scumbag ... He doesn't care about life, he doesn't care about others, he doesn't care about himself' (quoted by Watson, 2004: 234). After dwelling on Harris's crimes – he was sentenced for cold-bloodedly shooting two teenagers whose car he had hijacked – Watson quotes detailed accounts of Harris's appalling childhood, his parents' brutality and their complete lack of affection for him. The effect of this knowledge, in Watson's view, is not to suspend the 'reactive attitudes' but to call forth ambivalent attitudes; we are disposed to empathize with Harris as a victim at the same time as we condemn him as a victimizer. Norrie (2005) argues that such ambivalence is a common feature of responses to crime, and something with which legal categories of responsibility are unable to come to terms.

Cases like Harris's, however, illustrate the point that to understand harmful behaviour is not necessarily to forgive it. If, rather than quoting positivist studies

of child development, we try to understand in some depth the pattern of inter-
actions and decisions by which 'hard men' like Harris become what they are
(see e.g. Katz, 1988; Athens, 1989), we may come to see their ruthlessness, their
determination never to be humiliated again, to be feared if they cannot be loved,
as intelligible and even rational reactions to their situation. To paraphrase Marx,
such men make their own characters, but they do not make them just as they
please. To appreciate, and perhaps even empathize with, their reasons for acting
as they do, is not to say that those reasons should be exempt from moral censure (Downes and Rock, 1988: 100). Moral censure, which assumes that perpetrators have the capacity to behave differently, seems a more humane and
respectful response to serious wrong-doers than any of the likely alternatives. If
we see offenders 'as having a choice, if they see themselves as having the ability to make a choice, then we can provide supports that step by step undo an old
character and build a new one' (Lamb, 1996: 158).

But who is to censure them? If a judge presumes to punish Harris on behalf
of the state or of 'society', Harris might reasonably point out that this is the
same state that did nothing to rescue him from his appalling parents. How, he
might ask, can you punish me for being what I am, when you never gave me a
fair chance to become someone different? Whether or not any particular official
was negligent, Harris was left to endure what no child should have to endure,
and this was a grave injustice. What this calls into question is not so much
whether Harris was responsible for his actions, as whether the state had any
right to punish or censure him (as distinct from simply protecting others from
him) unless it also did what it could to make amends for that past injustice –
which, by sentencing him to death, it patently did not. This is not unrelated to
the issue of responsibility, since although people like Harris seem to be capable
of making choices for reasons, they hardly have the same capacity for 'reflective
self-control' – for understanding and acting upon moral reasons – as they might
have had with the benefit of a decent childhood (Wallace, 1994: 231–4).

A tenable view of someone like Harris is that he is (at least partially) responsible for his actions but that he has a 'right to rehabilitation', understood as an
educative process that would make him more fully capable of rational, morally
sensitive behaviour and would, as far as possible, overcome the harm done to
him in childhood (Rotman, 1990). The task for criminology is to understand how
(if at all) such rehabilitation can be effectively provided.

'Rotten social background'

In his remarkable dissenting judgement in *Alexander v US* 471 F.2d 923 (1973),
Chief Judge David Bazelon argued that in principle it should be open to a defendant to argue that what defence counsel called his 'rotten social background'

had left him unable to control himself when faced with racist taunts, just as he would (under the relevant law at that time) have had a defence of insanity if he was deprived of self-control by disease. The problem was, Bazelon pointed out, that people who are prone to explosive rage in the face of relatively common-place provocation need to be controlled, and if those with 'rotten backgrounds' were subjected to indefinite detention in the same way as the legally insane, the social injustice of which they were victims would only be aggravated.

In his excellent introduction to philosophical debates on responsibility, Matt Matravers (2007) argues that what troubles us in such cases is not necessarily whether or not the deprived person has 'reflective self-control' (cf. Wallace, 1994). Rather, we may 'think that at least some deprived wrong-doers have these powers, but that their pasts have inculcated the "wrong" values in them' (Matravers, 2007: 41). As criminologists from Merton (1957) to Young (1999) have argued, however, the 'wrong' values instilled into deprived offenders are closely related to the values of mainstream society, such as the desire for a big-spending consumerist lifestyle (with an emphasis on 'subterranean values' of hedonism and excitement) and the 'respect' due to them as men (see e.g. Wright et al., 2006). As Bourgois observes in his ethnography of crack-dealers, even behaviour 'that appears irrationally violent, "barbaric" and ultimately self-destructive to the outsider, can be reinterpreted according to the logic of the underground economy as judicious public relations and long-term invest-ment in one's "human capital development"' (1995: 24). The main issue here is, once again, what right the judge has, as the notional personification of 'soci-ety', to punish the offender for pursuing the very values that 'society' has instilled in him, while denying him access to legitimate means of achieving them; or for seeking to succeed in the informal economy when the formal economy has no use for him.

Antony Duff, who is committed to the idea that a legitimate criminal trial is a means by which a polity holds one of its citizens to account, writes:

> We rightly feel unease at realizing how many of those who are convicted and sentenced in our courts, receiving what are supposed to be their just deserts, have themselves been the victims of persisting and systemic injustice at the hands of the polity of which they are supposedly citizens (and thus at our hands as their fellow citizens). That unease sometimes motivates suggestions that serious (unjust) social disadvantage should be recognized as providing either a partial or a complete defense ... But we can more plausibly see the serious, systematic injustice that the defendant has suffered at the hands of the polity, not as a defence ... but as a moral bar to trial. If we fail to treat a person or group with the respect or concern due to them as fellow citizens, we may lose the moral standing to call them to account, to judge them or condemn them, for the wrongs that they commit as citizens. (Duff, 2007: 192)

But as Duff argues, to deny that the offender can be called to account at all would be to leave the victim without redress. He suggests that some form of restorative justice, involving not simply compensation to the victim but some attempt to restore civic relationships, may provide the best answer to this dilemma. The crucial question, in Duff's terms, is not *whether* unjustly deprived offenders are responsible, but *to whom* they can fairly be held responsible. Could there, for example, be forms of justice which, without verging on vigilantism, had some genuine claim to represent a local community – in particular, a community made up largely of the unjustly disadvantaged – rather than an abstract polity? (The forms of justice developed in some indigenous communities in Canada, New Zealand, Australia and elsewhere are of interest here: Stuart, 1996; Yazzie and Zion, 1996; Consedine, 1999.) By exploring questions like these, criminologists might be able to give the 'liberal idealist' vision of the criminal law a more radical edge.

Conclusion

From Maudsley (1874) onwards, criminologists have questioned whether individuals can be held fully responsible for their actions and suggested that in some sense society is responsible for crime. Although it is individuals who decide whether to commit acts of violence or dishonesty, when we study the spatial and temporal distribution of such events it can become apparent that they are the consequences of political and economic decisions. In Chapter 1 we discussed Danny Dorling's example of 'the man with the knife', whose actions can be traced through a succession of economic and political decisions all the way back to the former Prime Minister and those who voted for her (Dorling, 2004: 191).

There is no contradiction in holding both the individual murderer and the Prime Minister *morally* responsible for what happened, though of course it would be inconceivable in a democracy to hold an ex-prime minister, or her supporters, *criminally* responsible for a flawed economic policy. The man with the knife no doubt had reasons for what he did. Those reasons were a product of his social environment; and that environment was shaped by political decisions. The fact that one's social environment, or more precisely one's perception of that environment (reflecting, for example, a particular conception of masculinity), gives one certain reasons for action does not entail that acting on those reasons is morally acceptable. It does – and this, we would suggest, is the proper target of the socio-political critique of criminal law – call into question the right of those who pursue unjust policies with predictably criminogenic consequences to censure those who succumb to the pressures or temptations their policies create.

Judges, of course, are not generally responsible for social policy. But their claim to pronounce legitimate censure in matters that have nothing personally to do with them derives from a claim that they are in some sense 'speaking in the name and on behalf of the polity as a whole' (Duff, 2007: 53). If we regard the polity as a collective moral agent, of which punishment would ideally represent the moral voice, then that same collective moral agent must be held responsible for the social injustice that lies behind much interpersonal violence and small-scale property crime, and the legitimacy of punishment inflicted in its name is compromised. If, on the other hand, we deny that there is any such collective agent, then the judge is simply expressing his or her personal view (or that of a ruling elite) within the constraints of the law; and it is difficult to see why people should rot in prison for years just so that judges can broadcast their moral opinions more effectively.

A third possible view of the judge is that she is speaking on behalf of the victim. Whatever can be said about the social and economic background of offenders will not usually make it any less justifiable for the victims of crime to resent what offenders have done to them. The courts, it might be said, vindicate the victim's resentment and her rights by publicly censuring what has been done to her. At this point, the advocate of restorative justice will point out how little active role the victim plays in the process, and will argue that a genuine dialogue between offender and victim would be a far better way of expressing and clarifying moral values than a sentence handed down by the state.

We can sum up the arguments of this chapter in terms of three of the four critiques outlined in Chapter 1. The scientific critique accuses the criminal law of being dominated by a myth of free will. It advocates policies based on prevention, in which questions about a defendant's state of mind, though they could not be banished altogether, would be much less important than they are now. This now unfashionable view does not deserve to be dismissed as merely a relic of a discredited form of positivism. We have, however, defended the criminal law against this line of attack, drawing on a fairly orthodox, compatibilist account of moral and legal responsibility.

The socio-political critique of criminal law argues that it propagates a distorted image of social harm, by focussing on intentional wrong-doing rather than negligence that may be as or more immoral, and by neglecting the political and economic decisions that lead to crime. In so far as its target is the doctrine of criminal responsibility, we have found that critique to be overstated. Critics from this perspective would do better to concentrate their attacks on the state's right to punish, which thoughtful liberals like Duff (2007) concede is hard to defend where offenders are victims of social injustice.

Finally, the restorative critique argues that what calls for a response is the harm done to specific victims, rather than to 'society' at large, and victims should be much more involved in this process than they are now.

Summary

Criminal law censures conduct that is interpreted as freely chosen. The criminal law's commitment to some kind of 'free will' is not necessarily inconsistent with the kinds of causal explanation of conduct provided by the social sciences. Such explanations may tend to blunt the emotional force of 'reactive attitudes' of blame, resentment, etc. towards crime, though it is doubtful whether such attitudes ever could, or should, be eradicated. Doctrines of criminal responsibility reflect certain moral intuitions about who is an appropriate target for the 'reactive attitudes' and who is not. They have been challenged both 'internally' – on the ground that they draw the line in the wrong place – and 'externally', on the ground that any attempt to draw such a line is fundamentally misguided. The more tenable versions of the external critique, however, end up by accepting some form of responsible/irresponsible division and thus lead us back to the internal debate.

STUDY QUESTIONS

1. To what extent are assumptions about 'free choice' essential to criminal law? Are such assumptions compatible with criminological knowledge?

2. Explain the distinctions between intention, recklessness and negligence. Do you regard these distinctions as morally sound, or as ideological constructs which distract attention from major forms of social harm?

3. At what age do think young people should be treated as fully responsible for their actions, and why?

4. Is there a good case for replacing a punitive paradigm of criminal law with a preventive one? What changes in definitions of responsibility would this entail?

5. Do you share Antony Duff's 'unease' at punishing offenders who have suffered serious social injustice? If so, how many offenders does it affect and what are its practical applications? If not, why not?

FURTHER READING

A helpful introduction to the legal principles of criminal responsibility is C.M.V. Clarkson's *Understanding Criminal Law* (4th ed., 2005), Ch. 2. Matt Matravers's *Responsibility and Justice* (2007) is an excellent introduction to the philosophical debates about responsibility.

For a criminological perspective on philosophies of punishment, see Barbara Hudson's *Understanding Justice* (1996) and *Justice in the Risk Society* (2003). For a stimulating debate about youth justice, including the age of criminal responsibility, *Debating Youth Justice: From Punishment to Problem Solving?*, edited by Zoe Davies and Will McMahon, can be downloaded from http://www.crimeandjustice.org.uk/opus207.html

Notes

1 We follow Wallace (1994) in seeing resentment, indignation and guilt as the core reactive attitudes; Strawson himself used the term more loosely.
2 Gardner (2007) fits our profile of a 'liberal idealist' in some respects, but he rejects (in Ch. 10) the idea that criminal law has a single overarching goal.
3 In Humberside and some other police force areas, some drivers caught speeding are given the option of attending (for a fee) a seminar on the dangers of excessive speed as an alternative to prosecution. See http://www.humbersidesafetycameras.com/about-safety-cameras/speed-seminars (accessed 8 July 2009).
4 For examples see http://www.statewatch.org/asbo/ASBOwatch.html
5 See the partly dissenting judgement of Judges Rozakis and Costa in *T v UK* (1999) 7 BHRC 659, arguing that the period of detention faced by Jamie Bulger's killers was inhuman and degrading because it took no account of their 'transformation' due to increasing age.
6 While the ECtHR in *T v UK* (op. cit.) held that there was no agreed European standard as to the age of responsibility, five judges dissented on the ground that a norm could be discerned that the age of responsibility should be no lower than 13 or 14.

5

Responsibility and Homicide

Chapter Contents

OVERVIEW

Chapter 5 discusses the new law on homicide (which at the time of writing has yet to be debated by the House of Lords). The partial defences to murder - diminished responsibility, loss of control (formerly provocation) and infanticide - illustrate current debates over responsibility.

KEY TERMS

murder manslaughter diminished responsibility loss of control infanticide

In this chapter we continue our discussion of responsibility through an examination of the changes in the law of homicide in England and Wales which are going through Parliament at the time of writing (Coroners and Justice Bill, 2009). In addition to being topical, the legislation brings some of the moral issues discussed in Chapter 4 into focus, and provides a context for further exploration of the relations between legal and criminological accounts of responsibility.

As we saw in Chapter 4, to hold someone morally responsible is to regard them as an appropriate target for 'reactive attitudes' of praise and blame. To hold someone legally responsible is to regard them as an appropriate target of punitive sanctions. As one of the purposes of criminal punishment is to give institutional expression to those reactive attitudes that the state wishes to encourage, it is usually considered desirable that criminal responsibility, at least in serious cases, should track moral responsibility. When we hold people morally responsible, we take them to have acted for reasons, and our evaluation of those reasons prompts our reactions of praise or blame. We blame people who act for bad reasons and who disregard good reasons for acting otherwise. To be blameworthy, people must be able both to *recognize* and to *react to* the reasons that apply to them (Fischer and Ravizza, 1998). That is, they must be able to understand those reasons, and they must be capable of choosing to act in accord with them (defining the latter capacity precisely is extraordinarily difficult – Fischer and Ravizza make a good attempt but we doubt whether they succeed).

The distinction between recognition of reasons and reaction to them is an important one which illuminates some important divisions within both law and criminology. We can see this in the Victorian debates discussed in Chapter 4. The legal doctrine of responsibility was concerned almost entirely with the defendant's capacity to recognize the reasons for acting lawfully. In 1843 the judges formulated a definition of insanity that remains in effect to this day (*McNaghten's Case* [1843–60] All ER Rep. 229). According to this definition, defendants are responsible so long as they know the 'nature and quality' of their actions and know that they are legally or morally wrong, i.e. they can recognize the legal and moral reasons not to do them. Critics of the rules, like Henry Maudsley, complained that many insane people knew their acts were wrong but were 'irresistibly' impelled to do them – they *recognized* the reasons for refraining from crime but were unable to *react to* those reasons. As we have seen, Maudsley and other medical or criminological writers went on to argue that scientific observation of imprisoned criminals showed that many of them were also severely deficient in 'self-control'. They were aware of legal and moral reasons to refrain from crime but were too weak-minded to resist the temptations of the moment. As the difficulty of drawing any clear distinction between those who 'could not' and those who 'would not' react to reasons for refraining from crime became apparent, some criminologists argued for an abandonment of the responsible/irresponsible distinction, while many lawyers argued with renewed rigour for a traditional definition of responsibility on the basis of recognition to reasons. Modern positivist criminology has retained the image of the typical criminal as someone who reacts to short-term incentives and frustrations and ignores longer-term risks and goals (Gottfredson and Hirschi, 1990), but it has tended, as we saw in Chapter 4, to steer clear of philosophical puzzles about responsibility.

By contrast to the positivist approach, the kind of sociological criminology to which we are more sympathetic has tended to portray offenders as both recognizing and reacting to the reasons that apply to them. Conscious both of the economic or hedonistic advantages of crime and of the norms against it, actors respond by 'withdraw[ing] emotional support from the rules' (Merton, 1957: 136), by 'neutralizing' the moral bind of the law (Matza, 1969) or by 'empower[ing] the world to seduce [them] into criminality' (Katz, 1988: 7). People are portrayed as autonomously and creatively reacting to the reasons for and against breaking rules. To the occasional embarrassment of its practitioners (Cohen, 1979), this kind of criminology implicitly reaffirms the moral responsibility of the great majority of offenders. But it also tends, as we have seen, to highlight the moral and political responsibility of those who create the configuration of reasons to which criminal actors respond.

In this context, let us now look at the three defences to murder that the British government is trying to reform. They are all partial defences: they reduce what would otherwise be murder to a lesser offence but do not lead to a full acquittal. Diminished responsibility and provocation both reduce murder to manslaughter; infanticide is both a partial defence to murder and the offence of which those who successfully plead the defence are convicted.

Diminished responsibility

The Homicide Act 1957, a political compromise which sought, unsuccessfully, to fend off demands for the abolition of the death penalty (Christoph, 1962), provides in section 2:

> Where a person kills or is party to the killing of another, he shall not be convicted of murder if he was suffering from such abnormality of mind (whether arising from a condition of arrested or retarded development of mind or any inherent causes or induced by disease or injury) as substantially impaired his mental responsibility for his acts and omissions in doing or being a party to the killing.

The Act does not tell us what 'mental responsibility' means, but the Court of Criminal Appeal (the precursor of the Court of Appeal, Criminal Division) shed some light on the matter in the case of *Byrne* [1960] 2 Q.B. 396, stating that it 'points to a consideration of the extent to which the accused's mind is answerable for his physical acts which must include a consideration of the extent of his ability to exercise will power to control his physical acts' (403). Byrne was a 'sexual psychopath' who raped, killed and mutilated a young woman. There seems to have been no doubt that he knew what he was doing and knew he was breaking the law. In other words he was not insane in the legal sense. The basis of his defence was that his abnormal sexual urges were so strong that it was difficult or impossible for him to resist acting on them. That, according to the Court of Appeal, was an adequate basis for a defence of diminished responsibility.

Taylor (1976: 44) found that sexual offenders in the 1960s commonly offered 'accounts which talk of inner impulse', portraying the actor 'as an unhappy spectator during the operation of his own irreversible and uncontrollable urges'. Such 'vocabularies of motive' were, he argued, learned from accepted medical and legal accounts. The problem was not that deviant urges were innately uncontrollable, but that by *defining* them as uncontrollable, actors freed themselves to act on their desires and override the reasons for restraint. Rather than define offenders in a way that made their behaviour appear immutable and unavoidable, argued Taylor, we should criticize them for the choices they made: in other words, hold them fully responsible. Though he did not discuss homicide, his argument implicitly criticizes the kind of reasoning found in *Byrne*.

The use of diminished responsibility has declined in recent years, and it seems doubtful whether Byrne's defence would succeed today. Of those cases recorded as homicides in 1992 which resulted in homicide convictions, 15.8% were for diminished responsibility manslaughter, while the comparable figure for cases recorded in 2002/3 was only 2.6% (calculated from Povey, 2004, Table 1.02 and Povey, 2008, Table 1.02). The reasons are not entirely clear (Mackay, 2004) but seem to indicate an increasing medico-legal consensus in favour of holding most killers fully responsible for their actions. The majority of diminished responsibility verdicts do not result from jury decisions but from the prosecution agreeing to accept a plea of not guilty to murder but guilty to manslaughter, and the range of cases covered by this medico-legal consensus appears to have narrowed.

This trend toward greater responsibility was also reflected in the Law Commission's recent (2006) proposals that a diminished responsibility defence should result in a conviction for a new offence of second-degree murder, rather than manslaughter. As Quick and Wells (2006) argue, the Law Commission seems to have been influenced by a general mood of 'getting tough', and more specifically by prosecutors' accounts of the views of victims. The government has postponed a decision on the proposal for degrees of murder, but has followed the Law Commission's advice in proposing to replace the confused notion of 'mental responsibility' with a requirement that those who raise the defence suffer from an 'abnormality of mental functioning' arising from 'a recognized medical condition' that 'substantially impaired' their ability to understand the nature of their conduct, 'to form a rational judgement' or 'to exercise self-control' (Coroners and Justice Bill, 2009, clause 46).

The effect of these changes is a subtle but significant shift in the relations between the expert and the jury in cases where the plea is contested. The use of the term 'recognized mental condition' is designed to 'encourage reference within expert evidence to diagnosis in terms of one or two of the accepted internationally classificatory systems of mental conditions (WHO ICD10 and AMA DSM)[1] without explicitly writing those systems into the legislation' (Royal College of Psychiatrists, quoted by Law Commission, 2006, para. 5.114). The use of these classificatory systems for legal purposes is, to say the least, problematic. They are just that: systems of classification that enable medical professionals to communicate with one another about conditions of interest to them with a reasonable degree of confidence that they are talking about the same thing (Bolton, 2008). They are not designed to draw a 'scientific' boundary between health and illness, let alone between responsibility and non-responsibility.

The medical classification that causes probably the greatest difficulty under the existing law is 'alcohol dependence syndrome'. Until recently it was thought that alcohol dependence could not qualify as an 'inherent cause' or 'disease' within the meaning of the 1957 Act unless it had either caused organic brain damage or produced a condition in which drinking was 'involuntary' (*Tandy* [1989] 1 WLR 350). In *Wood* [2008] EWCA Crim 1305 the Court of Appeal decided that alcohol dependence syndrome was capable of being considered a 'disease' whether or not those conditions were met. While accepting a 'disease model' of alcoholism, the court in *Wood* recognized that the notion of 'involuntary' drinking – a complete inability to react to reasons not to drink – made little sense:

> Even a true alcoholic stops drinking sometimes. He will get dressed, or wash, or perform everyday functions without necessarily keeping a glass or bottle to his lips. He will stop drinking and go to bed. In one sense these actions all represent a deliberate choice not to drink and, if so, that implies that the defendant makes a further choice about when he will resume drinking. (Ibid., para. 37)

The question was not whether the defendant's drinking was involuntary but whether his dependence on alcohol 'was of such an extent and nature that it constitutes an abnormality of mind induced by disease or illness', and that was for the jury to decide (ibid., para. 41). Rather than a binary division between 'voluntary' and 'involuntary' drinking, *Wood* recognizes that the difficulty of refraining from drink is a matter of degree, and leaves it to the jury to decide whether that degree of difficulty is such as to amount to an 'abnormality of mind'.

Critics of the 'disease model' argue that a habitual drinker's decision to have another drink is merely one instance of the common phenomenon of people choosing short-term satisfactions in preference to longer-term goals (Fingarette, 1988; Rumgay, 1998). It is debateable whether this ever deserves to be called an 'abnormality of mental functioning', let alone a 'disease'. *Wood* leaves this difficult philosophical and criminological issue to be resolved by juries on a case-by-case basis, and so does the new law. This seems unnecessarily complex given that murder is what is called a 'crime of specific intent', meaning that the prosecution is required to prove that the defendant intended either to kill the victim or to cause serious harm. If the defendant caused the victim's death while too intoxicated to form such an intention he will be guilty of manslaughter rather than murder. Is there really a need for an additional defence for someone who clearly did have the requisite intention but would not have had it but for the effect of drink or drugs?

Under the new law, if the experts say that the defendant meets the criteria for alcohol dependence syndrome under DSM-IV or ICD-10, then unless their evidence for that conclusion is exposed as hopelessly flimsy, that would appear to settle the question of whether the defendant has a 'recognized medical condition'. The jury – if the case is contested – will then have to consider whether the disorder 'substantially impaired' the defendant's ability 'to exercise self-control'. Here what the Law Commission (2006, para. 5.119) envisaged was that the expert would explain the likely effect of the disorder and leave it to the jury to decide whether it amounted to 'substantial impairment'. It would be a bold jury that decided that a defendant who met the diagnostic criteria for substance dependence did not have a substantially impaired ability to control his alcohol consumption. The next question would be whether that impairment 'provides an explanation' of the killing. The Law Commission sees this as requiring 'an appropriate connection (that is, one that grounds a case for mitigation of the offence) between the abnormality of mental functioning ... and the killing' (2006, para. 5.124). The evaluative element of this concept of 'explanation' is not explicit in the Bill. If the defendant would not have killed had he not been drunk, and would not have been drunk but for his alcohol dependence, then his alcohol dependence seems to 'provide an explanation' for the killing. Whether it 'grounds a case for mitigation' is a different question. Similarly, the defendant's 'sexual psychopathy' in *Byrne* (above) provided an 'explanation' (of sorts) for his crime – he raped and killed a woman because he had an abnormally strong desire to rape and kill women. Whether that 'mitigated' the crime is quite a different question.

Provocation or loss of control

The most significant reforms proposed for English homicide are those proposed for the defence of provocation. The bill nominally abolishes the common-law defence of provocation and replaces it with a statutory defence of 'loss of control'. Like the old defence, the new one will reduce what would otherwise be murder to manslaughter (and not to the new offence of second-degree murder proposed by the Law Commission, 2006). By dropping the name 'provocation' the government presumably intends to make the defence less offensive to relatives of victims, whose 'provocative' conduct is implicitly blamed for their own deaths. The 'new' defence is unmistakeably provocation under another name, but with changes designed to make it less available to hot-tempered men and more suitable to desperate women striking back at their abusers.

The new law retains the concept of self-control, which the Law Commission described as 'a judicially invented concept, lacking sharpness or a clear foundation in psychology' (2004, para. 330). Self-control is a familiar concept to criminologists, having been a cornerstone of positivism from Ellis (1890) to Gottfredson and Hirschi (1990) (and given a critical spin by Morrison, 1995). Essentially, it is the ability or disposition to forego satisfaction of one's immediate desires in order to attain long-term goals or comply with moral values. When the defence of provocation first emerged in the seventeenth century, it did not depend on a 'loss of control' but rather on the sort of hot-blooded anger that a gentleman of honour was expected to display in certain circumstances (Horder, 1992; Spierenburg, 2008). Victorian judges, concerned to encourage greater self-control among working-class men, confined the defence to certain narrowly defined circumstances where a loss of self-control was considered to be understandable, such as catching one's wife in the act of adultery (Wiener, 2006). The Homicide Act 1957, s.3, removed these restrictions so that where the defendant claims that anything was said or done to cause him to lose his self-control, 'the question whether the provocation was enough to make a reasonable man do as he did shall be left to be determined by the jury', according to the effect that such a provocation would have on a 'reasonable man'. The new defence combines elements of the early 'righteous anger' and the later 'loss of self-control' models and tightens up the definition of provocative conduct.

The defence will apply to defendants who lose their self-control as a result of either or both of two 'qualifying triggers': fear of serious violence to themselves or other identifiable persons; or 'circumstances of an extremely grave character' that caused them to have 'a justifiable sense of being seriously wronged'. 'Fear of violence' allows the defence to be used in circumstances that come close to self-defence but where the use of force cannot be justified as 'necessary' and 'reasonable'. An example would be the well-known case of *Kiranjit Ahluwalia* [1992] 4 All ER 889. The defendant's husband, who had violently abused her for many years, had told her he would beat her in the morning; she poured petrol over him and set fire to him while he slept. It would be hard to argue that this was 'necessary' or 'reasonable' in order to avert a beating (but see Horder, 2001, for a careful argument that some women in a broadly similar position could make out a good case of self-defence). She would, though, appear to have had both a fear of serious violence and a 'justifiable sense of being seriously wronged'.

This second 'qualifying trigger' reflects what Kahan and Nussbaum (1996) have termed an 'evaluative' rather than a 'mechanistic' conception of the emotions. Becoming angry is not simply a physiological response to a stimulus; it *embodies* (in a literal sense) a strong negative evaluation of the person or situation that arouses anger, which may amount to a 'sense of being seriously wronged'. The evaluative character of anger is captured well in Katz's (1988) descriptions of 'righteous slaughter', where the actor responds to humiliation with lethal violence that he or she sees as a last desperate stand in defence of 'the right'. Kiranjit Ahluwalia's crime, for example, seems like a last stand in defence of her personal autonomy after years of humiliation.

Of course, the values that killers defend are not always those that the law is meant to uphold. They include, for example, sexual possessiveness and men's sense of entitlement to control 'their' women. The Bill makes the defence available only where the defendant's sense of being seriously wronged is 'justifiable'. In some situations the judge will be able to withdraw the question of whether the defendant had such a justifiable sense from the jury. The defence will not be available unless the circumstances are of 'exceptional gravity'. It is unlikely that, for example, the provocation offered in the leading case of *Morhall* [1996] AC 90 – a glue-sniffer being taunted about his glue-sniffing – would meet this test. The Bill also specifically provides that whether something said or done 'constituted sexual infidelity' must not be taken into account in deciding whether it was a 'qualifying trigger'. Suppose a wife finds her husband having sex with her teenage daughter – a jury could consider this an 'exceptionally grave' circumstance that gave her a 'justifiable sense of being seriously wronged' on the basis of the abuse of her daughter and her husband's betrayal of trust as a stepfather, without taking account of the element of infidelity. An apparent loophole in the Bill is that there is nothing to prevent the jury taking account of perceived sexual misconduct *not* amounting to infidelity. For example in *Mohamed* [2005] EWCA Crim 1880, the defendant, a devout Muslim, killed his unmarried daughter after finding a man in her bedroom. It could be argued that given the father's religious beliefs this was a circumstance of 'exceptional gravity' and he was justified in feeling seriously wronged. How far a defendant's religion or culture can be taken into account in determining what is 'justifiable' is not clear from the Bill.

The Bill also stipulates that the defendant must not have acted out of a 'considered desire for revenge'. In cases like *Ahluwalia,* distinguishing between a 'loss of control' and a considered act of revenge is not easy, and the Court of Appeal played down the evidence or Mrs Ahluwalia's purchases of caustic soda and petrol, which might suggest a premeditated crime (Nicolson, 1995: 195–6). The requirement under the old law for a 'sudden and temporary loss of self-control' (*Duffy* [1949] 1 All ER 932) caused particular difficulty in such cases. The Court of Appeal accepted in *Ahluwalia* that the requirement of 'suddenness' did not mean that the loss of control had to follow immediately on the last provocative act, and that the last act need not be the sole cause of the loss of control but might be the 'last straw' in a long course of conduct. In this way the old law could accommodate what Mrs Ahluwalia's counsel called the 'slow-burn' reaction to violence. Under the new law, there will be no requirement that the loss of control be 'sudden' at all. The provisions about infidelity and 'considered desire for revenge' should ensure that there will be no defence for the common type of murderer (Polk, 1995) who carries out the planned killing of his partner to punish her for infidelity or some other perceived transgression.

Instead of asking whether a 'reasonable man' might have been provoked to act as the defendant did, under the new law the test will be how 'a person of D's sex and age, with a normal degree of tolerance and self-restraint and in the circumstances of D' ('D' being the defendant) might have acted (clause 44(1)(c)). Rewording the test in this way avoids the troubling suggestion that killing under provocation can ever be a 'reasonable' act (cf. *Campbell* [1997] 1 Cr. App. R. 199: 207). It also appears to allow some characteristics of the defendant to be taken into account, so long as they do not relate only to 'tolerance and self-restraint'.

This point is of considerable importance in relation to 'battered woman' cases. In *Ahluwalia* the Lord Chief Justice accepted that if the defendant were in a state of 'learned helplessness', that would be a characteristic that could be taken into account in considering how the 'reasonable' woman would have behaved; but he rejected the defence on the ground that the defence had introduced no expert evidence (nor evidence from the defendant herself) that she was in fact suffering from 'battered woman syndrome'. (The court ordered a retrial on the basis that new psychiatric evidence could have supported a defence not of provocation but of diminished responsibility.) The courts' acceptance in this and some other cases that defendants' psychological characteristics could be taken into account in assessing the 'reasonableness' of their actions was highly controversial. It was endorsed by a majority of the House of Lords in *Smith (Morgan)* [2000] 3 WLR 654, but then disapproved by a special nine-member panel of the Privy Council in *Attorney-General for Jersey* v. *Holley* [2005] UKPC 23. Under *Holley*, which is accepted as stating the present law in England and Wales, personal characteristics can be taken into account only if they affect the gravity of the provocation. Under the current Bill, all of the defendant's circumstances can be taken into account 'other than those whose only relevance to D's conduct is that they bear on D's general capacity for tolerance or self-restraint' (clause 48(3)). Arguably, the kind of characteristics discussed in *Ahluwalia* are relevant to the gravity of the provocation or, under the new law, of the defendant's fear of violence or sense of wrong. A woman who feels confident enough to leave her husband before he beats her again has less reason to fear his violence, and may feel less humiliated by his threats, than one who feels herself trapped in a violent relationship. But such a feeling of being trapped could also be classed as a 'circumstance' of the defendant that should be taken into account in assessing how the 'person of ordinary tolerance and self-restraint' would have acted in the circumstances. It does not make her less tolerant or self-restrained but narrows the range of responses that is psychologically possible for her.

The danger in such arguments is that of portraying the defendant as a passive victim rather than an agent responding purposefully to desperate circumstances (Nicolson, 1995; Ballinger, 2005). Defendants like Ahluwalia are not mindless automata acting on blind impulses (Horder, 1992: 101, 177; Uniacke, 2007: 105); but they seem not to respond as they normally would to the legal, moral and prudential reasons for refraining from acting as they do. A person who is justifiably enraged by some serious wrong, or who is terrified, may be deprived of a fair opportunity to exercise reflective judgement on all the moral and legal reasons that should inform her response (Uniacke, 2007: 106–7). As Katz (1988: 43) puts it, rage (like terror) tends to 'block out' concern for the future. It is this 'blocking' of a person's ordinary capacities for reflection and foresight, we would suggest, that constitutes a partial excuse for killing.

Infanticide

Infanticide is one of two defences in English criminal law which is available only to women (the other being marital coercion[2]). Where a mother 'by any wilful act or omission causes the death of her child' before the child's first birthday, and if 'the balance of her mind was disturbed by reason of her not having fully recovered from the effect of giving birth to the child or by reason of the effect of lactation consequent upon the birth of the child', then rather than being guilty of murder she is guilty of infanticide, an offence which in practice usually results in a non-custodial sentence (Infanticide Act, 1938, s.1). The only effect of the current Bill is to make it clear that the Act applies only to acts or omissions which would otherwise have amounted to murder (reversing a surprising decision by the Court of Appeal in *Gore* [2007] EWCA Crim 2789).

Though the Infanticide Act seems a curious, and discriminatory, piece of legislation, it does make sense in its historical context (see Ward, 1999, 2002). In its original form, passed in 1922, the Act applied only to a woman who killed her *newly born* baby while the balance of her mind was disturbed. It was aimed at a type of case that aroused considerable public sympathy but where the defendants were *not* usually seen as 'mentally disturbed' in a medical sense. Typically they were young, poor, unmarried women who concealed their pregnancies because they were afraid of the stigma, and often the loss of employment, that they would face if discovered. They gave birth in secret and killed their babies shortly afterwards. Juries were reluctant to convict them of murder when they were assumed to have acted out of a combination of shame, panic and physical pain. It also seemed unfair that the mother should be sentenced to death (even if the sentence would never be carried out) while the man who had abandoned, or in some cases raped, her went scot-free. The Director of Public Prosecutions, who was involved in drafting the Bill, commented as follows on the phrase 'the balance of her mind was disturbed':

> No one can doubt what it means when one visualises the scene in the bedroom – the child crying, the woman possibly very inexperienced, a difficult labour, the umbilical cord to be dealt with and, if I may use the homely phrase 'the breakfast to be got ready as usual in the morning' ... so that she, under stress of circumstances and not being mistress of her actions, does what in cold blood she never would have done. (Bodkin, 1922)

After the 1922 Act was passed it became apparent that by limiting the defence to killers of 'newly born' babies, it actually excluded most of the cases in which mothers were found to be suffering from 'puerperal insanity', the symptoms of which (as in present-day puerperal psychosis) usually became apparent two weeks or more after the birth. To accommodate these cases the 1938 Act extended the age limit for the victim to one year. It also introduced the idea of the mother's mind being disturbed by lactation. In fact contemporary medical opinion did not attribute maternal psychosis to lactation alone, but rather to the combined effects of prolonged breast-feeding, malnutrition, anaemia and exhaustion (Ward, 2002). Singling out 'lactation' rather than poverty as the legally relevant cause made it politically acceptable to allow the mother a defence.

What this history suggests is that infanticide, which at first sight looks like a psychiatric defence with a very dubious medical basis, is really more akin to provocation. As in provocation, the killer is understood as acting under extremely stressful circumstances which produce an overwhelming emotional reaction and 'block out' the moral and prudential considerations that in ordinary circumstances would keep her from killing. Cases still occur which are quite close to those which the 1922 Act was aimed at: mothers who deny their pregnancy – probably even to themselves – give birth in secret and either kill their babies or allow them to die (Wheelwright, 2002). The *Gore* case which prompted the limited change to the 1938 Act in the current Bill was an example. In other cases the defence seems to reflect a simple inability to cope with a baby in difficult social circumstances (Mackay, 1993). It is not easy to see why, of all the people who commit offences as a result of difficult social circumstances and emotional problems, infanticidal mothers alone should be singled out for such very special treatment. Neither, on the other hand, is there any great clamour for such women to be given a life sentence. There seem to be good pragmatic reasons for leaving the infanticide defence alone.

Conclusion

Infanticide epitomizes the dilemma that the partial defences to murder pose for many criminologists. Our theoretical commitments lead us to emphasize the agency of the great majority of offenders, to understand them as choosing to act as they do for intelligible reasons, and to eschew medical explanations in all but extreme cases. That position seems to imply that most offenders can properly be held fully responsible for their actions. But to take that stance in the current penal climate is to condemn many people to harsh and – it seems to us – largely futile punishment. In a sense there is an easy – but politically unrealistic – answer to that dilemma: abolish the mandatory life sentence for murder. 'Mercy' killers, battered women, aggressive drunken men and professional killers are all responsible for their actions but vary greatly in their culpability, and a law which treats all alike is morally insensitive. But the dilemma for critical social scientists runs deeper than that, and one of the main messages of this book is to encourage our readers to face up to it.

Summary

The Coroners and Justice Bill introduces significant changes in the law of homicide, particularly with regard to the former defence of provocation, which will in future be called loss of control. The new law fails to resolve a number of difficult issues such as the effect of substance dependence on diminished responsibility; the extent to which individual characteristics, particularly those of victims of persistent abuse, may be taken into account in assessing loss of control; and the relevance of cultural and religious factors to a person's sense of being 'seriously wronged'. The new law also illustrates how a criminology which treats most offenders as autonomous agents can be taken to provide some support for narrowing the scope of some criminal defences, thus possibly encouraging the drift towards a more punitive system which most criminologists would oppose.

STUDY QUESTIONS

1. Has the Coroners and Justice Act come into force? Were the relevant provisions amended at all from the Bill discussed above?

2. See if you can find any examples of the new defences being raised in court. (Try newspaper websites, BAILII, or Westlaw and Lexis-Nexis if they are available.) Has the new law given rise to any difficulties?

3. Do our comments on alcohol dependence strike you as harsh? Under what circumstances, if any, should intoxication by alcohol or drugs constitute a full or partial excuse for crime?

4. Do you agree with the exclusion of sexual infidelity from the circumstances that can trigger a loss of control?

5. To what extent (if any) should cultural or religious factors be taken into account in assessing a defendant's 'sense of being seriously wronged'?

6. Is there any justification for retaining a separate offence of infanticide?

FURTHER READING

Belinda Morrissey's *Women Who Kill* (2003) provides an excellent and thought-provoking discussion of many of the issues we have covered. So, in a historical context, does Anette Ballinger's article '"Reasonable" Women Who Kill' (2005), freely available on the internet. In *Murder* (2006), Shani D'Cruze, Sandra Walklate and Samantha Pegg provide an interesting mix of historical and contemporary material, though their account of the law is unreliable. The changes we have discussed will render all current textbooks out-of-date, but Jonathan Herring's *Criminal Law: Text, Cases and Materials* (3rd ed. 2008), Ch. 5, leads the reader from basic definitions into the heart of the theoretical debates.

Notes

1 World Health Organization, International Classification of Diseases, 10th ed.; American Medical Association, Diagnostic and Statistical Manual of Mental Disorders, 4th ed., 1994 (usually abbreviated as DSM-IV).

2 This little-used defence is available only to a married woman who commits an offence in the presence of, and under pressure from, her husband. Unlike duress it need not involve a threat of violence: it is sufficient that the defendant's will is overborne by psychological pressure (*Shortland* [1996] 1 Cr. App. R. 116).

6

White-collar and Corporate Crime and the Law

Chapter Contents

OVERVIEW

Chapter 6:

- Outlines the reasons criminologists give for the relative neglect of white-collar and corporate crime by criminal law.

- Describes two broad strategies – differentiation and assimilation – through which the law approaches corporate wrong-doing.

- Explains why strict liability in criminal law is controversial.

- Traces the emergence and development of strict liability in criminal law.

- Discusses the desire to convict corporate bodies of 'traditional' criminal offences.

KEY TERMS

white-collar and corporate crime strict liability *mens rea* corporate criminal liability

Introduction

Some criminologists argue that a significant or even primary topic of criminological inquiry should be white-collar and corporate crime. These terms refer roughly to phenomena such as crimes (and analogous harmful acts) committed within businesses, by businesses, and by the respectable and powerful, along with environmental pollution, health and safety violations, money-laundering and large-scale frauds (Newburn, 2007: Ch. 18). In studying such phenomena, one of the first observations criminologists tend to make is that white-collar and corporate crime are relatively neglected by the criminal law. Although the social and financial harm arising from such crime is almost certainly much larger than that stemming from 'traditional' crimes committed by low-status people, much of it tends to go unpunished or to be punished relatively leniently.

Within criminology, various explanations for the relative neglect of white-collar and corporate crime by the criminal law have been suggested:

1   A lot of injurious behaviour identified by the label white-collar and corporate crime is not officially defined as criminal.
2   Even if it is officially defined as a criminal offence, it does not receive the attention by law enforcement agencies which it needs.

3   Even if they are prosecuted, powerful individual and corporate bodies can use their resources to avoid conviction.
4   Even if convicted, perpetrators of white-collar and corporate crime tend to receive comparatively lenient penalties.
5   Being designed with individuals in mind, traditional legal conceptions of criminal responsibility are difficult to apply to corporate wrong-doing.
6   Although much white-collar and corporate crime has individual victims, patterns of victimization do not match those of traditional crime.
7   Governments have self-interested reasons for not taking corporate crime seriously.

It is important to emphasize that much white-collar and corporate crime is handled in a different way to traditional crime, i.e. by regulatory agencies separate from the police. These agencies tend to perceive their task, not as the suppression of undesirable behaviour, but as the control of essential social activities such as production, trade and business with a view to ensuring that the safety and well-being of workers, consumers and the general public are protected. Their practical goal is to obtain compliance with regulatory codes rather than to punish wrong-doing (Richardson, 1987). To this end, they tend to use a variety of methods of obtaining compliance, including persuasion and advice. Criminal prosecution tends to be considered as one instrument among many for obtaining compliance.

Among the questions which criminologists and legal scholars have raised is whether this 'flexible' way of dealing with white-collar and corporate crime is effective and fair (Ashworth, 2006: 166; Newburn, 2007: 400). In this chapter, our main aim is to contribute to criminological discussion of these issues by describing various legal strategies for controlling white-collar and corporate crime. In addition, we want to look at how these efforts to tackle such problems have shaped the criminal law itself.

Differentiation and assimilation

Norrie (2001) provides a useful framework for thinking about this issue. He suggests that the basic concepts of contemporary criminal law were developed in the nineteenth century in the context of attempts to control 'working-class deviance'. The preferred form of control was one which focussed upon individuals, holding them personally responsible for their wrongful actions and the results of these actions. He suggests that those who shaped the criminal law in this period did not envisage it being applied to respectable people of the same social class as themselves. Nor did they envisage it being applied to corporate entities rather than individual human beings.

As awareness grew that corporate wrong-doing was a source of social harm as great as or even greater than that emanating from the wrongs of individuals from the lower social classes, attempts were made to apply the criminal law to corporate wrong-doing. Norrie suggests that two broad strategies were adopted: differentiation and assimilation. The former operates on the basis of a differentiation between corporate and individual crime. Corporate wrong-doing is regarded as quasi-criminal and dealt with through offences of strict liability which are quite different from ordinary offences in that they do not require proof of *mens rea*, i.e. proof that the 'wrong-doer' acted intentionally or recklessly (or perhaps negligently) in causing harm of a sort prohibited by the law. Assimilation operates on the basis that corporate wrong-doing is 'real crime' and attempts to define it using the standard concepts of criminal liability. In particular, it attempts to adapt the concept of *mens rea*, making it applicable to wrongs committed by corporate entities. Neither strategy, according to Norrie, succeeds in subjecting corporate wrong-doing to the sort of criminal condemnation that the law attaches to 'working-class deviance'.

In what follows, we will use Norrie's framework, looking first at strict liability and then at attempts to apply the concept of *mens rea* to corporate wrong-doing.

Strict liability

An offence of strict liability is one for which the prosecution need not prove *mens rea*, in order to secure a conviction, for some or all of the elements of the *actus reus* of the offence (Leigh, 1982: 1). Within contemporary criminal law scholarship these offences are generally seen as aberrations – departures from the general principle that a person may not be convicted of a crime unless they acted in a prohibited way (the *actus reus*) with a certain state of mind (the *mens rea*) such as 'knowingly', intentionally' or 'recklessly'.

This principle is widely regarded as being of crucial moral significance. Arguably it ensures that only those who *meant* to harm other people or violate their property rights, or did something dangerous with reckless disregard for the safety of other people or their property, are subject to the condemnation and stigma of criminal conviction and punishment. Those who cause such harm without meaning to, or without displaying recklessness, are not subjected to such condemnation. Hence, it is regularly suggested that *mens rea* plays the crucial role of ensuring that only those people who are proved to be at fault for harm resulting from their actions or omissions to act are punished for crimes (Herring, 2008: 146).

Because the creation of strict liability crimes dispenses with the requirement to prove *mens rea* – for at least one element of the *actus reus* – they are frequently criticized for flouting this basic principle of criminal justice. Dispensing with *mens rea* seems to allow 'the conviction of a person who ... is either free from moral fault, or who has not been proved to be so at fault' (Leigh, 1982: 7). For many criminal legal scholars such offences are therefore morally repugnant and should not exist. A few are willing to accept that strict liability might be acceptable for trivial offences which are widely regarded as 'not really criminal' and which 'do not carry the weight of moral censure that more serious crimes carry' (see Herring, 2008: 214). For such offences, economic considerations – such as the costs involved (e.g. time spent on investigations, court time) in requiring prosecutors to prove fault – may override moral objections to convicting people who have not been proved at fault. However, those who think strict liability may be acceptable in such cases tend to do so on the assumption that there is barely any social stigma attached to being convicted of such offences and the penalties are – relative to other criminal sanctions – mild (Ashworth, 2006: 169–70). Principles of justice are deemed to require that conviction for more serious offences – which can result in stigma and severe punishment such as imprisonment – should be on the basis of proof of *mens rea*.

Nevertheless, offences of strict liability are the most numerous offences in English criminal law (Ashworth, 2006: 164). Nor is strict liability reserved for conduct which is obviously 'not truly criminal' or for which the punishments are slight.

The emergence and development of strict liability

The use of strict liability in criminal law accelerated in the nineteenth century. This occurred in the context of the creation of a whole raft of legislation providing for the detailed regulation of activities such as manufacturing, food and drug production and sale, sewage disposal, construction of residential property and transportation. Some flavour of the nature of this regulation can be gained simply by looking at a list of key examples. The following come from a key period – the 1860s–1890s: the Factory Act 1878, the Liquor Licensing Act 1872, the Food and Drugs Act 1875, the Public Health Act 1875, the Rivers Pollution Prevention Acts 1876 and 1893, and the Regulation of Railways Act 1868. Inspectorates and similar regulatory bodies were given legal powers to enforce the regulations contained in such legislation.

These acts created a whole new field of criminal offences, since breaches of the regulations they contained were generally criminal offences which could result in criminal prosecution and punishment. The courts, however, were not given clear guidance on how to interpret such legislation when cases appeared before them. Leigh (1982: 16) suggests that, in the absence of such guidance, they tended to proceed on the basis of 'textual exegesis aided by a commonsense grasp of the public policy issues involved'.

Proceeding thus, the courts – especially from the 1870s onwards – began to interpret a number of offences involving matters such as selling adulterated tobacco and selling alcoholic drinks to drunken persons as offences of strict liability. In doing so, they may have been influenced by parliamentary debates surrounding the passage of legislation such as the Licensing Act 1872 and the Food and Drugs Act 1875 (although the courts were not supposed to refer to parliamentary debates in attempting to determine Parliament's intentions). In the case of the Food and Drugs Act, the Bill originally used the word 'knowingly' to qualify many of its offences (Smith, 1998: 212). However, as a result of claims that earlier legislation had been ineffective because of the difficulties of proving such knowledge, words such as 'knowingly' were struck out from many sections, and the resulting Act contained many offences which simply specified 'conduct' without mentioning any mental state. In this context, courts began to hold that Parliament had intended to create offences for which no proof of *mens rea* was required, and that – since their job in interpreting legislation was simply to give effect to what Parliament intended – they could not impose a *mens rea* requirement where Parliament had not intended to create one.

This move was highly controversial at the time, and has continued to be so. One counter position to the courts' approach described above is that, in interpreting statutory offences, the courts should presume that *mens rea* is required – and this presumption is only invalidated if Parliament expressly states that no *mens rea* is required. This viewpoint would eventually win out, although it has not stopped the courts treating many offences – some of them quite serious – as offences of strict liability (Leigh, 1982: 27). In the face of such resistance to the development of strict liability, some judges attempted to specify its precise scope and nature. This involved identifying the types of offences which could fall within the category of strict liability and determining what precisely the implications were of treating an offence as one of strict liability.

It is worthwhile looking a little more closely at a key case which demonstrates this approach: *Sherras v. de Rutzen* [1895] 1 Q.B. 918. The case involved an appeal by the licensee of a public house against conviction under the Licensing Act 1872 for unlawfully supplying liquor to a police constable on duty.

The offence occurred when a police constable who was on duty was served with liquor by the appellant's daughter, in his presence. Before entering the pub, the constable – in a blatant attempt to conceal the fact that he was on duty – had removed his armlet. The publican and his daughter took it for granted that police officers with their armlets off were off duty. The publican was convicted under s.16, sub-s.2 of the Act, which made it an offence to supply liquor 'to any constable on duty' and made no reference to any mental state, such as knowledge that the police constable was on duty. The prosecution's position was that since s.16, sub-s.1, which created a different offence of harbouring a constable on duty, did require such knowledge, Parliament intended sub-s.2 to create an *absolute* prohibition against serving a police constable whilst on duty. The word 'knowingly' was deliberately omitted from sub-s.2 by the legislature, it was argued, because it was intended that a publican serving a police constable should do so at his own risk. Behind these formal legal arguments, we can surmise, is the concern that if it is necessary to *prove* that the publican knew a police constable he served was on duty, convictions would be extremely hard to obtain.

In this case, the court held that the conviction ought to be quashed. Day, J. based his opinion on the fact that the appellant 'had no intention to do a wrongful act; he acted in the bona fide belief that the constable was off duty'. In other words, the appellant lacked *mens rea*. For Day, J., proof of *mens rea* was required; the only effect of the omission of the word 'knowingly' from sub-s.2 was to shift the burden of proof from the prosecution to the defence, i.e. instead of the prosecution having to prove that the publican knew the constable was on duty, the publican would have to prove that he did not know this.

Day, J.'s opinion is clearly sympathetic to the idea that criminal liability requires *mens rea* unless Parliament expressly states otherwise. At first sight, Wright, J. – who gave the second opinion in the case – is in straightforward agreement. He too thought the conviction should be quashed. He starts by saying he is of the same opinion as Day, J. and goes on:

> There is a presumption that *mens rea*, an evil intention, or a knowledge of the wrongfulness of the act, is an essential ingredient in every offence . . .

However, Wright, J. then went on to qualify this position, by indicating three types of case which were exceptions to the general principle – where the presumption of a *mens rea* requirement could be 'displaced'. They are:

1 acts which 'are not criminal in any real sense, but are acts which in the public interest are prohibited under a penalty';
2 public nuisances; and
3 cases where 'although the proceeding is criminal in form, it is really only a summary mode of enforcing a civil right'.

It is the first of these exceptions that concerns us here. In this seemingly trite case, Wright J. is – if not quite inventing – at least referring explicitly to the existence of a new legal entity. He is suggesting that there is a new type of legal wrong – an offence which is not really a crime. Because these offences are not really crimes, it is not necessary to prove what one has to prove in order to convict somebody of a real crime, i.e. that the accused person acted with 'evil intention' or 'knowledge of the wrongfulness of the act'. But the converse also seems to be implied, i.e. if an offence is one of strict liability, then the behaviour in question cannot be truly criminal (it must fall within one of Wright, J.'s three exceptional categories and none of these looks 'truly criminal'). The behaviour in question is clearly wrong in some sense – it is contrary to the public interest and needs to be prohibited under penalty. But it is not criminal in any real sense.

It seems, then, as if criminal proceedings are being used as a convenient, available method of dealing with a new class of wrongful acts – even though such acts are not considered really criminal. In the twentieth century, criminal proceedings would be used more and more to deal with these new 'offences'. Eventually, approximately half of the cases where criminal proceedings are used would be such cases, i.e. offences which do not require proof of *mens rea* and hence seem not criminal in any real sense. Yet, a *clear* differentiation between the two types of legal wrongs – 'offences which are not really criminal' and 'true crimes' – is never drawn.

Strict liability and white-collar and corporate crime

A great deal of the conduct which criminologists call 'white collar and corporate crime' is handled by the criminal law as offences of strict liability. One advantage of this is that it should make it easier to convict the perpetrators of such conduct of criminal offences. However, this advantage comes at a cost. When an offence is one of strict liability it tends to be represented and understood as conduct which is legally wrong but not really criminal. This could affect the court's attitude towards sentencing. But just as important, it can result in criminal conviction failing to perform effectively one of its most important functions: conveying strong social censure and stigma. Usually, to describe something as a crime is to do more than depict it as something prohibited in the public interest – it is to depict it as something particularly immoral or disreputable. By convicting perpetrators of white-collar and corporate crimes of offences without proving *mens rea* the law enables them to regard and represent their conduct as technical infringement rather than real criminal wrong-doing. They can say to themselves and others, 'we have been convicted of a criminal offence, but we are not real criminals. What we have done – even if it has caused enormous harm – is in a quite different *moral* category to (say) a common theft, burglary or personal assault'.

The enforcement of strict liability offences

The rather formal criticism of strict liability outlined above becomes more meaningful when we consider how those who decide whether to prosecute perpetrators of strict liability offences make such decisions in practice. A significant amount of research has been done on how regulatory agencies use offences of strict liability (e.g. Carson, 1970; Richardson, 1987; Rowan-Robinson et al., 1990; Alberini and Austin, 1999). A key question in such research is if they use their discretionary powers over whether or not to prosecute those who commit strict liability offences to prosecute only those they consider to be blameworthy. Overall, the answer seems to be that they do. In practice, for a number of reasons, regulators rarely prosecute 'blameless innocents' (Richardson, 1987: 303). Rather, they tend to understand their task as being to obtain maximum compliance with regulations, they use a range of methods to achieve this goal, and prosecution tends to be used only where these other mechanisms have not succeeded. For instance, a company with a long-standing unacceptable attitude towards safety is more likely to be prosecuted if it is caught breaching safety regulations than is a company which has a good attitude.

These findings clearly have implications for the claim that strict liability in criminal law is unjust. In addition, the research suggests that many of those who are prosecuted for strict liability offences are in fact prosecuted because a particular breach of a regulation is not an isolated incident but one part of a more general tendency to fail to comply with the law, to put profit ahead of safety, to fail repeatedly to correct situations that are known to be dangerous, and so on. Yet, because the offences for which they are prosecuted and convicted are strict liability offences, their offences tend to be regarded both by them and others as 'not real crimes'. This prompts Andrew Ashworth, among others, to argue:

> No-fault offences which are followed by low penalties on conviction are almost counterproductive, resulting in the imposing of derisory fines on large organizations. Indeed, if regulation in such spheres as industrial safety had been harnessed to relatively serious offences requiring proof of fault, then those offences might now be taken much more seriously, integrated into peoples' thinking about offences against the person rather than being regarded as 'merely regulatory' and 'not real crime'. (Ashworth, 2006: 168–9)

Corporate criminal liability

Rather than advocating strict liability, critical criminologists may seek to bring more white-collar and corporate harm within the scope of criminal law by advocating prosecution of its perpetrators for offences for which it is necessary to prove both *actus reus* and – for each element of the *actus reus* – *mens rea*. Although the need to prove *mens rea* may make conviction more difficult, if successful it should also make it far harder for those convicted to view and represent their offence as 'not really criminal'. However, this approach encounters a particular difficulty if the significant perpetrators of crime are considered to be not actual people – including members of corporate bodies acting on behalf of those bodies – but corporate entities such as companies themselves. Here, one runs up against what Moran (1997) calls the law's anthropomorphic imagination.

The idea of making companies liable for harm at criminal law has gathered momentum in recent decades. To some extent, this was in response to a series of disasters within a short period of time in which substantial numbers of people were killed and seriously injured and where it transpired that a company's failure to put in place adequate protective measures was a significant cause of the disaster. A particular low point was 1987–8. In March 1987 the car-passenger ferry *Herald of Free Enterprise* capsized killing 193 people; in November 1987 the King's Cross tube station fire killed 31 people; in the Piper Alpha oil platform explosion of July 1988, 167 people died; and in the Clapham Junction rail crash of December 1988, 35 people died and 500 were injured. In all of these cases, subsequent inquires revealed that – whatever the immediate cause of the disaster – the underlying causes were a whole host of failings on behalf of corporate bodies to put in place mechanisms to reduce the risks of such disasters occurring.

This took place, moreover, in a particular political and cultural climate. Providers of public services and regulatory authorities had experienced fierce budget cuts. There was a fairly widespread perception that Britain was becoming the sort of place where private companies pursue profit at all costs and in particular scrimp on expenditure on safety and undertake increasingly risky activities. In such a context, to construct these events as corporate *crimes* – and to portray them as serious wrongs committed by greedy and reckless companies pursuing profit at the expense of the lives of their workers and customers – began to seem fitting. But rhetorically portraying events as corporate crimes is one thing. It is a significant step further actually to charge companies with crimes, prosecute them, convict them, and punish them through the criminal law. Yet, since the 1980s in particular, there has been a strong movement towards doing precisely this. The enactment of the Corporate Manslaughter and Corporate Homicide Act 2007 is simply one significant event in this movement for corporate criminal liability (Horder, 2007).

Why criminal law rather than civil law?

It is easy to understand the *desire* to hold companies to account for their failings which resulted in so much death and injury. What is not quite so obvious is that – as a practical strategy – criminal proceedings are the best or most appropriate way to hold corporate bodies to account. An alternative would be to hold them to account through civil law proceedings. For instance, they might be sued for the tort (private wrong) of negligence. After all, the usual substance of the argument is that as a result of negligence – failing to take reasonable steps to protect others from foreseeable risk of harm – companies have caused death and serious harm to their employees, customers and other members of the public. For victims of negligence, the usual route to legal redress would be through private law action in which compensation is sought from the negligent party for the harm suffered. If successful, those injured can obtain compensation which materially benefits them. The idea that it is negligent companies, rather than merely negligent managers or employees, who should be the target of such civil law actions is of course particularly useful for those seeking redress since – unlike the individuals – the companies may have the resources to pay the large amounts of compensation which would be deemed appropriate given the scale of harm caused by their negligent conduct.

The idea that redress for such wrongs should be through criminal law is therefore not an obvious one; although such is the 'clamour for corporate liability' (Herring, 2008: 762) that it has quickly come to be seen as an obvious move with the only problem being how to overcome political inertia and the technical difficulties involved in holding companies to account through criminal law. Neither, on the other hand, is it obvious that negligence is a matter only for civil and not for criminal remedies (Hart, 2008: Ch. 6). The call for corporate criminal liability seems particularly problematic, however, when one considers the different purposes of tort law and criminal law. Whilst both share a concern to provide victims of wrong-doing with redress and to allocate responsibility for harm resulting from wrong-doing, they operate according to different logics.

In tort law, a primary function of legal action is to obtain compensation for those wrongly harmed from those responsible for the harm. It is not a central concern to ensure that those who cause harm should have something unpleasant inflicted upon them in return for doing something that is disapproved of. Whilst paying compensation may be experienced as unpleasant, this is not the primary purpose of ordering it. Hence, it concerns us little that compensation tends to paid in practice by insurance companies, rather than directly by those responsible. To the contrary, we tend to insist that those who engage in risky activities should have insurance that will enable them to pay any compensation they are ordered to pay for harm they might cause.

Criminal law is quite different. There, ensuring that those who suffer harm receive compensation is at most a secondary aim. A primary concern is to ensure that those who wrongfully cause harm suffer something unpleasant in return. Hence, there is a concern to ensure that those who are ordered to undergo punishment actually undergo it. For instance, if a person is sentenced to imprisonment, a relative or friend of that person would not be permitted to go to prison in their place. It is worth noting that this makes fines, despite their widespread use as punishment, problematic as a form of punishment; we can never be sure that the person who is ordered to pay the fine is actually the person who pays it – a fine can be paid by a friend or relative and the person we want to punish may not experience any hardship (cf. Young, 1987).

Looked at in this light, in the aftermath of a harmful event, the strategy of targeting corporate bodies (rather than individual employees) through tort law makes sense. Establishing that corporate bodies were negligent, whilst not always easy, seems feasible, since to establish negligence one does not have to prove some 'state of mind' (see below). Moreover, corporate bodies are more likely to have the resources to pay the amounts that will be required to compensate multiple victims who have suffered serious harm.

The point of targeting corporate bodies through criminal law is less obvious. If the purpose is to make those responsible for harm suffer something unpleasant in return, one runs up against the fact that corporate bodies are not real persons and cannot have unpleasant experiences in the same way that human beings can. Corporate bodies, in short, cannot really feel pain. A criminal sanction imposed upon a corporate body may certainly cause some *people* to have an unpleasant experience. Managers, shareholders, employees and others may all feel the effect of a punishment imposed upon a corporate body. But the corporate body itself seems to be beyond the reach of punishment. This is not, of course, to say that corporate bodies are beyond moral censure. The question is why such censure cannot be appropriately imposed by civil rather than criminal courts (for example by exemplary damages or by judicial criticism of the defendant corporation). The important practical effect of moral censure is that it damages a corporation's public image, and that sort of damage can be inflicted by civil suits as well as by criminal prosecutions (Hans, 2000: 4–5; cf. Clarkson, 1998 who opposes the view that we should use civil rather than criminal law as a route to redress from companies that cause social harm).

The mind of the corporate body

The question of whether corporate entities are the sorts of things that are suitable targets for criminal law has other dimensions. In particular, there is the question of whether corporate bodies have the sorts of *minds* which are required if it is to make sense to deem them the authors of crimes.

An entity must possess a mind – or something similar to a mind – in order to commit a ('real') crime. As we have seen in earlier chapters, this is because 'crime', at least as traditionally conceived in legal scholarship, has at least two ingredients: a 'conduct element' and a 'mental element'. An entity must make some sort of mental decision to do what is prohibited, or to bring about harm, for that conduct to be officially condemned as criminal. This tends to be recognized by those who advocate greater criminal liability for corporate bodies. Gobert and Punch, for instance, base their case for corporate criminal liability on the claim that companies are organic entities with their own personalities, which are quite distinct from those of the individual human beings who direct, manage or work for the companies or profit from their activity:

> A company has its own distinctive goals, its own distinctive culture, and its own distinctive personality. It is an independent organic entity, and, as such, should be responsible in its own right, directly and not derivatively, for the criminal consequences that arise out of the way its business is conducted. (Gobert and Punch, 2003: 39)

Other theorists of corporate liability point to the tendencies of corporate bodies to develop their own agency which is not reducible to that of associated individuals, and of bureaucratic structures of corporation developing into intelligent, computer-directed decision-making systems (see Sullivan, 1996).

Whatever the value of such perspectives, the courts in England have found it difficult to conceive of companies as entities possessing a mental state (Wells, 2001: 84). In their efforts to imagine the corporate body as an entity possessing a capacity for criminal action, the English courts have tended to think more in terms of deriving corporate criminal liability from the actions and decisions of real people associated with the corporate body. In what follows, we will very briefly review the development of corporate criminal liability in England and Wales.

The development of corporate criminal capacity

Prior to the nineteenth century, corporations tended to lie outside the scope of criminal law (Turner, 1962: 70). If a crime was committed on the orders of a corporate body, criminal proceedings could be taken against its members in their personal capacity, but not against the corporate body itself. The main reason for this was in fact the rule that in criminal courts prisoners were required to stand at their bar and could not be represented by attorneys (ibid.). But arguments that corporate bodies did not possess minds (and could not therefore have a 'guilty will') and bodies (and so could not be subject to usual criminal punishment such as hanging) were also put forward in support of the rule.

During the 1840s, however, the courts began to hold that a corporate body could be indicted by the corporate name and have fines imposed upon it (Turner, 1962: 71). Initially, indictments were allowed against corporate bodies for 'non-feasance', i.e. omitting to do something it had a duty to do. This was on the ground that as it was only the corporate body itself – rather than individual employees – who had such a duty, the only way the wrong could be dealt with was by criminal proceedings against the corporation. But by the mid-1840s indictments were being allowed for misfeasance: obstructing a highway. By the 1880s, it had became established – by the Interpretation Act 1889 – that where the word 'person' appeared in a statute it included a 'body corporate' unless a contrary intention appeared in that statute (Turner, 1962: 71; Wells, 2001: 86–7).

However, it was generally held that corporations could be prosecuted only for offences which could be punished by a fine (Turner, 1962: 71). Moreover, it was widely thought that corporate bodies could not be prosecuted for offences – such as manslaughter and burglary – which could be punished by a fine, but which were considered too grave for a fine to be the usual punishment. If such crimes were committed by somebody acting under the orders of a corporate body, the appropriate course of action was to indict the actual persons who ordered the actions, provided it could be proved that they instigated the offence (ibid.: 72). Attempts were also made to hold companies vicariously liable for certain acts committed by their employees acting within the scope of their employment, under an old doctrine of vicarious liability which enabled 'masters' to be held criminally liable for certain acts of their 'servants' (ibid.; Leigh, 1982). The development of this mechanism in English criminal law was very patchy (Wells, 2001: 90–3), although in the United States vicarious liability remains a common way of holding companies criminally liable (Clarkson, 1998: s.4iv).

In the 1940s a series of cases established the principle that a corporate body could be directly (as opposed to vicariously) responsible for crimes requiring proof of *mens rea* 'by the fiction that the elements of criminal liability present in the responsible agent of the corporation can be "imputed" to the corporation itself' (Turner, 1962: 72; Wells, 2001: 93–5). Here we will consider two of these: *Director of Public Prosecutions v Kent and Sussex Contractors, Limited* [1944] K.B. 146 and *ICR Haulage Co., Ltd.* (1945) 30 Cr. App. R. 31.

DPP v Kent and Sussex Contractors concerned a company which was charged with offences that involved making false mileage returns in order to obtain extra petrol coupons under the motor fuel rationing scheme established during World War II. The offences with which it was charged required proof of a mental element: the statements had to be submitted 'with intent to deceive' and those charged would have to make a statement which 'they knew to be false'. The justices who heard the case held that the company could not be guilty of the offences because the offences involved 'an act of will or state of mind which could not be imputed to a body corporate'. The DPP appealed, arguing that a company 'must be assumed to have that kind of fictitious mind which ... can have knowledge and an intent to deceive and so can be held guilty of the offences charged'. The appeal was allowed. In brief, the reasoning of the Divisional Court, which heard the appeal, was that a company could 'have knowledge and form an intention through its human agents' (per MacNaghten, J.). In certain circumstances, the knowledge and intention of somebody acting as an agent of a company (in this case it was the company's transport manager) could be imputed to the company itself (ibid.). The crucial innovation here was that the company was not held vicariously liable for the acts of its agents; rather, the acts – *and accompanying mental states* – of the company's agents were attributed to the company itself.

In *ICR Haulage* the Court of Criminal Appeal considered whether a limited company could be indicted for conspiracy to defraud. By this stage, it was accepted that a limited company could be indicted for some, but not all, criminal offences. The controversy over corporate criminal liability was about 'where and on what principle the line must be drawn' (per Stable, J.). The appellants argued that companies could not be indicted for offences which required proof of *mens rea* because 'a company, not being a natural person, cannot have a mind' (ibid.). The Crown argued that companies could be indicted for such offences. According to the Crown, the offences for which a company could not be indicted were restricted to those which could by their nature only be committed by a natural person, such as bigamy, and those for which the only punishments available could not be imposed upon a company, such as murder – 'where the only punishment the Court can impose is corporal' (ibid.). The court dismissed the company's appeal, and affirmed that as a general rule a company could be indicted for criminal acts of its human agents, i.e. criminal acts of a company's agents could be attributed to the company itself.

The principle under which corporate bodies are held liable at criminal law for some criminal acts of their officers or agents has come to be known as the 'identification doctrine':

> If an individual who is sufficiently senior within the corporate structure as to represent metaphorically the 'mind' of the company commits a crime within the course of his/her employment, that act and *mens rea* can be attributed to the company. The company can be 'identified' with these acts and held directly accountable. In such cases it will always be possible to bring a prosecution against both the company and the individual. However, a company cannot be identified with a crime committed by a person lower down in the corporate hierarchy. His or her acts are not the company's acts and thus the company cannot be held liable. In such cases a prosecution can only be brought against the individual concerned. (Clarkson, 1998: s.4i)

While the identification doctrine operated initially to expose corporate bodies to the possibility of prosecution for criminal acts committed in furtherance of their goals, it has subsequently been criticized as too narrow given the complex nature of corporate criminality. Clarkson, among others, suggests that the doctrine enables corporate bodies to avoid criminal liability for much wrong-doing that they are arguably responsible for. There are several reasons for this. In large companies it is unlikely that senior managers will actually commit the *actus reus* of an offence (they will ensure that it is only others lower down in the hierarchy who get their hands dirty). Also, given the complex structure of many companies, it is often impossible for outsiders to ascertain which individuals did what. The most significant criticism of the identification doctrine, however, is that it fails as a mechanism for holding corporate bodies responsible for wrongs which emerge, not so much from the clearly wrongful deeds of specific individuals who work for the corporate body, but from the policies and operational procedures of the corporate body itself, i.e. from systematic failings which are seldom attributable to any specific individual. The collapse of the prosecution of P&O for manslaughter, in respect of the deaths that occurred as a result of the capsize of the *Herald of Free Enterprise*, is often used to illustrate this point (see Lacey et al., 2003: 667–72 for 'the *Herald of Free Enterprise* story'). As Clarkson puts it:

> The main cause of the collapse of the prosecution in the P&O case was the fact that P&O had no director in charge of safety and no clearly articulated safety policies, particularly in relation to open-door sailings. The various personnel involved in the capsize of the *Herald of Free Enterprise* were each doing their own job ...; the real cause of the capsize and resultant deaths was the lack of co-ordination between them as a result of an absence of safety policies. The Sheen Report investigating the capsize was in no doubt where the true fault lay: the company itself, with its absence of safety policies and failure to give clear directions, was 'infected with the disease of sloppiness' ... In such cases, despite clear blame being directed at the company, the identification doctrine precludes any successful prosecution of the company. (Clarkson, 1998: s.4i)

Criticism such as this has led to various efforts to devise other mechanisms by which corporate bodies can be held liable at criminal law for wrong-doing and resultant harm. These include the 'aggregation' or 'collective knowledge' doctrine which aggregates acts and mental elements of various persons within a company to see if together they constitute a criminal offence (ibid.: s.4ii); a reactive corporate fault approach (based on the ideas of Fisse and Braithwaite, 1993), which is complex but basically involves companies being ordered to take certain measures in the aftermath of wrong-doing and being prosecuted for the original offence if they fail to comply with such orders; a 'management failure' model (Clarkson, 1998: s.4v); the creation of specific corporate offences such as the offence of corporate manslaughter contained in the Corporate Manslaughter and Corporate Homicide Act 2007 (Horder, 2007); and a corporate *mens rea* doctrine which is very complex but works on the idea that since *mens rea* is always necessarily *inferred* from conduct and surrounding circumstances (since we cannot have direct access to a person's thoughts and intentions) there is no reason why we cannot devise distinctive principles for inferring *mens rea* from corporate conduct and surrounding circumstances (Clarkson, 1998: s.4vi; Wells, 2001).

These competing approaches to corporate criminal liability have had the effect of unsettling an area of law that, in the early 1990s, seemed to be quite settled (Jefferson, 2000). What does seem clear is that, at least in the UK, those who favour criminal liability as a response to corporate wrong-doing, as opposed to civil liability or other alternatives outside of the criminal law, are now the dominant voice in the debate. Indeed, the debate about corporate liability is now very much one that takes place amongst those who favour criminal liability and is about the best mechanism or set of mechanisms for achieving this. The idea that the solution to white-collar and corporate crime may lie outside of the criminal law is now quite muted. Quite strangely, although there are some notable exceptions (especially Braithwaite, 2002) many critical scholars who tend to be highly sceptical about the value of criminalization and punishment, as methods of dealing with complex social problems involving anti-social behaviour, seem to have little doubt about their value as a method of handling corporate and white-collar crime.

Critical scholars such as Slapper and Tombs (1999) are, of course, well aware of this irony. They respond by suggesting a number of reasons why deterrence through criminal sanctions is potentially more effective and fairer when applied to corporations than to individual 'street' criminals. Corporations, they argue, are the sort of rational, calculating entities that are amenable to deterrence; their crimes are often continuing states of affairs that would be amenable to detection given increased investigative resources; the deterrent 'message' of criminal sanctions would be relatively easy to communicate to likely offenders; and increased deterrent punishment of corporations is unlikely to result in social injustice (Slapper and Tombs, 1999: 185–8). Tombs (1995: 255–7) acknowledges that many corporations are not, in reality, the rational actors they represent themselves as being, but suggests that if they fail to respond to incentives to improve standards there will be a strong case for 'rehabilitative' strategies which would impose better management upon them.

It is difficult to assess the merits of a deterrent strategy because of the dearth of relevant empirical research (Geis and DiMento, 2002). If the aim of the criminal law in this field is solely to deter, then strict liability may be a sensible mechanism since it provides an incentive to minimize the *risk* of infringing the law. If, on the other hand, the aim is to communicate a symbolic message about what constitutes really serious wrong-doing, it may be more appropriate to concentrate on either criminalization or more effective civil remedies for corporate negligence.

Summary

Criminologists frequently observe that white-collar and corporate crime are relatively neglected by criminal law. This chapter contributes to this discussion by exploring legal strategies for controlling white-collar and corporate crime. To do this we draw upon Norrie's (2001) useful distinction between strategies of differentiation and assimilation. Differentiation involves creating strict liability offences to control corporate wrong-doing. Assimilation involves prosecuting the perpetrators of corporate wrong-doing for 'traditional' offences for which it is necessary to prove *mens rea*.

The idea of making companies liable for harm at criminal law has gathered momentum in recent decades. However, there are numerous problems in holding companies responsible for 'traditional' crimes. To overcome these problems, various legal doctrines have been developed to attribute the actions and mental states of corporate agents to the corporate body itself. The movement to subject corporate wrong-doers to criminal sanctions continues to gather strength.

STUDY QUESTIONS

- Why does white-collar and corporate wrong-doing tend to escape effective criminalization?

- What are the drawbacks of differentiation as a strategy for ensuring corporate wrong-doing is criminalized?

- What are the pros and cons of using criminal law rather than civil law to hold corporate wrong-doers to account?

- If we accept that companies are different from individual human beings in that they do not possess physical bodies or minds, what difficulties does this create for attempts to convict them of 'traditional' criminal offences?

FURTHER READING

Chapter 18 of Newburn's *Criminology* (2007) is a very useful guide to the criminological literature on white-collar and corporate crime. Turning to the law, Wells' *Corporations and Criminal Responsibility* (2nd ed.) (2001) is the leading criminal law book about the criminal liability of corporations. Again, the chapter on 'Strict and Corporate Liability' in Norrie (2001) is invaluable. Jonathan Herring's *Criminal Law: Text, Cases and Materials* (3rd ed. 2008) has chapters which provide accessible accounts of the law and theoretical debates concerning strict liability and the criminal liability of corporations.

7

Proving
Criminal Guilt

Chapter Contents

OVERVIEW

Chapter 7:

- Outlines the development of the criminal trial in England, focussing in particular on the jury and adversarial procedure.

- Considers the strengths and weaknesses of the form of procedure that had emerged by the mid-nineteenth century.

- Examines the erosion of this form of procedure by the growth of plea-bargaining and summary justice.

- Explains some key aspects of the law of evidence.

KEY TERMS

jury adversarial procedure summary trial plea-bargaining hearsay confessions expert evidence

In this chapter we turn from the legal definitions of criminal offences to the procedures used to establish the 'facts' of criminal cases. In ordinary parlance the word 'fact' commonly means 'Something that has really occurred or is actually the case' (*OED*), but when lawyers refer to 'the facts' of a reported case, they usually mean the matters that the court treated as having occurred for the purposes of its decision on the law. Facts, as the great legal theorist Hans Kelsen (1961) pointed out, are 'made' rather than (as lawyers usually say) 'found'. The subject of this chapter, then, is the making, or social construction (McBarnet, 1981) of legal facts.

As in Chapter 2, we start by presenting a long-term historical account, this time of the English criminal trial, and an ideal-typical model of what is ostensibly the central institution of common-law criminal procedure, the adversarial jury trial. Although this model is far removed from the routine practices of the modern criminal justice system, it continues, we shall argue, to underpin the principles of evidence law.

Trial by jury

The ending of ordeals

The birth of the present law system of criminal justice can be dated to the year 1215, when Pope Innocent III abruptly withdrew the Church's support from the system of trial by ordeal. Irrational though it might seem today, trial by ordeal made good sense within the world view of early mediaeval Europe. Whether a person was guilty or innocent was not simply a question about past events; it was a question about the state of that person's soul. The ordeal revealed that underlying spiritual reality by a physical sign. The spiritually pure person would sink into consecrated water; his or her hand would heal cleanly after carrying a hot iron. If people who had almost certainly done what they were charged with – and without strong suspicion, they would not be subjected to the ordeal (Groot, 1988) – were found to be innocent, that was because true repentance had cleansed the guilt from their souls (Olson, 2000; Ho, 2004).

McAuley (2006) argues that Innocent III's withdrawal of support from the ordeal was part of a wider package of reforms which reflected the emergence of a criminal law based on the deterrence of wrong-doing rather than the settlement of private disputes. In the Church courts, and in the secular courts of much of Europe, a more inquisitorial form of justice emerged, in which the judge was seen as conducting an inquiry to find out the truth. In England, the courts adjusted in a different way to the end of ordeals (Bartlett, 1986). The judges, forced to improvise a new procedure, turned to an existing institution, the jury of presentment: a body of local men whose task had been to present for trial those 'truly suspected' of crime, whose guilt would then be determined by ordeal (Green, 1985: 4–11). To the jury now fell the task of making the judgement of guilt or innocence itself.

In crucial respects, the jury retained something of the character of the ordeal (Haldar, 1998). The 'inscrutability of the jury's verdict was reminiscent of ordeal procedure' (Bartlett, 1986: 139). It resolved disputes in a manner which – at least until the Court of Criminal Appeal was created in 1907 – could not be challenged. It also mitigated the harshness of a criminal law that prescribed capital punishment for every felony (Green, 1985; Olson, 2000). Conviction rates of 20–25% appear to have been the norm for English felony trials until an upturn in the 1430s (Bellamy, 1998: 91–5). That successive rulers and their judges accepted this state of affairs suggests that they were willing to allow the law to be tempered by community sentiment (Green, 1985; Groot, 1988). Arguably the jury still plays this role today.

From self-informing to impartial juries

At first, trial juries appear to have been largely or entirely 'self-informing' (Klerman, 2003): jurors relied on their own knowledge of local events and personalities, not on the testimony of witnesses. By the early fourteenth century, testimony from accusers, witnesses and the accused was a significant feature of some trials (Musson, 1996: 191–5), and by the sixteenth century it was essential. Under a statute of 1555 accusers and their supporting witnesses were required to attend the trial and could be fined if they failed to do so (Langbein, 1974: 35). This was a significant step towards a modern system of criminal law where the state, rather than the complainant, is in control of proceedings.

Although jurors today are not expected to have any knowledge of the specific events at issue or the individuals involved, they are expected to bring with them a vast amount of background knowledge about social behaviour, folk psychology and morality which is essential to reach a decision (Anderson et al., 2005, Chs. 7 and 10; Burns, 1999). By refusing to admit expert evidence on matters which are deemed to fall within the 'common knowledge' of the jury, the courts have retained something of the jury's character as a self-informing repository of community knowledge.

The concept of fact

It was in the sixteenth century, according to the *Oxford English Dictionary*, that the word 'fact' entered the language. It derived from the Latin *factum*, thing done, and was most commonly used to mean a crime or evil deed. In law, it referred to any human action of legal significance, and particularly the act constituting a crime (Shapiro, 2000: 10). Such facts had to be proved to the jury's satisfaction by evidence. Barbara Shapiro (2000) argues that the common experience of jury service among men of middling rank influenced the ways in which questions of fact and evidence were addressed in science, religion and many other spheres of English intellectual life.

Juries were to return their verdicts 'according to conscience' (Green, 1985). 'The process by which the conscience was to become "satisfied" was a rational, not an emotional one' (Shapiro, 2000: 22). In the tradition of classical rhetoric, judgements of probability depended on the overall persuasiveness of arguments, which yielded opinion, rather than knowledge (Shapiro, 2001). From the late seventeenth century development, however, probability came to be thought of as a graduated scale, the highest level of which was sometimes called 'moral certainty' (Shapiro, 1991: 8). The 'satisfied conscience' or 'moral certainty' were common formulations of the standard of proof later expressed as 'beyond reasonable doubt' (or nowadays, being 'sure').

In continental Europe, the Roman-Canon law of proof made the establishment of guilt 'a complex art' obeying 'rules known only to specialists' (Foucault, 1977: 37). In the sixteenth and seventeenth centuries, however, courts were often able to evade the formal requirements of the law of proof and impose non-capital punishments on the basis of a free judicial evaluation of the evidence (Langbein, 1977). What Foucault (1977) calls the 'rule of common truth', according to which courts based their claims to truth on standards that any rational subject was considered able to understand, seems to have arrived earlier and more gradually than he supposes. The English juror also followed a 'rule of common truth', relying on his own reason and conscience. Reason might lead different men's consciences to different conclusions, as Chief Justice Vaughan recognized in his celebrated decision in *Bushell's* Case (1671) Vaughan 135, that a juror could not be fined for reaching a verdict which the judge deemed contrary to the evidence. (The principle underlying *Bushell* has recently been reaffirmed in the House of Lords' ruling that a judge cannot direct a jury to convict: *Wang* [2005] UKHL 9.)

The broad discretion allowed to jurors made it possible to take account of social factors such as the perceived character of the accused and the punishment the jury considered appropriate. King (1988) argues that the pattern of verdicts on early eighteenth-century property offences indicates that juries reached 'principled' decisions by taking account of such matters as the price of food, whether offenders had families to support, and the need for stern discipline of wayward servants. To take such factors into account in the determination of guilt, however, was at odds with enlightenment ideas of legal certainty and equality before the law.

The bulwark of our liberties

It was in the late seventeenth century that the English jury came to be seen as 'the principal bulwark of our liberties' – a view which Blackstone ([1768] 1979: 350) erroneously ascribed to the authors of *Magna Carta*. *Bushell's* Case, in which the jury refused to convict two Quakers for preaching, was one of a series of trials for political and religious offences in which juries refused to accept the judges' view of the case. The record of the jury, however, was uneven; many cases went the government's way, in part because government and judges found ways of ensuring that compliant jurors were selected (Cornish, 1968: 129–33).

Central to the debate over the jury's powers was the difficult distinction between questions of law – the province of the judge – and questions of fact. In trials for seditious libel, for example, the judges insisted that whether the words of a publication were seditious was a question of law, and the only question of fact was whether the defendant had published them. Defence lawyers and some juries resisted this view of the law, which was finally overturned by Fox's Libel Act of 1792. The opponents of judicial power argued that *'ex facto jus oritur,* all matter of law arises out of matter of fact, so that till the fact is *settled,* there is no room for law' (Hawles 1785 [1680]: 15). What the jury had to 'settle' was not simply a question of 'brute fact', such as whether the defendant's hand had held the pen which made certain marks on a sheet of paper, but the interpretation and classification of those facts as, for example, the writing of a libel. The classification of facts is not easily distinguishable from the interpretation of law (MacCormick, 2005: 141–2) and so there is a sense in which the jury – today as in the eighteenth century – is involved in determining the scope of the law on a case-by-case basis (Burns, 1999; Hildebrandt, 2006). For example what exactly is 'dishonesty' for the purpose of theft, 'gross negligence' in manslaughter, or a 'reasonable' belief in consent to sexual intercourse? 'Fact-finding' in such cases involves an important normative dimension (Duff et al., 2008).

For most of the jury's history, property qualifications ensured that questions of this sort would be answered by 'respectable' men who had a stake in preserving private property. As Hay (1988) shows, the eighteenth-century 'palladium of liberty' was drawn from no more than a quarter of the adult male population. Female householders were admitted to jury service in 1919. Although inflation gradually eroded the effect of the property qualification, those living in the poorest housing were excluded (Cornish 1968: 28–9) until property qualifications were abolished in 1974.

The adversarial system

The common-law system of trial is commonly described as an adversarial one, in contrast to the inquisitorial model favoured in many civil law systems. The adversarial model has five fundamental features (Landsman, 1990; Vogler, 2005):

1 The factfinder adopts an essentially neutral and passive role during the proceedings, not that of actively leading an inquiry into the truth. In English trials this is especially true of juries (which rarely ask questions, and can only do so through the judge) but it is also true of judges by comparison with their civil law counterparts.

2 Responsibility for the production of evidence and arguments rests primarily on the parties. In modern systems this means, in practice, that it rests on the prosecution and defence lawyers.

3 Before the trial both the prosecution and the defence engage in processes of 'case construction' (McConville et al., 1991) which are unashamedly partisan. The police, who obviously command the lion's share of resources in most cases, are not expected to pursue inquiries at the behest of the defence, as they sometimes do in the more inquisitorial Dutch system (Fennell et al., 1995). Conversely, the defendant

is generally under no obligation to assist the police inquiry (the 'right to silence'). Inequality and secrecy in the pre-trial process are somewhat mitigated, in the modern system, by provisions for disclosure of documents (Ashworth and Redmayne, 2005, Ch. 5).

4   Adversarial procedure accords primacy to the public trial, rather than the building-up of a dossier through a series of investigative steps (Damaska, 1986; Vogler, 2005). Great weight is given to the witness's oral evidence and answers to questions at trial, as opposed to their statements recorded in writing at an earlier stage. When the adversarial model is combined with a system of jury trial, this allows the jury to play a more central role than is possible in an inquisitorial system (cf. Munday, 1993).

5   The trial is in the nature of a contest governed by a fairly elaborate set of rules, including rules which restrict the use of evidence which *prima facie* has some probative value but the use of which is deemed to be in some way unfair, or to risk unnecessarily prolonging the trial.

The adversarial system grew up in England during the eighteenth century. Before that, felony trials appear to have followed a pattern that differed quite markedly from either an adversarial or an inquisitorial model. The judge played a very active role in questioning the witnesses and guiding the course of the trial, assisted by the depositions (written statements) taken by magistrates in pre-trial proceedings. Jurors also 'joined in the conversation, to ask questions, or to make observations' (Langbein, 2003: 319). The trial took the form of an 'altercation' in which the prosecutor (typically the alleged victim) and defendant spoke for themselves without the assistance of lawyers; the participation of defence lawyers in felony trials (as distinct from those for treason or misdemeanour) was limited to making submissions of law. There were relatively few rules governing this contest, which was 'nasty, brutish, and essentially short' (Cockburn, 1972: 109). By present-day standards, the procedure was thoroughly unfair to defendants. The onus was effectively placed on them to rebut the presumption that the charges against them were true, and yet they and their witnesses could not testify under oath. Nevertheless, about a third of felony defendants secured an acquittal (Beattie, 1986: 481–2; Langbein, 2003: 14; King, 2000: 231), and many others were convicted of lesser offences than the capital crime charged. The high (but very imprecise) standard of proof and the willingness of juries to exercise discretion 'in favour of life' were deemed adequate safeguards of the defendant's interests (Langbein, 2003: 33, 56–9).

In the 1730s, the judges began to relax the rule restricting the participation of defence counsel in felony trials (Landsman, 1990: 544; Langbein, 2003: 106–7). Langbein interprets this change as a response to two developments in the conduct of prosecutions. One was the growing use of solicitors and counsel to prosecute cases, on behalf either of private individuals or of official agencies such as the Mint. The other (also emphasized by Landsman, 1990) was the system of rewards which acted as an incentive to the production of perjured evidence. The introduction of defence lawyers 'evened up' a system that was becoming too obviously unfair, and protected the court against being hoodwinked by dishonest prosecutors and shady solicitors. Extending a measure of 'due process' to the defence was a form of crime control at a time when prosecutions not uncommonly amounted to criminal conspiracies.

The period c. 1730–1800 also saw the emergence of some key rules of evidence (Beattie 1986; Langbein, 2003). Hearsay evidence – evidence of something said outside court, which could not be tested by cross-examination – was received with increasing caution, and Blackstone ([1768] 1979: 368) considered it an established rule that hearsay evidence 'shall not be received as to any particular facts'. Similarly there was increasing caution over confession evidence extorted by threats and/or promises, for example by employers who promised their servants not to prosecute if they confessed, and then reneged on their promises. We discuss the modern forms of these rules below.

While the problem of dishonest prosecutions appears largely to explain the moves towards adversarialism in the 1730s, Landsman (1990) argues that it cannot explain the continuing trend towards more adversarial practices later in the eighteenth century. In the most controversial prosecutions of this period, such as the libel cases mentioned above, zealous defence advocates appealed to the jury over the head of the judge. In such cases it was the adversarial attitude of the bar that enabled the jury to play a genuinely independent role (Landsman, 1990: 591).

Apart from its role in politically contentious cases, the jury remained important in limiting the application of the death penalty. Defence counsel assisted the jury in this respect by helping to uncover any 'circumstance in favour of the prisoner' which could justify an acquittal, or a conviction for a lesser offence than the one charged (Langbein, 2003: 315). Langbein's interpretation of this process as manifesting a reluctance to pursue the truth – 'too much truth brought too much death' (2003: 337) – is highly debatable (cf. Vogler, 2005: 142). The 'circumstances favourable to the prisoner', after all, were aspects of the truth. Perhaps more truth brought more doubt, and therefore less death. Of course, the exclusionary rules of evidence and the beyond-reasonable-doubt standard of proof 'assured not only that some innocent defendants would be spared, but also many culpable ones' (Langbein, 2003: 336), but it was precisely the point of the procedure that it should be seen to prefer errors 'in favour of life' over errors that killed. The priority accorded to avoiding convictions of the innocent is now seen as one of the most fundamental principles of modern criminal procedure (Stein, 2005).

The next stage in the development of the adversarial trial was the removal, in 1836, of the rule that forbade defence counsel to address the jury. As Cairns (1998) argues in his account of the 1836 reform and its effects, the arguments for allowing speeches by counsel focussed on their importance in helping the jury find the truth (or, perhaps more accurately, in discerning why the truth was doubtful):

> A speech would enable defence counsel to point out the improbabilities and inconsistencies of the prosecution case, to simplify their cross-examinations, to ensure the prisoner's case was fully argued, and to guide the judge and jury through labyrinthine evidence ... all of which would contribute to the discovery of the truth ... The objective was right verdicts, not prisoners' rights. (Cairns, 1998: 84, 88)

Drawing on Foucault's analysis, Cairns argues that the 'rule of common truth' – the requirement that guilt be proved by evidence that would satisfy any reasonable person –

> describes a specific instance of the need for harmony of the law and public feeling recognised by early nineteenth century reformers ... The spectator must leave court in no possible doubt of the correctness of the verdict ... [T]he consideration of the evidence had to match the standard of proof – all the facts had to be disclosed, all their complexities discussed and all possible defences raised by them considered ... [A]dversarialism ... offered a comprehensive investigation of the truth within a procedure sufficiently fair to deprive the prisoner of any sympathy from judge, jury or spectators. (Ibid.: 94)

The adversarial trial became, above all, a contest between narratives. The case of *Palmer,* which Cairns (1998: 163) calls the 'apotheosis' of the adversarial trial, was won by prosecution counsel's skill in organizing a mass of circumstantial evidence into a single, coherent story – a feat which so impressed the novelist Wilkie Collins that it inspired the narrative technique of his masterpiece, *The Woman in White* (Sutherland, 1998). Palmer's counsel, though he tenaciously probed the weaknesses in the prosecution case, was unable to marshal the evidence into a coherent alternative theory. Though we cannot know the jury's thought-processes, it seems likely that they engaged in what present-day psychologists of the jury call 'explanation based decision-making' (Hastie and Pennington, 1996).[1] If there is one, and only one, coherent story that fits the evidence, and it also fits the legal categorization of an offence, that is what a jury will usually accept as 'beyond reasonable doubt'. Where there is a coherent, plausible story consistent with innocence, there will be a reasonable doubt.

Another effect of counsel's speeches, however, was to encourage silence on the part of defendants, who were under much less pressure than before to present their own account of events to the jury. Many (probably on legal advice) said merely 'I leave it to my counsel' (Langbein, 2003: 266–73). Defendants were not permitted to give sworn testimony (Cairns, 1998: 175). It was thought that this removed the pressure that prisoners would otherwise be under to perjure themselves, and protected 'ignorant and terrified' defendants against being bullied into incriminating themselves by prosecuting counsel or partisan judges – the latter being a particular bugbear of Irish nationalist MPs who tenaciously resisted attempts to make the defendant a competent witness (Jackson, 1990; Allen, 1997). When this reform was finally enacted in 1898, it was coupled with the rule that the defendant could not be *compelled* to testify. Until 1994, the judge was required to direct the jury that no adverse inference could be drawn from the defendant's silence.

The criminal trial: ideals and realities

We can now present an idealized model of the English criminal trial as it had evolved by the end of the nineteenth century. Our formulation of this model owes much to the Victorian jurist James Fitzjames Stephen (1860, 1863; see also Ward, 2004). Though only a small minority of criminal trials today bear much resemblance to this model, the model is helpful in criticizing the existing law and in understanding the law of evidence.

1 Central to the model is the institution of the jury. The jury's claim to legitimacy rests on two characteristics: it is independent of the state (and of the investigative process) and it is in some sense representative of the community. Historically, it was taken to represent the morality and sense of fairness of a respectable, law-abiding, male section of the community, whose values the law aimed to instil into the lower strata of the population. In its present form it ostensibly represents a cross-section of the local community as a whole. The jury's verdict lends some credibility to the idea of conviction as a judgement of the community, not just the state (Burns, 1999; Dubber, 2004; Duff et al., 2008). The price the state has to pay for this is the acquittal of a certain number of people who defy the law, or the state's interpretation of it. The acquittal of two protestors who attempted to damage planes in order to prevent war crimes in Iraq (Norton-Taylor, 2007) is a good illustration both of the jury's independence of the state and its exercise of moral judgement.

2 The jury's task is largely one of allocating the risk of error. It is logically impossible to provide absolutely certain proof of past events, in the sense that '2 + 2 = 4' is certain.

But if the jury is unanimously (or, since 1967, by at least a 10–2 majority)[2] satisfied 'beyond reasonable doubt', or so that it is 'sure' of the defendant's guilt, the risk of error is deemed small enough to be borne by the defendant. The sense of being 'sure' is largely an intuitive one for which no reasons are given (Stephen, 1863: 207; Burns, 1999). The judge's task is to ensure that there is a rational basis on which a jury *could* be sure: that the evidence is such that a reasonable jury could regard it as proving guilt (*Galbraith* [1981] 1 WLR 1039). But the jury is never obliged to convict. Even when the admitted facts are such that, on the judge's interpretation of the law, there can be no doubt of guilt, the jury can 'perversely' acquit an accused whom it does not believe to deserve conviction (Matravers, 2004). Although some see the jury verdict as an essentially irrational process for deciding on guilt (Nobles and Schiff, 2000), and others as an ineffable form of holistic understanding (Burns, 1999), we think it is more accurate to say that jury verdicts are, inevitably, underdetermined by reason (Ward, 2006a). Many, perhaps most, cases decided by juries could reasonably be decided either way.

3　The function of the jury and that of counsel in the adversary system are complementary. In order for the jury to play a genuinely independent role it is important that the adduction of evidence should not be entirely under the control of the state. It is also essential that the jury comes 'cold' to the evidence, without prior knowledge of the investigation (Doran et al., 1995: 21). In order for the jury's sense of being sure to be an adequate guarantee that the risk of error is low enough to convict, every possible ground for reasonable doubt should be presented by the defence, and every disputed piece of prosecution evidence rigorously tested.

Even in this idealized form, the adversarial trial has a number of serious limitations, all of which stem from a central feature of the trial, that it is not designed to *search* for truth, but rather to *test* a version of the truth put forward by the prosecution.

From the defendant's point of view, the adversarial contest is often an unequal one. In theory both the police and the defence 'are able to dig out their own evidence; but in reality it is only the police who have any spades with which to dig' (Spencer, 2002: 626).

The system's reliance on cross-examination places severe burdens on victims and other witnesses, who are subjected to what can be an extremely gruelling and distressing process, often directed at sowing confusion rather than establishing truth (Rock, 1993; McEwan, 1998).

From the point of view of the community, the functions of the trial might be thought of as authoritatively establishing the truth and calling wrong-doers to account (Duff et al., 2008). In both respects the adversarial trial has limitations. Because it depends on testing the credibility of oral testimony, it often either excludes or marginalizes forms of evidence that may be more reliable than oral testimony but are not amenable to cross-examination, e.g. what the witnesses said when their memories of the incident were fresh. (The rules in this respect have, however, been significantly relaxed by the Criminal Justice Act 2003.) As for calling wrong-doers to account, this seems to imply that those who have done what they are accused of should admit it and either apologize or explain their rejection of the law. The options they are offered, however, are to lie, to keep silent, or to 'get it over with' by mouthing the word 'guilty' and leaving it to a lawyer to make some stereotyped expression of remorse. In some situations, such as 'date rape' allegations, the incentives to lie are almost irresistible, and completely counterproductive as a way of getting wrong-doers to accept that they have done wrong.

For all that, the trial, particularly the jury trial, has much to be said in its favour. It offers significant protection against state power, and jury service is an important, educative and, for many jurors, rewarding element of citizenship (Matthews et al., 2004, Redmayne, 2005). Unfortunately, the routine work of modern criminal justice bears little relation to these ideals.

Since the mid-nineteenth century an ever-increasing proportion of crimes have been dealt with by summary proceedings (see Chapter 3), which now account for about 96% of prosecutions. If cautions, fixed penalty notices and other alternatives to prosecution are taken into account, the proportion of cases tried by jury is even smaller. Summary trials are heard either by district judges (formerly stipendiary magistrates), who are professional lawyers, or by lay magistrates, who are reasonably representative in terms of gender and ethnic origin, but are drawn overwhelmingly from the professional and managerial classes, and two out five of whom are retired from full-time employment (Morgan and Russell, 2000). Magistrates cannot claim the democratic legitimacy of the modern jury (Sanders, 2002), but are closer to the jury's historic role of representing local elites or the 'respectable' classes. Indeed, Vogler (2005: 213) argues that it was precisely the 'democratization' of the jury that lost it its 'traditional support among the elite classes' and facilitated reductions in the scope of jury trial.

The principle that the prosecution has to prove its case beyond reasonable doubt is subject to numerous exceptions. We have encountered two examples: the defences of insanity and diminished responsibility, which have to be proved by the defence on the balance of probabilities. Ashworth and Blake (1996) calculated that of 540 offences triable at Crown Courts in 1995, 219 placed the onus of proof on the defendant in some respect. Since the Human Rights Act 1998 came into force a number of these presumptions have been challenged (Dennis, 2007). Some of these challenges have succeeded, while in other cases the courts have accepted that it is fair to place the burden of proof on the defendant: for example in areas where businesses ought to take precautions against infringing the law and to keep records to show they have not done so.[3]

Only a small minority of defendants receive an adversarial trial. In 2005–6, 4.8% of defendants prosecuted by the CPS in the magistrates' courts were convicted after a trial and 2% were found not guilty. The rest either pleaded guilty (62.4%), were tried in their absence, mainly for motoring offences (15.6%), failed to appear, or had their cases discontinued. In the Crown Court, 64.3% pleaded guilty, nearly five times as many as were convicted by juries (12.9%). Most acquittals (13.2% of CPS prosecutions) were ordered by the judge because the prosecution presented no evidence (CPS, 2006, Annex A).

The 'mass production of guilty pleas' (McConville et al., 1994; Sanders and Young, 2006) depends on providing strong incentives for defendants to plead guilty. The 'guilty plea discount' has been set by the Sentencing Guidelines Council (2004) at a third of the sentence where the defendant pleads guilty at the first reasonable opportunity. The real discount is greater than this in triable-either-way offences, because those who plead guilty at the first reasonable opportunity normally do so at the Magistrates' Court, where sentences are typically much less severe than at Crown Court (Sanders and Young, 2006: 391–3). As the Sentencing Guidelines make clear, pleading guilty is *not* a mitigating factor (courts no longer pretend it has anything to do with remorse). It justifies a reduction in sentence because it 'avoids the need for a trial (thus enabling other cases to be disposed of more expeditiously), shortens the gap between charge and sentence, saves considerable cost, and, in the case of an early plea, saves victims and witnesses from the concern about having to give evidence'. It is difficult to reconcile a 'just deserts' approach to sentencing with a rule that makes punishment so dependent on factors unrelated to the gravity of the crime, and penalizes people so severely for exercising their right to a fair trial.

The guilty plea system almost certainly leads to substantial numbers of innocent people being convicted. In Zander and Henderson's (1993) study, 11% of Crown Court defendants pleading guilty claimed to be innocent, and in 6% of cases defence counsel were concerned that their client's pleas were false. There are no recent data from magistrates' courts but Dell (1971) also found that about 11% of those pleading guilty claimed to be innocent. Of course, not all those who claim to be innocent are so, and often guilt or innocence is not a cut-and-dried matter but depends on the application of flexible standards like 'dishonesty' or 'reasonable force' – the very questions that juries are thought ideally qualified to determine. At the very least, however, these data and the obvious coercive pressures on defendants are enough to rebut any suggestion that a plea of guilty is equivalent to proof of guilt beyond reasonable doubt. In fact, if guilty pleas were subject to the law of evidence, they would have to be declared inadmissible under the Police and Criminal Evidence Act 1984, s.76, as confessions made under circumstances that tend to make them unreliable. In short, the majority of people punished by the courts are convicted on the basis of no reliable evidence whatever.

For many of those who plead guilty, their conviction reflects not a fair or accurate assessment of what they can be proved to have done, but some kind of bargain as to the seriousness of the charge, the number of charges, or the way the facts will be presented to the court (Sanders and Young, 2006). Again, this bears little relation to 'just deserts' and it also negates any possibility of serious moral dialogue between the defendant and the court (let alone the victim). Instead of focussing on what the offender has done, the reasons why she should regret doing it, and whether she actually does regret it, the 'facts' on which the offender is sentenced are the product of a bargaining process between two teams of lawyers. Such 'fact bargains' are encouraged by the Court of Appeal's guidance that prosecution and defence counsel should agree in writing the factual basis of a possible guilty plea before seeking an indication from the judge of the sentence such a plea would attract (*Goodyear* [2005] 3 All E.R. 117, para. 66). The idea, beloved of philosophers of criminal law, that the law serves to express solemn moral censure of wrong-doing, is difficult to reconcile with the realities of the criminal justice game.

Evidence in the adversarial trial

It is, then, only in the roughly 1% of cases dealt with by contested jury trials that the criminal justice system makes any serious attempt to live up to its historic ideals, and it is for these trials that the complex rules of evidence are designed. Although the same rules apply, for the most part, to the magistrates' courts, Darbyshire (1997: 111) observes that 'The contents of a tome on evidence have a similar informative bearing on proceedings in magistrates' courts to the contents of *Larousse Gastronomique* on a bucket of Kentucky Fried Chicken.'

It is widely believed that the law of evidence has grown up largely as a result of judicial distrust of juries (Thayer, 1898; Schauer, 2006). Juries supposedly cannot be expected to understand the difficulties of inferring guilt or innocence from hearsay, character evidence, confessions, etc., so they have to be shielded from it by having the evidence declared inadmissible. This rather patronizing view of laypeople is an easy target for critics of evidence law. In his *Review of the Criminal Courts*, Lord Justice Auld (2001: 547) recommended 'that the English law of criminal evidence should, in general, move away from technical rules of inadmissibility to trusting judicial and lay fact-finders to give relevant evidence the weight it deserves'.

Critics of the law of evidence generally assume that the proper purpose of the rules is to maximize the number of factually accurate verdicts, a purpose which many of the rules do not serve in any obvious way. The law has, however, at least three other purposes: to avoid unnecessarily lengthy proceedings, to allocate the risk of error between the State and the defendant, and to promote other moral values, such as an abhorrence of torture and 'state-created crime' (e.g. *A v Home Secretary* [2005] UKHL 71; *Looseley* [2001] UKHL 53). In briefly examining three aspects of the law, our aim is not to explain all its intricacies, but to show how these rules are thought to contribute to achieving a fair trial.

Hearsay

The rule against hearsay, often seen as one of the most arcane and technical rules of evidence, stipulates that a statement made out of court is not admissible as evidence of the truth of what the speaker said, as distinct from evidence of the fact that she said it. The rule is subject to numerous exceptions which have been codified, but by no means simplified, in the Criminal Justice Act 2003. Although a number of rationales for the hearsay rule have been advanced, by far the most cogent is that it exists to protect the right to cross-examine witnesses (Law Commission 1996, para. 3.17). If someone who could have been called as a witness is instead allowed to testify at second hand through an out-of-court statement, the opportunity to test their evidence by cross-examination is lost. There is therefore a risk that the jury will place undue reliance on the evidence because flaws that would have been exposed by cross-examination will remain undiscovered. For example, the evidence of many prosecution witnesses would no doubt sound much more convincing if it were given through the mouths of police officers who could edit out any inconsistencies or equivocations. On the other hand, excluding hearsay may lead to error by depriving the jury of important evidence. When the party seeking to rely on the evidence could reasonably have been expected to call the original witness, it is fair that they should bear the risk of error if they fail to do so. If the other party is responsible for the witness's unavailability – for example if prosecution witnesses will not testify because they have been intimidated by the defendant – then the party responsible should bear the risk. Harder questions arise when the witness is dead or unavailable for reasons beyond either party's control. These are the situations for which the complex rules on hearsay provide.

These rules do not apply to civil cases, where the fact that evidence is hearsay is a matter of weight rather than admissibility: the judge will hear the evidence but may decide that because of the lack of cross-examination little reliance can be placed on it. Judges – whose professional socialization encourages them to place a high value on the adversarial testing of evidence – clearly are considered more likely than jurors to take an appropriately sceptical view of hearsay evidence. Such judicial scepticism sets some limits to attempts to circumvent the hearsay rule by dealing with alleged criminal behaviour through civil procedures such as ASBOs and Closure Orders (by which householders can be evicted on the basis of allegations of drug dealing). The High Court has advised magistrates considering applications for Closure Orders to look critically at 'anonymous hearsay witnesses stating that they do not wish to identify themselves for fear of reprisals without, in many cases, being at all specific about the reasons for their fear', and to be prepared to give little or no weight to such evidence (*R (Cleary)* v *Highbury Corner Magistrates' Court* [2006] EWHC 1869 (Admin), para. 30).

Confessions

The admissibility of confession evidence is technically an exception to the hearsay rule, since it allows an out-of-court statement by the accused to be produced as evidence of the truth of what is stated. Concern about a series of miscarriages of justice attributable to false confessions led the introduction of a relatively strict regime regulating confessions in the Police and Criminal Evidence Act 1984. Section 76 provides, in essence, that if the prosecution wish to introduce a confession into evidence they must be able to prove beyond reasonable doubt that it has not been obtained by oppression or by conduct (such as breaches of procedures laid down in codes of practice) of a kind that is likely to result in unreliable confessions. The question is not whether the particular confession is likely to be false, but whether anything said or done (usually but not necessarily by the police) would be likely to make *any* confession made as a result unreliable. The courts are instructed not to take account of whether the confession may have been true, and at least one murder conviction has been quashed even though the defendant's lawyers accepted that her confession was true (*McGovern* (1991) 92 Cr. App. R. 228). In addition confessions can be excluded under s.78 of the 1984 Act, which gives judges a discretion to exclude prosecution evidence on the ground that it would be unfair to the defendant.

Clearly the law accepts that the acquittal of some defendants whose confessions were true is preferable to the conviction of defendants whose confessions were false. It is the police, in most cases, who control both the questioning of defendants and the keeping of records, such as video recordings of interviews, to show that nothing improper was done,[4] so it is considered reasonable that the police should bear the burden of satisfying the judge that the confession was not improperly obtained. In these respects English procedure compares very favourably with practices Hodgson (2005) describes in France, where prosecutors tolerate violence to suspects during questioning and defence lawyers are not permitted to be present; but it bears repeating that this vigilance regarding confession evidence is in stark contrast to the unquestioning acceptance of guilty pleas.

Character evidence

The question of when the defendant's previous convictions should be put in evidence is probably the aspect of evidence law to which criminological research is most relevant. Unfortunately the issue is also extremely complex, and we can do little more than sketch the key questions here.

We can start with two obvious points. First, previous convictions can sometimes be relevant evidence of guilt. Take the alleged shoplifter who claims to have taken goods without paying through sheer absent-mindedness. It would be hard to deny that evidence of his 20 previous convictions for shoplifting made this defence less plausible.[5] Second, there is a risk that previous convictions will prejudice a magistrate or jury against a defendant. The Law Commission (2001) has distinguished two types of prejudice:

> 'reasoning prejudice', the tendency to give bad character evidence undue weight in determining whether the defendant is guilty as charged, and 'moral prejudice', the tendency to convict through distaste for the defendant without being truly satisfied that he or she is guilty as charged at all. (2001: para. 6.33)

If these two forms of prejudice are abhorrent to the legal system, it is hard to understand why evidence of 'good character' (which in practice often means nothing more than an absence of previous convictions) has always been admissible as evidence both of the defendant's credibility and the unlikelihood of his committing the offence charged. Historically, a major function of the jury was to exercise 'moral prejudice' in favour of defendants of good character, who as we have seen were often acquitted, or convicted of lesser offences, despite strong evidence against them. It is not obviously irrational to take character into account in deciding what constitutes 'reasonable doubt'. A conviction for shoplifting might be much more damaging to someone who sees herself as a paragon of respectability than to someone with a long criminal record, and on utilitarian grounds one might argue that there are stronger reasons for giving the former defendant the benefit of any possible doubt. Such reasoning, however, offends against the principle of equality before the law, which may be one reason for keeping character evidence from juries or magistrates. Conversely, an unacknowledged feeling that the wrongful conviction of people of 'bad character' is really no great tragedy may be one factor that makes a relaxation of the rules on character evidence appear acceptable.

To show that bad character evidence gives rise to 'reasoning prejudice' it would have to be shown not only that juries and magistrates are more likely to convict if they know of a defendant's previous convictions, which they almost certainly are (Lloyd-Bostock 2000, 2006), but that this does not reflect the genuine probative value of the evidence. Redmayne (2002a: 76) argues that in light of the evidence from reconviction studies, 'it looks as though the problem with Lloyd-Bostock's subjects is that they increase their guilt likelihoods by *too little* when confronted with a recent similar previous conviction, rather than by too much'. As Redmayne (2002b) acknowledges, however, reconviction studies can only tell us that, for many offences, those with a previous conviction are much more likely to be *convicted* of a further similar offence than those without. This ignores the 'dark figure' of offences for which people are not convicted,[6] and the darker figure of wrongful convictions, although it is probably safe to assume that most 'officially identified career offenders' have real criminal careers (D. J. Smith, 2007: 643). Crucially, it also ignores the likelihood that a high proportion of *innocent* accused have prior convictions for similar offences. There is no doubt that people with previous convictions have a greatly elevated risk of being charged with further offences (see e.g. McAra and McVie, 2007), but we know of no reason to suppose that, among those charged, those with similar previous convictions are more likely than those without to be guilty.

Despite these difficulties, reconviction figures might be thought to provide some support for one of the most controversial provisions of the Criminal Justice Act 2003. Before the Act, evidence of previous convictions was admissible in a number of situations where their probative value was considered to be greater than their prejudicial effect (Tapper, 2004; Roberts and Zuckerman, 2004). What was not permitted was the use of previous convictions merely to show that the defendant is the kind of person who commits offences of the same general type as the one charged. In some respects the 2003 Act restates the previous law, but it also makes evidence of past misconduct admissible to show that 'the defendant has a propensity to commit offences of the kind with which he is charged' (s. 103 (1) (a)). Offences of the same 'kind' include all offences in either of the two broad categories, one of offences against property and the other of sex offences defined by the Criminal Justice Act (Categories of Offences) Order 2004. So, for example, armed robbery is the same 'kind' of offence as shoplifting, although the Court of Appeal has indicated that an offence of shoplifting would not normally amount to evidence of a propensity for robbery (*Hanson* [2005] EWCA Crim 824). Evidence of previous convictions (or 'other reprehensible behaviour') can also be used to show that the defendant has 'a propensity to be untruthful' (s. 103(1) (b), 112(1)).

Let us now consider two objections to the use of criminological evidence to support the 2003 provisions. First, drawing on Stein's discussion (2005: 183–9), it can be argued that even if it is true that convicted thieves or sex offenders are more likely than other people, on average, to commit further similar offences, there is still a form of prejudice involved in applying this generalization to individual defendants. The prejudice consists of assuming that what is true *on average* of members of a category is true of an individual member of that category. For example, however strong the evidence that black people in certain areas commit a disproportionate number of mobile phone robberies (Harrington and Mayhew, 2001), surely no judge would tell a jury to regard a black defendant as more likely than a white one to have stolen a phone, in the absence of evidence that the specific perpetrator was black. And even advocates of free use of character evidence might hesitate to argue that since 'career' offenders tend to be versatile rather than specialized (D. J. Smith, 2007: 647), a criminal record should be considered as evidence of a general propensity to commit *all* kinds of crime. Even if such reasoning increased the overall proportion of accurate verdicts, it would be unfair to innocent black defendants, or innocent defendants of 'bad character', because they would bear a disproportionate risk of wrongful conviction. The objections are harder to sustain where the defendant's record gives unequivocal evidence of a relevant propensity (e.g., five convictions for the same offence in the last year) or where there is clear evidence that the offender and the defendant have some peculiarity in common (such as an unusual *modus operandi*). The Court of Appeal's judgement in *Hanson* (above) gives some reassurance that character evidence will not be used to base very broad generalizations on a single conviction. The Court stresses that whether a previous conviction shows a relevant propensity depends on the particular circumstances of each case, not simply on whether the conviction is in the same broad category as the offence charged, and that a single conviction will often fail to demonstrate propensity. Arguably this is a narrower – but also a fairer – interpretation of the law than the government intended (Waterman and Dempster, 2006). The *Hanson* guidelines, however, leave a great deal to the discretion of trial judges, and to magistrates who will have heard the evidence even if they eventually decide to exclude it (Darbyshire, 1997).

The second objection to the Act is that it gives an incentive to the police and prosecutors to bring prosecutions on weak evidence, bolstered by the defendant's previous convictions (House of Commons, 2002, paras 114–16; Munday, 2005). As we have seen, anyone charged with an offence, guilty or innocent, is subject to strong pressures to plead guilty, and these will be exacerbated by the prospect of previous convictions being introduced in a context where it is difficult to predict how judges or magistrates will exercise their discretion[7] or how damaging previous convictions will be to the defence. Judges may decide to exclude character evidence where they suspect it is being used to bolster a weak case (*DPP* v *Chand* [2007] EWHC 90 (Admin)). Defence lawyers, however, do not always challenge weak cases as forcefully as they should (McConville et al., 1994) and faced with the added threat of bad character evidence they may well encourage clients to plead guilty. That, of course, will give the clients more bad character to be used against them next time the police 'round up the usual suspects'.

The merits of evidential rules are too often discussed solely with reference to their use in jury trials. If we really had a criminal justice system in which the prosecution had to prove its case beyond a reasonable doubt to an impartial lay tribunal, there might be a good case for relaxing the rules on character evidence and trusting jurors and magistrates to decide what weight to give it. In the system we actually have, in which most convictions result from coerced guilty pleas and the key decision makers are the police, the CPS and defence lawyers, the Act appears much more dangerous.

Conclusion

Perhaps the most important distinction between the civil-law inquisitorial system and the common-law adversarial jury system is that the former embodies a high level of trust in state officials to seek out the truth (Hörnle, 2006). The latter, on the other hand, views state prosecutions with a degree of distrust and insists that they be subject to rigorous and independent public scrutiny. In his excellent comparative study of criminal procedure, Vogler argues that although the 'professionalism, rigorous truth-finding and deductive reasoning' of the inquisitorial system is 'highly seductive', history shows that 'the consequences of unrestrained inquisitoriality are catastrophic' (2005: 20–1). While the investigation of crime inevitably has an inquisitorial character, its results should not be taken on trust but need to be kept in check by adversarial trials and lay decision-makers. For those who are not disposed to place blind faith in the State's processes of criminal investigation, the most serious flaw of the adversarial system is not the nature of the trial but that it allows trials to be avoided if one side can be persuaded to give up without a fight. The 'mass production of guilty pleas' may create an impression of efficiency, but it hardly deserves to be called a system of justice.

Summary

Over a long history, English common-law developed a distinctive form of criminal procedure characterized by adversarialism and lay adjudication. These aspects of criminal procedure have serious drawbacks but also some important strengths. The processing of the great majority of cases, however, bears little relation to the historic ideals of criminal justice.

STUDY QUESTIONS

- If the adversarial system were on trial for perverting the course of justice, what would be the main points for the prosecution and defence? If you were a juror, what would be your verdict?

- Would you consider yourself competent as a juror to deal with a major criminal case such as a murder, rape or commercial fraud? Who, if anyone, would you consider better qualified to decide such cases?

- In descending order of importance, list what you consider to be the four or five most important goals of the criminal trial and the law of evidence.

- Should the guilty plea discount be abolished?

FURTHER READING

Andrew Sanders and Richard Young's *Criminal Justice* (2007) provides an extremely informative and critical account of all aspects of criminal procedure and evidence. For an in-depth discussion of the normative framework of the criminal trial see the three volumes of *The Trial on Trial*, edited by Antony Duff, Lindsay Farmer, Sandra Marshall and Victor Tadros (2004, 2006, 2008). Paul Roberts and Adrian Zuckerman's *Criminal Evidence* (2004), though not easy reading for beginners, is both an excellent textbook and a robust defence of a liberal view of criminal procedure. Richard Vogler's *A World View of Criminal Procedure* (2005) is highly recommended for comparative and historical perspectives.

Notes

1 Note that this speculation about the jury also fits the 'story model' (as explanation-based decision making is also known). The story according to which the jury convicted because the prosecution story was convincing is coherent – it fits the evidence we have about the trial – and plausible, because it matches what we 'know' about how juries commonly behave.
2 Or 9–1 if the number of jurors is reduced to 10: Juries Act 1974, s. 17.
3 E.g. *Johnstone* [2003] 3 All ER 884 (trade mark offences); *Davies* [2003] ICR 586 (safety regulations); *R (Grundy & Co.)* v *Halton Magistrates* [2003] EWHC 272 (unlicensed tree felling).
4 There are, of course, loopholes in this system, such as the possibility of unrecorded conversations prior to the recorded interview (Moston and Stevenson, 1993).
5 This is an illustration of the long-established principle that evidence of previous convictions may be relevant to show whether an action was 'designed or accidental': *Makin* [1894] AC 57.
6 The best estimate from the British Crime Survey is that 3 per cent of offences against individuals or their property result in a conviction or caution (Barclay and Tavares, 1999: 29).
7 The Court of Appeal has stressed that 'the trial judge's "feel" for the case is usually the critical ingredient of the decision at first instance' and the circumstances in which it will interfere with the judge's discretion are limited: *Renda* [2006] 2 All ER 553 at [3].

8

Punishment

Chapter Contents

OVERVIEW

Chapter 8:

- Discusses criminal law's distinctive 'power to punish'.

- Analyses and develops contemporary criminological conversation about 'penal excess' and 'penal moderation'.

- Explains and distinguishes instrumentalist and retributivist thinking about the purpose of punishment.

KEY TERMS

punishment penal excess penal moderation instrumentalism retributivism

Introduction

A distinctive feature of criminal law, compared with other bodies of law which regulate conduct, is that those who are convicted of contravening its provisions can be punished by the state. Accordingly, an account of criminal law as a social institution might be advanced through discussion of its distinctive power: the power to punish.

However, judicial punishment is an extremely broad and complex topic and we want to avoid providing a bland and over-simplified account of it. To this end, we are going to concentrate upon a central theme within contemporary criminological conversation about punishment: the theme of 'penal excess'. In the context of discussing 'penal excess' we will introduce some fundamental questions concerning the purpose and justification of judicial punishment.

Over the last few decades, we have witnessed a 'punitive turn' (Hallsworth, 2000). A long period of slowly progressing humanization and civilization of the practice of punishment seems to have come to a halt and gone into reverse. The state is now punishing more people than it used to, and it is using harsher and rougher methods of punishment. This has been accompanied by the rise of 'ill-tempered forms of public talk about crime, offenders and how to punish them' (Loader, 2007: 4).

Some of the more dystopian accounts of current penal trends have been questioned (e.g. Zedner, 2002). Warnings have been sounded about the dangers of assuming that what has happened in the USA is typical of other modern societies, mistaking political rhetoric for actual change in policy and practice, and overlooking trends that point in a different direction. However, such questioning is generally regarded as qualifying, rather than negating, the notion that – at least in the field of crime, justice and punishment – we live in 'dark times': we have 'a highly politicized, over-dramatized and "hot" penal climate' (Loader, 2007: 9).

The words just quoted come from Ian Loader, a particularly prominent figure in contemporary criminological conversation about penal excess. Loader has led a call for 'penal moderation' (ibid.). The task, as he puts it, is 'to inculcate a sense of restraint in how our society talks about and delivers punishment' (ibid.: 3).

In this chapter, we seek to advance this conversation about penal excess and moderation. We start with a summary of how criminologists generally describe and explain penal excess and look at the nature of their calls for penal moderation. However, we then note that levels of punishment that criminologists routinely assume to be excessive are actually regarded by many people as quite acceptable. For many, if there has been an increase in criminalization and punishment, this is simply correcting a tendency towards over-tolerance of anti-social conduct and over-leniency in the use of judicial punishment.

Given the existence of such views, if criminologists are to succeed in their goal of curbing and reversing the punitive turn, they need to be much clearer about the basis of their own judgement that contemporary punishment is excessive. Such a judgement could in fact rest upon two quite different forms of reasoning about punishment: instrumentalism and retributivism. Criminologists tend to be vague about the basis of their judgement, but often invoke instrumentalist reasoning. We suggest that in doing so they are neither properly representing their concerns, nor intervening in a way likely to be politically effective. We argue that retributivist reasoning – which is often seen as associated with punitivism – is in fact an essential resource for justifying and persuading others of the view that contemporary punishment is excessive.

We conclude with the suggestion that there may be a positive aspect to demands for more criminalization and punishment. Rather than simply asking people to moderate such demands, it might be more productive to see them as expressing in very crude terms an important critique of the institution of state punishment. Through a creative alliance with, rather than dismissal of, those who voice such criticism, it might be possible – instead of arguing over levels of punishment – to arouse interest in radically different ways of approaching issues of crime and justice.

The criminological analysis of 'penal excess'

In the UK, the origins of the punitive turn are generally traced to the 1979 general election – the first in which 'law and order' was a central issue. However, a crucial turning point is considered to be the early-mid 1990s when the Labour Party attempted to shed its image of being the party which was soft on crime by declaring its intention to be 'tough on crime, tough on the causes of crime' and Conservative Home Secretary Michael Howard declared that 'prison works' (Newburn, 2007: 14–5). The criminological response to the punitive turn has included writing books and articles with titles such as *Tough Justice* (Dunbar and Langdon, 1998), *The Expanding Prison* (Cayley, 1998), *The Exclusive Society* (Young, 1999), 'Emotive and Ostentatious Punishment' (Pratt, 2000), *The Culture of Control* (Garland, 2001), *Harsh Justice* (Whitman, 2003) and *Addicted to Incarceration* (Pratt, 2009).

In what follows, we will pull out some themes from such literature. However, we are also going to focus specifically upon the fairly recent deliberations of the Commission on English Prisons Today (CEPT). This is an independent commission made up of criminologists and penal reformers. It was established to investigate, among other things, what is driving up the prison population and what can be done to reverse this trend (http://www.prisoncommission.org.uk/). The term 'penal excess' and similar terms crop up frequently in their discussions. Such terms evoke a range of phenomena.

One development is the number of new criminal offences being created by statute. According to CEPT, 'over the past ten years the Labour government has created more new criminal offences than were introduced in the previous 100 years' (CEPT, 2007: 5). It is important to point out that, although this is significant in its own terms, it need not mean that the reach of criminal law is actually being extended; that depends on the nature of these new statutory offences (e.g. is behaviour which was previously lawful being criminalized, or is much of it simply re-defining existing offences?) and the way they are being used by law enforcement agencies. Indeed, in one of the contributions to CEPT discussions, David Faulkner suggests that much of this legislation 'has been too detailed and complicated; much of it has had little effect' (Faulkner, 2007). However, the general assumption of CEPT is that this legislative activity has resulted in more and more conduct being met with state punishment. As they put it, in a sentence containing a magnificent 'typo': 'the impact of this legislative activity can be found directly in the ever-growing numbers behind bards' (CEPT, 2007: 5).

In the wider literature referred to above, other developments are pointed to which are likely to extend the range of conduct that is met with criminal justice intervention. These include the emergence of zero-tolerance policing schemes, the growth of surveillance, and – crucially – an erosion of important procedural rights previously enjoyed by those suspected of committing crime or behaving anti-socially. At a more general level, it tends to be suggested that modern society is becoming increasingly intolerant of marginalized people and bothersome conduct that previously would have been tolerated. Also, it is suggested, society is resorting more quickly and exclusively to criminalization and punishment as standard methods of dealing with people and conduct deemed troublesome.

In addition, the term 'penal excess' suggests that the penal sanctions used are becoming harsher. Again, there are various aspects to this. More and more people who could, given the nature of their offences, be kept in the community are being sent to prison and the length of prison sentences has increased (Coyle, 2007). Within prisons, conditions are much worse than they used to be. Constructive goals, such as 'rehabilitation, skills, reintegration and other goals aimed at challenging recidivism are marginalised' (Hoyle, 2007: 15). Even when offenders are kept in the community, the policy seems to be to ensure that they are *punished* rather than subjected to anything more constructive. Indeed, there is now a tendency to take seriously proposals to revive cruel and humiliating punishments – so-called shame sanctions – which, not so long ago, were considered obsolete (Johnstone, 2002: 123–4).

This latter development points to another meaning of 'penal excess'. It is not simply that more people are being punished and that the punishments being imposed are more severe. There is also a change in the manner of punishment and in the attitudes behind it. Punishment and penal discourse have become extravagant, impetuous, ill-tempered and over-enthusiastic. Some of this is captured in John Pratt's phrase 'emotive and ostentatious punishment' (Pratt, 2000). The suggestion here is that there has been a resurgence of penal practices that are designed, not simply to sanction and control unacceptable conduct, but to humiliate offenders and to express straightforwardly the way people feel about them – with the assumption that the dominant feelings are anger, rage, indignation, hatred and resentment (cf. Braithwaite, 2006: 403). All sorts of fanciful and gruesome methods of punishment and control – which not so long ago were deemed to be largely extinct in the modern world – are being considered for revival and to some extent actually being revived. Punishment, and more generally talk about crime and offenders, is becoming 'de-civilized' (Hallsworth, 2000; Pratt, 2002).

Explaining 'penal excess'

As well as pointing to penal excess, criminologists are concerned to explain why the punitive turn occurred. These explanations are of interest here, in that they seem to take for granted that the explanatory task is to account for an irrational or pathological change in the public and governmental reaction to crime. Hence, the emphasis tends to be upon 'factors' that might have produced such a change rather than on the arguments of those who have consciously promoted it.

A typical criminological explanation of the punitive turn will start by pointing to 'economic, cultural, and political transformations that have marked late twentieth-century social life' (Garland and Sparks, 2000: 1). It is suggested that these transformations have disturbed moral and social cohesion (Pratt, 2007). They have left the ordinary people of modern societies feeling that they are surrounded by dangers and risks over which they have little control. This makes people fearful, anxious and on edge. Crime has become the symbolic focus of such concerns – hence people feel an urgent need to do a something about it. Their reactions, though, are not guided by cool rational thinking. Rather, their responses to crime become a vehicle for giving vent to all of their fear, anxiety and rage. They 'take it out' on people whom they identify as tangible causes of their problems. At the same time, they are easily duped into thinking that this 'works'. This is because most ordinary people are ignorant about the causes of crime, the circumstances of offenders, the reality of penal practices, and the actual effects of penal sanctions.

Much of the punitive turn, then, is driven by populist fears and ignorant beliefs (Pratt, 2007). But, these are in turn fuelled and exploited by a sensationalist media and cunning politicians. For the media, sensationalizing crime sells and so do calls to get tough – and this is even more important in an increasingly competitive industry. Ordinary people, who rely heavily on the popular media for information and framing of problems, find their anxieties and punitive mindsets confirmed and amplified in the media. For politicians, a focus on crime as *the* problem deflects attention away from other causes of contemporary ills – which they are either unwilling or unable to identify and tackle. And harsh justice as the solution enables them to appear as strong, willing to take tough measures when required, and able to do *something* at a time when the capacity of national governments to control what happens within their territories is increasingly eroded by forces of globalization. Politicians, accordingly, increasingly see an advantage in fuelling, exploiting, and meeting the demands of popular punitiveness. The political debate about punishment has accordingly become reduced to questions of who is the toughest.

Penal moderation

Faced with the punitive turn, many criminologists have become deeply pessimistic and dystopian (Zedner, 2002). Some seem to think that – in the current climate in which academics are kept at arms length from the policy-making process (Faulkner, 2007) – all that criminologists can do is expose what is happening and hope that people see sense. Others, however, refuse such a despairing stance. These include the members of the Commission on English Prisons Today.

In his CEPT discussion paper, Ian Loader suggests that the Commission needs a 'big idea' to link its specific recommendations and to ensure that it transforms the terms of public debate about crime and punishment (2007: 1) As a candidate, he suggests 'penal moderation'. The term suggests limiting and restricting the use of punishment and making it less violent, severe and intense. For Loader, penal moderation has three key elements: restraint, parsimony and dignity.

One goal is 'to inculcate a sense of restraint in how our society talks about and delivers punishment' (ibid.: 3). Loader suggests that many citizens are morally ambivalent about punishing and that, in order to inculcate a sense of restraint, it is necessary 'to bring this ambivalence to the surface of public discussion – and find ways of institutionalizing it' (ibid.). The ambivalence to which Loader refers is at two levels. First, with regard to punishment specifically, citizens feel angry and resentful towards criminal wrong-doers and have a passionate desire to inflict harm on them. Yet, they also seek repair, forgiveness and reconciliation and feel regretful and uncomfortable about punishing people. More generally, Loader suggests that the intense desire to punish is also at odds with the English self-image as a society which is 'tolerant, forgiving and pragmatic'. As we understand it, the core of Loader's proposition here is that if we can call the attention of citizens to the fact that they have deep value-commitments which are at odds with penal excess, they will begin to feel ashamed of it and be motivated to reverse it.

A second goal is to make a case for parsimony as a principle governing penal policy. In order to make this case it is necessary to make society understand that the punishment of offenders, and especially imprisonment, (a) can contribute little to solving problems of crime and disorder, (b) is very costly and (c) should therefore be used sparingly, as a last resort and in strict proportion to the harm done (ibid.: 4–5).

A third goal is to instil a culture of moderation within the occupational outlooks and working practices of penal institutions. To this end, it is suggested that it is important to ingrain the idea that all who are under the 'care and control' of the penal system remain citizens (even if non-UK nationals) with human rights – especially to dignity – that should be recognized and protected.

Beyond penal moderation

Loader does acknowledge a problem with 'penal moderation': that for something which is meant to be a 'big idea' it seems purely negative. The message it seeks to inject into public debate is that we need to use the power to punish less, more cautiously and with regret and even shame. It does not offer much by way of positive alternative solutions to problems of crime and disorder. Nor does it offer much by way of support to those working within the penal system who are trying to do more positive things – 'work, training, education, drug treatment and other rehabilitative programmes' (Loader, 2007: 6) – but struggle for recognition and resources. Loader acknowledges, then, the need to reconcile penal moderation with proposals for more positive penal interventions and alternative ways of handling problems of crime and disorder.

Amongst these alternative – more positive – interventions, restorative justice has succeeded most in capturing the public, professional and political attention in recent years (cf. Johnstone, 2002; Johnstone and Van Ness, 2007). Another member of CEPT, Carolyn Hoyle (2007), explores the extent to which restorative justice can provide solutions to the penal crisis. She suggests – albeit rather cautiously – that more thorough and imaginative use of restorative justice, which currently exists only on the periphery of criminal justice, could help reduce prison numbers.

What follows is largely sympathetic to the goal of penal moderation and the development of imaginative alternatives – especially restorative justice – to conventional penal approaches to crime. However, we also want to sharpen up and in some ways redirect some of this argument.

Is contemporary punishment excessive?

We have seen that many criminologists take it for granted that contemporary societies use the power to punish excessively. However, it is crucial to recognize that what many – perhaps most – criminologists deem to be a move to penal excess is regarded by others, including large swathes of the public, as the correction of a previous tendency to over-tolerance of anti-social conduct and over-leniency in the use of punishment.

This is made clear by David Faulkner in his contribution to CEPT discussions (Faulkner, 2007). He shows that the developments which are denounced by most criminologists as 'penal excess' have been urged and welcomed by many people who regard the criminal justice system as one of many failing social services. On this view, the criminal justice system has long been failing in its job of protecting ordinary hard-working people and innocent victims from those who choose to prey upon them. The perceived failings of the system include the following: a great deal of anti-social behaviour, that makes people's lives a misery and goes unchecked because it is outside prevailing legal definitions of crime; existing criminal laws which are inadequately enforced; a misplaced concern for the human rights of suspects which results in many offenders avoiding conviction; sentences imposed which are inadequate to protect the public and to demonstrate that anything meaningful is being done about crime; prisoners who are pampered rather than punished; and actual prison sentences imposed which are rarely served.

Overall, from this perspective, the criminal justice system favours the criminal rather than the victim and the public. This failure is bound up with the fact that the system is controlled and operated by professional elites – judges, civil servants, managers, academics – who because of their comfortable social position have been relatively unaffected by the upsurge in crime and anti-social behaviour (Johnstone, 2000).

To dismiss such claims as reactionary strikes us as inadequate. Criminologists, if they wish to join in the public debate about punishment at all, need to provide those who think this way with strong arguments to the effect that (a) expanding criminalization and punishment is not only bad policy but is incompatible with the moral and political principles which ought to guide and constrain the use of punishment; and (b) there are alternative ways of handling crime which will better meet the demand that something *meaningful* be done about conduct which is making the lives of many people – but especially those who are already relatively deprived and powerless – miserable.

Examining the notion of penal excess

The basis of the judgement that contemporary societies punish excessively is seldom made clear. In order to sustain this claim, we would in fact have to address questions about the proper purposes of punishment, the levels of punishment needed to achieve these purposes, and factors which should constrain our use of punishment even if such constraint means failing to achieve certain important goals. This requires us to think philosophically about punishment in a manner which is not prominent in much contemporary criminological conversation.

There are, of course, very different ideas about the purpose of punishment. It is common to divide these into two broad schools of thought: instrumentalism and retributivism (with other schools espousing various 'mixed theories': see e.g. Hart, 2008, discussed in Chapter 4). These two schools offer radically different ways of thinking about what constitutes an appropriate amount of punishment – and hence what might constitute penal excess. In what follows, we will provide a very brief account of the core ideas of each school and the ideas about penal excess that flow from them.

Instrumentalism

An instrumentalist (there are probably no pure instrumentalists, so this is an abstraction) tends to think of the purpose of social policies and practices as being to achieve certain ends – some desirable state of affairs – and judges them primarily in terms of their effectiveness and efficiency in achieving those ends. So, punishment (and various penal methods) is thought of by the instrumentalist as a tool which we use in an effort to bring about a desirable state of affairs. Usually, it is assumed that the 'end' to be achieved is crime reduction – either the prevention of further offences by a particular offender and/or lower crime rates within some territory. But, punishment might be regarded as a mechanism for bringing about other desirable states of affairs such as the recovery of crime victims from trauma, reduced fear of crime in society or even the satisfaction of vengeful feelings which could have resulted in the offender suffering acts of private vengeance which are more harmful to them than state punishment.

A crucial point is that, within this way of thinking, the practice of punishing people has no intrinsic moral merit – we do not have an obligation to punish wrong-doers because it is inherently ethical to do so or unethical not to do so. Rather, punishment is simply a method we use in an effort to engineer a desirable state of affairs.

However, on the face of it, any individual act of punishment will actually achieve something undesirable. Punishment brings harm and pain to the person punished and indeed to what we might call the offender's micro-community: those who are emotionally attached to or dependent upon the offender. Also, most of the penal methods we use are expensive, and the money could be used to achieve other things that are desirable (such as better health and social services or lower taxes). So if we assume that bringing harm and pain to people is – looked at in isolation – undesirable, and that spending a lot of money on it makes it even more undesirable, it is not obvious why an instrumentalist would advocate punishment.

In fact, for the instrumentalist a justification of punishment must take the form of a cost-benefit analysis. To be justified, punishment must achieve some benefit – some desirable state of affairs – which is sufficiently valuable to justify its human and fiscal costs. Moreover, punishment must be the most effective and efficient way of achieving this benefit. This is in fact a common way of thinking about why we punish and why we are justified in doing so. If we assume that punishing a person will result in less crime in the future, and that the crime that is prevented would have caused more misery than is created by the act of punishment, then punishment is justified – at least for the instrumentalist. Or, to be more precise, it is justified provided there is not any other more economic method of preventing the crime.

The classic utilitarian doctrines concerning punishment, developed by 'pioneers in criminology' such as Beccaria and Bentham (see Monachesi, 1960; and Geis, 1960 respectively) exemplify this instrumentalist way of thinking. And it is crucial to recognize that these doctrines played a vital role in establishing and justifying the notion that the penal system of the late eighteenth century was *excessive* in its use of punishment.

Classic utilitarian penal theory encouraged us to think about punishment in economic terms: as an investment rather than as a moral obligation (see Moberly, 1968: Ch. 2). And, for the utilitarians, punishment 'should not be regarded as settling an old account but rather as opening a new one' (ibid.: 44). In doing so, we should ask 'what profit is our investment going to yield?'. Decisions about how much to punish should be governed by principles of prudent investment (ibid.: 46). The prudent investor is one who invests only where there is a reasonable expectation that the initial expenditure will result in long-term profit, and will not be wasted. So too with punishment. The prudent punisher is one who punishes only when, and only to the extent that, it is likely to bring future benefits in terms of human happiness. Anything beyond that is excessive.

What is important here is (a) that for classic utilitarianism, penal excess was wrong because it was wasteful, and (b) there was a clear principle by which one could judge whether punishment was in fact excessive (although translating this into an actual calculation would be immensely complicated). As Leon Radzinowicz explained it, the position of classic utilitarianism was that the severity of punishment:

> ... must be strictly limited. Whilst it should be proportionate to the crime, it should not go beyond the point necessary to prevent the criminal from injuring anew his fellow-citizens and to deter others. This could be secured by ensuring that the evil inflicted on the offender exceeded any advantage derived from his crime: 'all beyond this is superfluous and consequentially tyrannical'. (Radzinowicz, 1966: 10–11; the words quoted are Beccaria's)

Crucially – as Moberly (1968) and Foucault (1977) make clear – although the penal excesses of the eighteenth century were frequently condemned by utilitarians on the basis of an appeal to 'the rights of man', the main basis of the claim that they were excessive was based largely in instrumentalist reasoning.

Some limits of instrumentalism

Instrumentalism provides a form of reasoning which criminologists can use to justify and communicate their claims about contemporary punishment being excessive. Indeed, if criminologists do attempt to justify rather than simply assert the claim of penal excess they often do so by resorting to instrumentalist reasoning.

Instrumentalism does, however, have significant limitations as a basis for denouncing penal excess:

1 Those who think purely in instrumentalist terms must concede that, if it could be demonstrated that a move towards 'tough justice', 'penal expansion' etc. *did* result in a desirable state of affairs, e.g. crime did decrease and victims felt more satisfied,

then the critique that this is 'penal excess' would lose much of its force. It is difficult to explain, in instrumentalist terms, why we should not expand and intensify the use of judicial punishment if it does work. Given the enormously complex methodological issues involved in carrying out research and in analysing the limited evidence available, it would, at any rate, be beyond our expertise to provide a rigorous argument as to why *some* 'excessive' methods, such as selective incapacitation of recidivist minor offenders or a massive use of capital punishment, would not work. And if this is such a daunting task even for relatively well-informed commentators, what is the general public to make of it? Since criminologists have achieved very little demonstrable success in controlling crime, and little consensus among ourselves, there is no good reason to expect the public to trust our supposed expertise on what works and what doesn't.

2   Even if it is accepted that harsh justice is not effective in achieving crime reduction, it may be effective in achieving other desirable outcomes. For instance, if 'emotive and ostentatious punishments' significantly increases the happiness of the majority of people who are not subject to them (because they enable them to express their feelings in a way they find highly satisfactory) then for a pure instrumentalist this would be a perfectly good reason for using such punishments, even if they are not good at reducing crime.

3   Most importantly, we guess that instrumentalist reasoning actually fails to capture the real reasons why many criminologists regard contemporary punishment as excessive. Rather, the real or at least core objection to increasing criminalization and so on is that it involves the state interfering with personal freedom in areas in which it has no right to interfere. And, at least part of the core objection to 'harsh justice' is that it oversteps the boundaries of morality, decency and civilized conduct. The basis of claims of penal excess is, in short, moral and political. What criminologists really want to say is that the contemporary use of criminalization and punishment is politically intrusive and morally repugnant – not that it is bad policy, although it may be that as well. Hence, they need a language which can justify such claims. One element of this language may be retributivism.

Retributivism

Retributivists think about punishment in a very different way to instrumentalists. For the retributivist, the punishment of offenders is less a method of producing some desirable state of affairs, more a morally appropriate and – in some versions – morally obligatory response to wrongful behaviour. Those familiar with the retributivist critique, which emerged in the 1970s, of treatment-oriented sentencing (von Hirsch, 1976) will hardly be surprised by our invocation of retributivism as a resource for countering penal excess. However, many criminologists will still find this strange. Despite the revival of retributivism in legal and moral philosophy since the 1970s, it still tends to be regarded within criminology – and in particular within the discourse of restorative justice – as little more then a secularized version of theories of divine vengeance in which wrongs must be paid for in the currency of pain, suffering and even death. It is still quite common in criminological conversation to hear the punitive turn being *attributed to* the retributivist revival.

Whist retributivism is not without its problems, it also has certain advantages. One advantage is that, precisely because it refuses the notion that punishment can be justified by reference to constructive results that it might bring about (insisting that it must be justified on the ground that it is deserved), it is wary of the enthusiasm to do good which can fuel penal excess even more than the desire to impose suffering on those who wrong us.

Another advantage of retributivism, compared with instrumentalism, is that it tends to take the question of people's *rights* seriously (which is not to say it succeeds in its goal of squaring punishment with respect for rights). To explain: one objection to instrumentalist thinking about punishment is that it seems unaware of the point that, even if punishment does prevent more misery than it causes, and even if it is the most efficient way of preventing such misery, it is not thereby morally justified. If intentional infliction of pain and suffering on another human being against their will is on the face of it morally wrong, then it is difficult to see how it can be justified (shown to be morally right) simply on the ground that it saves others from misery. To leave the argument there is to suggest that the individuals punished either have no *rights* or (what seems to be much the same thing) their rights can be overridden simply on the ground that the greater good requires it.

So, if we believe that individuals have certain rights (e.g. to life, bodily integrity, freedom of movement, freedom of conscience) that ought to be respected and protected, then to justify punishment we surely need to show something more than that it prevents more misery than it causes. What we seem to need is a justification of punishment that shows that punishing people is consistent with taking their rights seriously. A strength of retributivism is that – at least in some versions – it seeks to provide such an account.

Retributivism is in fact a very complex way of thinking about punishment. In what follows, we will attempt to explain some of its basic features. This is necessary in order to achieve our purpose: to show that retributivism provides a very different basis for making and justifying claims about the excessiveness or otherwise of punishment.

It is useful to distinguish two versions of retributivism, although not all retributivists make such a distinction and these can be combined. One is 'weak retributivism', which claims that the legitimate authorities in society have a *right* to punish those who commit crime. The other is 'strong retributivism', which claims that the authorities in society have an *obligation* to punish those who commit crime where there is a reasonable opportunity to do so.

As we have indicated, one of the questions weak retributivism addresses is that of how punishment can be consistent with respecting people's rights. One retributivist response to this question involves arguing that offenders somehow *consent* to being punished. At first sight this seems absurd. Whilst some offenders may deeply regret their actions and agree that they should suffer for them, many do not feel or express remorse. Even if they do feel remorse, most offenders do not – on the face of it – consent to the punishments that are imposed upon them (some of course may submissively undergo punishment, but submission is a far cry from consent). Indeed, if most offenders did obviously consent to being punished, we would need a much smaller criminal justice and penal apparatus than we have. Imagine for a moment how this might work. We could have the equivalent of 'swear boxes' placed in convenient places, and those who broke the law could go along to them and deposit the appropriate 'fine'. For those who committed serious crimes, we could provide prisons (with regimes of varying harshness) where they could voluntarily go to atone for their wrongs. For those who committed very grave wrongs and believed in the death penalty, we could provide 'assisted suicide'.

Punishment, then, would look a bit like a secular version of *penance* in the Christian faith (we voluntarily go along to somebody to confess our crimes, they tell us what hardships we must undergo to atone for what we have done and hence restore our relationship to the community, and we then voluntarily undergo these hardships). The fact that this connection between state punishment and religious penance seems so implausible (perhaps outside the confines of very small close-knit communities) makes us baulk at the idea that offenders consent to being punished.

So, what are retributivists saying? In fact, they have two plausible arguments:

1 We tacitly consent to being punished for crimes we commit by availing ourselves of the benefits of living in a society in which people generally obey the law.
2 A rational person would consent to the general idea that people should be punished for crimes, so when offenders actually do not consent they are not behaving rationally. We respect their rights as rational people when we punish them.

This second idea, we should note, is not as implausible as some may think, at least when it is limited to those crimes that every reasonable person would agree are wrong. Many offenders strongly subscribe to the general idea that wrongdoing should be met with punishment. Also, we do often make ourselves suffer for doing wrong – we can subject ourselves to very painful feelings of guilt when we fail to live up to what we recognize as justifiable demands about how we should behave. In the form we have stated it, however, the argument is clearly question-begging. The retributivist needs to explain *why* a rational person would consent to punishment. We shall not attempt such an explanation here.

What we have called 'weak retributivism' argues that punishment of offenders (provided it can be shown to be deserved) is morally permissible. However, it does not argue that we *must* punish offenders if we have a reasonable opportunity to do so. Hence, one could accept 'weak retributivism' and still contend that there are often good (instrumentalist) grounds for not punishing. For instance, it might be argued, as indeed it was by some defenders of the South African truth and reconciliation process, that insistence on punishing perpetrators (even of gross human rights violations) can be an obstacle to the achievement of desirable states of affairs (see Tutu, 1999; Chapter 9 below).

Many retributivists, however, also advocate what we might call 'strong retributivism': the authorities in society are morally obliged to punish those who commit crime where there is a reasonable opportunity to do so. This explains, for instance, why retributivists are often highly critical of the truth and reconciliation process in South Africa (cf. Tutu, 1999: Ch. 4). Again, the problem with this position is how to justify punishment in terms that are neither instrumentalist nor question-begging.

Retributivism and penal limits

Although retributivism has its limits and problems, we suggest here that it provides an important basis for thinking and communicating about the issue of penal excess. Further, since a significant amount of the public demand for more punishment is presented in retributivist language, there is perhaps a greater chance of influencing people if one talks this language. We should make it clear, however, that we do not suppose that retributivism can answer questions of precisely how much we should punish. Moreover, the language of retributivism can be used to justify very severe uses of punishment, as well as being a force for penal moderation. The value of retributivism, in this context, lies in the *approach* which it suggests we take to such issues.

From a retributivist perspective, our use of punishment should – as a matter of moral and political principle – be limited in at least three ways. To the extent that it exceeds these limits, punishment is morally wrong and tyrannical, i.e. an unjustifiable interference with our rights and liberties.

(a) Limits to the extent of criminalization: Although retributivism has little specific to say about the content of criminal law, there are reasons for supposing that a retributivist criminal law would be much more restricted in scope than an instrumentalist criminal law. The logic of retributivism is consistent with punishing conduct that is considered immoral, but sits uneasily with the use of punishment to sanction behaviour that is simply a public nuisance or a public danger. In other words, a retributivist would arguably tend to find problematic the vast expansion in the scope of the criminal law, since the nineteenth century, to encompass much conduct that is not really depraved or wicked – even though it may need to be controlled.

(b) Limits to the severity of punishment: For the retributivist, punishment is only justified insofar as it is deserved. This suggests that the amount of punishment imposed upon an offender will be determined by asking questions such as 'what punishment is *merited* for doing that?' We are of course aware that – especially in a 'hot penal climate' – people may think that those who commit certain crimes deserve to be punished far more severely than they currently are; so retributivist logic could result in many offenders receiving very harsh justice. However, there are two other aspects of retributivism that we wish to highlight.

First, it tends to regard the imposition upon people of more severe punishment than they deserve, in order to achieve forward-looking goals such as crime prevention, as wrong. So, for example, if it the prevalent view is that muggers deserve to be sent to prison for up to three years, with the precise sentence depending on how bad the mugging was, it would be quite wrong – for the retributivist – to sentence a mugger whose offence was relatively mild to the full three years on the ground that mugging is on the increase and we need to make an example of someone.

Second, although retributivism is consistent with a highly moralistic stance, whereby individuals are held fully responsible for their bad conduct no matter what their circumstances, its focus on desert does (or at least should) invite us to ask more complicated questions, such as how the existence of limitations on a person's capacity to choose how to behave or to control their conduct affects the question of what they deserve when they behave badly. As Jeffrie Murphy (1973) once argued, retributivism – when combined with a critical theory of the causes and roots of criminal behaviour – can actually lead to the conclusion that punishment lacks moral legitimacy in societies such as ours. We developed a similar argument regarding some offenders in Chapter 4.

(c) Limits to the intrusiveness of penal sanctions: For retributivism, when it comes to determining the severity of punishment, the question is 'what does the offender deserve?' This is quite different from the question 'what is required in order to reform the offender?' Somebody who commits a minor offence may require a long period of penal intervention to be 'reformed' and this may need to include the imposition of various forms of therapy and behaviour modification techniques. Hence, seemingly humane reformist or rehabilitationist approaches to punishment can actually lead to much longer and more intrusive penal sentences than can be justified by reference to retributivism.

To make ourselves clear, we are not suggesting that encouraging people to think about punishment in retributivist rather than instrumentalist terms will result in penal moderation. As we have seen, instrumentalism has its own sense of penal limits, which can be valuable. Also, it would be just as mistaken to equate retributivism with penal moderation as it is to commit the more common error of equating it with a harsh, punitive approach to offending. Our point is simply that retributivism, properly understood, contains within it ideas which can be developed into a forceful case against penal excess. The key messages of retributivism are that those who behave wrongfully ought to be punished – i.e. we ought intentionally to inflict pain or suffering upon them – but only to the extent that they deserve this. Retributivist talk makes intuitive sense to many people and hence may be the sort of talk we need to use to engage people about crime and punishment.

Of course, this pragmatic argument for using retributivist talk does not establish that retributivism is a philosophically sound position. As one of us argued some time ago (Ward, 1986), there is a temptation for radicals or reformers who don't really believe in retributivism to adopt it as a 'noble lie' in an attempt to 'sell' relatively humane penal policies to a sceptical public. We would suggest, however, that those who espouse 'penal moderation', rather than penal abolition, must have some reasons for regarding 'moderate' punishment as legitimate, and that if they articulate those reasons carefully it may well turn out that they are at least weak retributivists. Our own position in this respect will become somewhat clearer in the next chapter.

Conclusion: From penal moderation to alternative images of crime and justice

To conclude, we want to return to the 'popular' critique of the failings of a criminal justice system outlined earlier. The critique is of a system dominated by social and professional elites, and unresponsive to the needs and demands of those whom the system claims to serve: people's whose everyday lives are made miserable by unchecked anti-social conduct. The critique is of a state-run system of criminal law that often fails to provide a meaningful – let alone effective – response to conduct that arguably is intolerable. Such a critique is often combined with calls for the authorities to get much tougher on crime and offenders.

One criminological response to this popular critique is to urge those who make it to be more moderate in their penal talk and to urge policy-makers to be more moderate in their penal policies. What we have suggested above is that this response can be strengthened by making it much more clear why contemporary penal talk and policy are regarded as excessive, and that this requires rigorous thinking about the basis of this judgement. In particular, it is necessary to demonstrate that 'tough justice' is not only bad policy but may also be inconsistent with retributive values which many people hold dear.

However, in common with the Commission on English Prisons Today, we think it is also necessary to suggest alternatives which genuinely address the concerns behind this popular critique. A starting point, however, is to try to recognize the radical elements within the popular critique. The term 'penal populism' tends to be used in criminology to denote something very reactionary – a development to be checked and opposed. But, as Barry Vaughan (2008) suggests (in a review of John Pratt's book *Penal Populism*), populism has more productive features. Its resentment – both of those who through persistent anti-social behaviour destroy the quality of people's lives and of 'an elite cocooned from ordinary experience' who do nothing much about it – may be a promising basis on which to start a serious conversation about how we can develop a *meaningful* response to crime and anti-social conduct.

The popular critique calls for action to be taken – against crime and anti-social conduct – which provides justice and security. Rather than pleading for moderation, a more fruitful 'way in' for criminologists may be to demonstrate that contemporary forms of criminal justice and punishment, no matter how tough they are made, will always be inadequate as routes to justice and security. It might be better to supplement and to some extent replace them with alternative ways of construing crime and justice – such as restorative justice. But here, restorative justice should not be understood or presented simply as a 'more constructive' response to offending conduct. What needs more emphasis is the 'tough' side of restorative justice: its refusal to 'let off' those who disregard the rights of others with 'mere punishment' and its insistence that they be confronted with the human misery they cause and play an active role in making amends for doing so.

Summary

Over the last few decades, criminalization seems to have expanded and punishment seems to have become tougher and less civilized. Criminologists tend to denounce 'penal excess' and call for a return to penal moderation. However, in public discourse, what criminologists denounce as penal excess is often regarded as the correction of a previous tendency to over-tolerance of anti-social conduct and over-leniency in the use of punishment. In the light of this, we suggest that criminologists need to articulate more clearly the grounds on which they *judge* contemporary punishment to be excessive. We explore two very different styles of reasoning in which such a judgement might be based: instrumentalism and retributivism. We also endorse the arguments of those who suggest that calls for penal moderation need to be accompanied by the exploration of alternative ways of construing crime and justice.

STUDY QUESTIONS

- What precisely is meant by the punitive turn and when and why did it start?

- How would you respond to somebody who argued that as a society we are too tolerant and too lenient towards those who behave anti-socially?

- What are the key differences between instrumentalism and retributivism?

- Can either provide a satisfactory justification for punishing offenders?

- How might the idea of restorative justice transform public debate about crime and justice?

FURTHER READING

Early in this chapter, we mentioned a number of books written in the wake of the punitive turn which are all worth reading. We suggest, in particular, David Cayley's *The Expanding Prison* (1998) and David Garland's *The Culture of Control* (2001). John Pratt's *Punishment and Civilization* (2002) is also very interesting. The discussion papers of the Commission on English Prisons Today are a useful way in to contemporary debates – available at http://www.prisoncommission.org.uk/. There are a great many books on the philosophy of punishment. One classic work, which is excellent for bringing out the spirit of utilitarian and retributivist thinking, as well as identifying their limitations, is Sir Walter Moberly's *The Ethics of Punishment* (1968). For a more up-to-date review of the subject, the Stanford Encyclopedia of Philosophy entry on 'Legal Punishment' is useful; it is available at http://plato.stanford.edu/entries/legal-punishment/. Restorative justice as an alternative way of construing crime and justice is the subject of Gerry Johnstone's *Restorative Justice: Ideas, Values, Debates* (2002).

9

State Crime and Criminal Law

Chapter Contents

OVERVIEW

This chapter critically examines the use of criminal proceedings as a response to state crime. Criminal proceedings may take place in international courts or tribunals; in the courts of the state where the crimes took place (often after a change of a regime); or in the courts of another state exercising extra-territorial jurisdiction. The appropriateness of conventional criminal justice notions of individual responsibility, procedural fairness and retributive or deterrent punishment to large scale human rights abuses can be questioned on a number of grounds, which are discussed in the chapter.

KEY TERMS

international criminal justice transitional justice universal jurisdiction war crimes crimes against humanity genocide

When we adopt the kind of long-term historical perspective that we did in previous chapters, the key criminological trend, at least in Europe, is clear. Homicides and, probably, other kinds of serious interpersonal violence have declined massively over the past eight centuries or so (Eisner, 2001). To be more accurate, homicides *unauthorized by those in power* have declined. Violence has not disappeared but has been monopolized by states, whose capacity for slaughter has grown to an awesome extent (Tilly, 1992; Elias, 2000 [1939]). Rummel (1994) calculated a 'mid-range' estimate for the number of people murdered by governments from 1900–87 of over 169 million, not counting the 35 million or so killed in wars.

To people accustomed to thinking of criminal prosecution and punishment as the appropriate response to serious wrong-doing, it seems natural to demand that government-instigated murder and mayhem should be subject to criminal sanctions. In the same way that the 'vengeance and compensation' model for settling disputes gave way to a centralized system of justice, it might seem that the time has come for the 'anarchical society' of states (Bull, 2002) to give way to a cosmopolitan legal order: one in which every individual is a 'citizen of the world' entitled to legal protection of his or her basic rights (see Held, 1995; Habermas, 2000.)

Since the end of the World War II, there have been some significant moves in that direction (Ishay, 2004). Prominent German and Japanese military and political figures were prosecuted and punished by death or prolonged imprisonment. The Universal Declaration of Human Rights was signed in 1948, followed by binding covenants on Civil and Political Rights and Economic Social and Cultural Rights (1966), which have been signed by most of the world's states. Regional Human Rights courts have been established for Europe, Africa and the Americas, though they do not impose criminal punishment. Since the end of the Cold War there has been a growing impetus towards criminal prosecution, with special tribunals established to deal with war crimes, crimes against humanity and genocide in the former Yugoslavia, Rwanda and Sierra Leone, and an International Criminal Court, established under the Rome Statute of 1998, seeing the start of its first prosecutions.

From the point of view of criminology these developments are important in at least one respect. They place it beyond dispute that war crimes, crimes against humanity and genocide are indeed *crimes* (Mullins et al., 2004). In fact they make up most of the world's serious violent crime; and there is no good reason to exclude the perpetrators and victims of these crimes, and the enforcement or non-enforcement of the legal and social norms against them, from the purview of criminology (Green and Ward, 2004). But if we view these developments from the perspective of a criminology even mildly critical of criminal law, many difficult questions immediately come to mind.

- Will it do any good? It is notoriously difficult to demonstrate that domestic criminal punishments have any deterrent or rehabilitative effect, so what reason do we have to suppose that international punishments will be any more effective?
- Can international or transitional courts deliver retributive justice? Domestic criminal law is notoriously loaded against the poor and powerless (Reiman, 2007). Won't international law be the same? One law for the great powers, another for the little people; punishment for the vanquished and propaganda for the victors?
- Is criminal law, with its focus on individual culpability, a suitable mechanism for dealing with crimes by state agencies? We have seen how difficult criminal law finds it to get to grips with crimes by corporations; crimes by governments seem to pose equal or greater difficulties.
- Can criminal courts ensure fair trials for those accused of international crimes while also being fair to their alleged victims and dealing with cases within a reasonable time?
- Will the 'theft' of conflicts by international courts and tribunals deprive societies of the chance to address their own conflicts in ways that might be more constructive? (Christie, 2004)
- Are we seeing the emergence of a global sovereign which will seek to impose a monopoly of organized violence on the whole planet (Hardt and Negri, 2000)? Will 'policing' global crime simply become a new justification for war?

This chapter will address these questions in relation to three types of judicial response to state crime:

- *International criminal law*: the body of international law that defines the crimes for which individuals can be prosecuted in international tribunals: the International Criminal Tribunals for former Yugoslavia (ICTY) and Rwanda (ICTR) and the International Criminal Court (ICC). There have been many proposals to create a category of 'international wrongful acts' for which states rather than individuals would be criminally liable (see Jorgensen, 2000) but all have proved highly contentious and none has been adopted.
- *Universal or extra-territorial jurisdiction*: the trial and punishment of crimes against international law by states other than those in whose territory they occurred (see Reydams, 2003).
- *Transitional justice*: crimes committed under a previous regime within the state where they are tried, where the trial is legitimized by appealing to international or ostensibly universal norms. Transitional justice does not always take either a cosmopolitan or a criminal form: the successor regime may rely on domestic laws which it maintains were valid at the time of the act, or it may resort to non-criminal forms of justice such as truth commissions. Where criminal law is used, it may be administered by national courts or 'hybrid' bodies which derive their authority and personnel from both domestic and international sources (see, for example, Horovitz, 2006; Reiger, 2006).

The main types of crime we are concerned with are the following:

Crimes against peace: i.e. waging or preparing to wage aggressive war contrary to international law.

War crimes: i.e. violations of the laws and customs of war (international humanitarian law).

Crimes against humanity: these include murder, rape, torture, illegal deportation or imprisonment, and persecution (the deprivation of basic human rights on grounds of ethnicity), when they are committed as part of 'a widespread or systematic attack against a civilian population' (a phrase used in many ICTY and ICTR judgements; see Mettraux, 2005: 155).

Genocide: this embraces a range of acts (usually but not necessarily involving killing) committed with the intention 'to destroy, in whole or in part, a national, ethnical, racial or religious group, as such' (Convention on the Prevention and Punishment of the Crime of Genocide, 1948).

All these definitions raise difficult legal issues, some of which we will touch on in discussing the critical questions set out above.

What good will it do?

Advocates of international criminal justice, and international tribunals themselves, often assume that it will deter potential perpetrators of international crimes (e.g. Robertson, 2000; *Rutaganda*, ICTR-96-3-T para. 456). As Drumbl (2005) argues, this assumes that the perpetrators are able to make rational choices of a kind which seem implausible in a context of collective paranoia, fear and hatred. Even if individuals are able to make rational choices, the risk of punishment for most individual perpetrators is likely to be fairly slight (Wippman, 1999). For some perpetrators, 'the value of killing or dying for a cause actually exceeds the value of living peacefully without the prospect of punishment' (Drumbl, 2005: 590). For those less strongly committed, the psychological pressure to obey orders or go along with what others are doing may be far stronger than that stemming from a distant prospect of punishment (Tallgren, 2002). For the people best placed to make rational calculations – military and political leaders – the risk of punishment will be much greater if they lose power, so the rational course may be to remain in power at all costs, or else to try to trade peace for an amnesty (Fichtelberg, 2005: 35).

As in the case of ordinary criminal justice, a more plausible case can be made for international or transitional justice as a symbolic form of censure which may have significant (though not readily measurable) effects in reinforcing social norms. By using criminal law, 'the international community (and its component States) are constructing a normative discourse that expresses deep condemnation of the behaviour and support for its victims' (Sadat, 2002: 52). Risse et al. (1999) present a series of case studies to support their 'spiral model' of human rights norms, by which governments which make a rhetorical commitment to human rights find that actual compliance with human rights norms becomes increasingly important to their domestic legitimacy and international respectability. A government which prosecutes its predecessors for human rights abuses by the due process of law is making a strong public commitment both to human rights and to the rule of law, which helps to embed those norms in that country's political discourse. This is an argument for trying people in their own country, rather than in international courts; but international courts serve as a symbol of the 'international community's' commitment to human rights standards (Ralph, 2007) and international trials are often highly publicized in the countries where the alleged crimes occurred.

There are a number of other reasons why trials, or some kind of transitional process, may be considered important. One is to protect offenders from summary justice or revenge (Borneman, 1997; Minow, 1998: 11–12), or simply to separate former oppressors from their victims. The Norwegian criminologist Christie (2004) remarks that it would have been unthinkable after Norway was liberated to have met Quisling on the streets of Oslo; and Stover (2007: 110–1) found that many ICTY prosecution witnesses saw trials as 'the most expedient means of removing war criminals from their communities'. The main reasons Stover's interviewers gave for testifying, however, were: that trials and convictions would serve as 'a message to others'; that they had a 'moral duty' to 'bear witness' on behalf of friends and neighbours who had been killed; and a desire to confront their former tormentors (ibid.: 112).

Just punishment?

For Hannah Arendt, 'to the question most often asked about the Eichmann trial: What good will it do?', there was 'but one possible answer: It will do justice' (Arendt, 1977: 254). Yet there was, Arendt argued, great difficulty in applying retributive justice to crimes 'committed under a criminal *law* and by a criminal *state*' (ibid.: 262). Although these difficulties did not prevent Arendt from concluding that it was right to hang Eichmann on retributive grounds, Carlos Nino (1996) and Mark Osiel (2001), both writing about transitional justice in Argentina, have developed her arguments in rather different ways.

Nino draws on Arendt's earlier argument that the worst crimes of totalitarian states exemplify a kind of 'radical evil' that humankind 'can neither punish nor forgive' (Arendt 1968 [1951]: 459). Arendt borrowed the term 'radical evil' from Kant, but used it in a completely different sense, to mean an 'absolute evil' that is not explicable 'by the evil motives of greed, covetousness, resentment, lust for power and cowardice' (ibid.). Nino (1996: 141) takes Arendt's point to be that retributive justice breaks down in such cases because the perpetrators, by treating their victims as 'subhuman' have rendered themselves 'unfit for dialogue'. They may justifiably be punished for preventive purposes, but retributive punishment 'may be unsuitable for radical evil' (ibid.: 142). Fichtelberg (2005), on the other hand, uses a similar argument to justify a draconian form of retributivism: the only fitting punishment would be permanent exclusion from all human society – a fate intended to be worse than death.

Some of the worst atrocities, where degradation, suffering and death are inflicted not as a rational means to an end but for their own sake, or to give expression to a view of their victims as unworthy of life, do seem to fit Arendt's characterization of 'radical evil' (see, for example, Green and Ward, 2004: 181–2). It is reasonable to assume that *at the time they commit their crimes,* the perpetrators are not in a fit frame of mind to enter into moral dialogue. It hardly follows that moral dialogue is impossible when they are eventually brought to trial. It would be difficult to enter into meaningful dialogue with a defendant who said 'I am not a murderer because those I killed were not truly human', but we know of no war crimes defendant who has adopted this line. However inadequate and banal their denials or excuses may be, they generally do enter into a form of dialogue which is premised on a recognition of their alleged victims' humanity, and one reason why they are willing to do this is presumably the threat of punishment. Perhaps Arendt's and Nino's point is that *honest* dialogue is impossible because the perpetrators could never acknowledge their true motives. As we have already suggested (Chapter 7), the criminal trial is not, in general, a forum that is conducive to honest dialogue. The case for trials is that even a seriously flawed public dialogue is preferable to silence.

Osiel (2001) develops Arendt's argument in a way that is more consistent with her views on the Eichmann trial. The difficulty in punishing Eichmann was not that he was 'radically evil' in Arendt's sense. On the contrary, his evil was 'banal', prompted by the most ordinary motives of personal advancement (which is close to what Kant meant by 'radical evil'). Eichmann's conviction was problematic on legal grounds because he had acted under orders, which would give him a defence unless the orders were 'manifestly illegal'. In Nazi Germany, no order that could be traced to the will of the Führer could be illegal, because the will of the Führer was the highest law. The Israeli judges who tried Eichmann maintained that genocide offended against 'a feeling of lawfulness that lies deep within every human conscience' (quoted by Arendt, 1977: 293). It is, argue Arendt and Osiel, psychologically naïve to expect 'every human conscience' to be immune to an official morality that makes murder a duty. Eichmann's conscience seemed to be clear (or at least, Arendt did not think the contrary had been proved); and Osiel, while doubting Arendt's assessment of Eichmann, thinks this was true of the Argentine officers he interviewed. Following the ultra-reactionary Catholic ideology endorsed by an element of the junta and its supporters in the Church, they considered torture and murder to be justified by a kind of 'higher law' that sanctioned all necessary measures in the struggle against 'international communism'; and they assumed that Argentine law would be interpreted accordingly.

Even if perpetrators considered their acts morally and legally justified, this is not a convincing objection to prosecution, but arguably makes prosecution all the more necessary. There is little doubt that both the Nazi and the Argentinean leadership understood very well that they would be regarded as criminals if they fell from power (Arendt, 1977: 266–7; Osiel, 2001: 86–7), and in this sense they had fair notice that they were rendering themselves liable to punishment. Argentinean officers knew that they belonged to a 'subcultural community' at odds with secular society, which Osiel (2001: 139) acknowledges might put them on notice of the criminality of their actions in the eyes of civil society. Many Rwandan murderers seem to have believed even after they were captured that they were acting in self-defence to pre-empt the Tutsi plot portrayed in government propaganda (Mamdani, 2001; Drumbl, 2007). Such an attitude might be thought to make it all the more necessary that they are publicly confronted by the reality of what they have done, although the huge numbers involved make mass prosecutions, even through the relatively informal and reconciliation-oriented *gacaca* tribunals, a formidable task.

There are, however, cases where the defendants have a strong case for asserting that their actions were legally justified. A particularly controversial instance is that of the former East German border guards who were tried after reunification for shooting people trying to escape to the west. Most of those shootings were, on the face of it, legally justified under an East German law authorizing the use of deadly force to prevent a felony at the border (Quint, 2000: 501–2). Moreover, both the reunification treaty between East and West Germany and the federal constitution enshrined the principle *nullum crimen sine lege* (no crime without law, i.e. a law in force at the time of the crime). To avoid these restrictions the German courts invoked the formula coined after World War II by the jurist Gustav Radbruch to the effect that 'extreme injustice is no law' (Borneman, 1997: 143; Alexy, 2001). This is a form of what is known in legal theory as natural law or legal idealism: the claim that the validity of a law depends upon its moral merits, not merely on its being made by an authoritative source (Alexy, 2002). Similar arguments were invoked in Argentina to justify prosecutions for acts legalized by the junta (Nino, 1996: 66).

The opposing view in legal theory, that the validity of a law depends on the criteria actually used by officials of the system, not on its moral merits, is known as legal positivism (though it has little if anything to do with positivism as understood in the social sciences). Positivism as such takes no position on questions of transitional justice, except to insist that what to do is a moral and political question which cannot be resolved by appealing to a definition of law (Ward, 2006b). For a positivist, laws which punish actions that were legal at the time are plainly retrospective but it does not necessarily follow that they are morally wrong (Hart, 1958). The objection to retrospective laws is that they diminish human freedom by depriving citizens of the ability to plan their lives in the confidence that, so long as they do not break the law, they will not risk punishment (Woozley, 1968). It is difficult to see how human freedom is enhanced by assuring people that they are free to torture and murder so long as the tyranny they live under permits it.

To punish people for *obeying* the law, or doing what they took to be their duty, may seem paradoxical, but precisely because excessive obedience is the root of the crime, it may be appropriate to use the law to teach a moral lesson about the limits of its own authority. Osiel (2001: 35) argues that expecting people to disobey unjust laws shows a 'complete lack of sympathetic understanding of the institutional and socio-economic constraints within which less fortunate people labor' and a 'remoteness from the human experience of subordination'. The same could be said about many criminal punishments. It is a characteristic of criminal law that it sets very high standards of individual moral responsibility, which in some circumstances are difficult for ordinary mortals to attain (see Chapter 4). People who fall short of those standards in exceptionally difficult circumstances may merit little or no punishment, as the German courts recognized in imposing suspended sentences on almost all the border guards they convicted (Elster, 2004). Sometimes, however, there are good reasons why the law should at least call them to account.

Another objection to retributive justice is that the sheer scale of many international crimes renders the idea of proportionate retribution meaningless. Nils Christie remarks of the execution of Rudolf Höss, the commander of Auschwitz-Birkenau:

> I have never been able to understand it. One life against one and a half million! One broken neck against all those suffocated, starved to death, or plainly killed in that camp. To me, the execution became a sort of denigration of the 1.5 million victims. Their worth became, for each of them, 1.5 millionth of the worth of the Commander. (Christie, 2004: 87)

For opponents of retributivism like Christie, state crime provides a kind of *reductio ad absurdam* of the retributivist case. The retributivist must believe that the infliction of deserved suffering somehow makes the world a better place (Gardner, 2008: xv). But can anyone believe that the world would be a better place if all those complicit to a greater or lesser degree in the horrors of Rwanda, former Yugoslavia or East Timor got what they deserved (if their desert were measured on the same scale by which criminal justice systems punish ordinary offenders)? Christians have a name for a realm where everyone gets their just deserts: Hell. That is not to deny – and even Christie does not deny – that giving selected individuals a punishment that is much less than commensurate with their crimes (by conventional standards) may in some cases serve important symbolic or emotional purposes.

Phelps (2004) argues that the true value of retribution lies not in the harm inflicted on the perpetrator but in the vindication of the worth of the victim that the perpetrator's act has denied. State crimes such as torture symbolize the state's superiority over its internal enemies. In settings such as truth commissions:

> The victims regain dignity and autonomy by correcting for themselves the false message about their worth, which seems far superior to the state's doing so. The victims themselves, with the support and acknowledgment of the state, repudiate the message that the state's violence fostered. (Phelps, 2004: 61)

In this sense, Phelps argues, public storytelling can itself be a form of retribution. That may be an odd use of the word, but it makes the point that even those who are not retributivists in the usual sense can regard criminal (or restorative) justice as serving certain purposes that are intrinsically, rather than instrumentally, valuable. To call people to account, to insist that they answer for their actions or at least listen to those who accuse or condemn them, may be considered an intrinsically worthwhile exercise. So may the public vindication of human rights and repudiation of oppression. Achieving these goals may not require the infliction of suffering beyond the humiliation intrinsic to the process (which according to Hamber (2002: 71) some of the victims attending meetings of the South African Truth and Reconciliation Commission considered 'to be the best "revenge" possible'). It may be wise to focus on these intrinsically worthwhile features of international and transitional justice rather than speculating on their instrumental benefits.

In making this point we must at once concede the two great limitations of such a quest for justice. First, people are called to account either by people who have power over them, or by people with whom they have entered into some form of voluntary relationship. 'Winners do not punish their own' (Elster, 2004: 197), though they may set up some form of inquiry into their own, as in the case of the African National Congress in South Africa (Hayner, 2001: 121). Secondly, the value of recognition for victims of oppression, though real, is limited in the absence of social justice (Stanley, 2005). Stover found that:

> most of the ICTY witnesses ... resisted a definition of justice that focussed solely on the punishment of suspected war criminals, though they viewed retributive justice as a key component in rebuilding their communities. Instead, they said that justice had to include an array of social and economic rights for the persecuted, including the right to live where they wanted and to move freely and without fear; the right to have the bodies of loved ones returned for proper burial; and the right to receive adequate treatment for [their] psychological trauma ... These are all components of social justice. (2007: 119–20)

Individual accountability for collective crimes

International criminal law is concerned solely with the responsibility of individuals, not of corporations or state agencies. Yet the law also defines international crimes in such a way that they can only be committed as part of an organized action of some kind.

Many crimes against humanity involve the same actions as ordinary crimes such as rape and murder, but to be committed 'against humanity' rather than merely against a specific individual, they must form part of a concerted attack on a civilian population. The crime may be committed for purely personal motives but the perpetrator must know he is contributing to a mass crime (*Tadić*, ICTY case IT-94-1-A, appeal judgement, 15 July 1999, para. 250).

Similarly, a war crime must have some connection to a war (which may be either an international or a civil conflict, although many provisions of the

Geneva Conventions apply only to international conflicts). The crime itself need not have been ordered or planned by anyone, but 'the existence of an armed conflict must, at a minimum, have played a substantial part in the perpetrator's ability to commit it, his decision to commit it, the manner in which it was committed or the purpose for which it was committed' (*Kunarać*, ICTY case IT-96-23/1-A, appeal judgement, para. 58). The crime of genocide requires not merely that there be a systematic attack aimed at destroying an ethnic group, but that the individual offender personally intends to destroy the group, 'in whole or in part'.

To convict someone of genocide or a crime against humanity is, therefore, to censure a collective enterprise as well as that individual's part in it. Since, in most cases, only a minority of participants in mass atrocities are likely to be punished, there may seem to be a degree of unfairness in such proceedings in that selected individuals are made to shoulder the guilt for a collective crime.

Drumbl (2007) argues that because of their collective nature, mass atrocities are not 'deviant' in the same way that ordinary crimes are, and that this creates a barrier to dealing with them adequately by the procedures of ordinary criminal law. We think that Drumbl overstates this contrast, partly because his view is shaped by his experiences in Rwanda, where the 1994 genocide, perhaps more than any other mass atrocity, was carried out by ordinary people in their ordinary environment doing what was demanded of them by people in authority (Prunier, 1995; des Forges, 1999). More typically, genocide, torture and war crimes take place in 'enclaves of barbarism' (de Swaan, 2001): segregated spaces (ranging from prisons to entire regions) where the ordinary rules of social behaviour do not apply. The actor enters temporarily into an enclave where all manner of violence is permitted, but returns to a world where ordinary norms of civilized conduct are still observed. Conforming within the enclave he is at the same time a deviant from the perspective of the wider society, and various mechanisms of neutralization, denial or 'doubling' (Lifton, 1986) may be necessary to allow perpetrators to move between these two moral worlds (Alvarez, 2001; Cohen, 2001; Green and Ward, 2009). Moreover, as Drumbl acknowledges, many ordinary cases of street and white-collar crime are also explicable in terms of conformity to the norms of some social enclave, be it an inner-city *barrio* (Bourgois, 1995) or a corporate boardroom.

We must not confuse the *sociological* concept of deviance with the *moral* concept of individual responsibility or culpability. Individuals deserve moral censure because what they do is morally wrong – because they act for bad reasons and contrary to good reasons – not because it is deviant. It is far from obvious that conformity makes wrongful actions any less reprehensible, because conformity of itself is not a good reason for action. 'Everybody else was doing it' is not a valid excuse for murder or cruelty. It does provide a reason for parsimony in punishment, because in a situation where only a minority of wrong-doers can be punished at all, mild punishments are more equitable than severe ones (Braithwaite and Pettit, 1990), and where an attempt is made to put all major perpetrators on trial, as in Rwanda – where the number of accused could eventually reach one million, or a third of the adult population – universal severity would produce appalling consequences (Schabas, 2005). But that is a different point from whether it detracts from the perpetrators' moral guilt.

While the pressures placed on people by authoritarian political cultures cannot justify or excuse participation in atrocities, they do arguably diminish individual perpetrators' responsibility for their actions. Fletcher (2002) argues that states which promote a culture of intolerance erode their citizens' power of critical reflection and hence their ability to make responsible decisions. On this view, the effect of prolonged exposure to a climate of authoritarian hatred is akin to a mental disability (cf. Chapter 4 above), and reactions to the pressures it exerts cannot be judged by objective standards of reasonableness. Arguments on these lines may be plausible in some cases, such as those of children forcibly recruited as soldiers, or even 'voluntarily' recruited as a result of propaganda and poverty (Brett and Specht, 2004). They are less plausible with regard, for example, to the Rwandan intellectuals and clergy who abandoned their critical faculties in the lead-up to genocide (Gourevitch, 1999).

The degree of individual agency involved in many so-called crimes of obedience should not be underestimated. As Fine (2000: 304) argues, 'the very act of following a rule involves a degree of interpretive endeavour and moral evaluation'. But torture and genocide often involve something much more creative than mere interpretation. In Rwanda, for example, 'the care with which thought was given as to ways to inflict maximum physical suffering and to sow maximum psychological terror defies belief' (African Rights, 1994: 335). These were not the actions of people in an 'agentic state' (Milgram, 1974), behaving as if they were passive tools of those in authority. They were, however, almost certainly the actions of people who lacked the capacity, in the midst of a chaotic situation, to stand back and reflect critically on what they were doing. In the aftermath of such actions, it seems essential to create settings that do promote critical moral reflection. As noted in Chapter 7, criminal trials are not ideally suited for this purpose, particularly when they are adversarial and threaten people with heavy punishment. Even when a degree of remorse and self-criticism are elicited, as in the case of Albert Speer at Nuremberg (Sereny, 1995), there will always be room for doubt over how far they are the product of a tactical calculation. The same goes for truth commissions where, as in South Africa, co-operation is the price of amnesty.

Whether or not one considers the culpability of individual perpetrators to be mitigated, it does seem fair to say that direct or indirect responsibility is characteristically shared by many others in their societies: those who took crucial political decisions, stirred up ethnic or political hatreds, or simply did nothing.

Drumbl (2007) sees this as an argument for some form of 'collective responsibility', and sees some of the more controversial doctrines developed by the ICTY, such as the concept of the 'joint criminal enterprise' as flawed attempts to provide for a degree of collective responsibility within an individualistic system of justice. Under this doctrine, anyone who participates in a collective criminal act can be held individually responsible for any action committed as a natural and foreseeable consequence of the joint enterprise. This allows rank-and-file perpetrators to be convicted of murders carried out by other participants in the same attack and commanders to be convicted in circumstances which fall outside the more established doctrine of command responsibility (Schabas, 2003). Command responsibility applies where a subordinate commits a crime and the commander 'knew, or had reason to know that the subordinate was about to commit such acts or had done so and the superior failed to take the necessary and reasonable measures to prevent such acts or to punish the perpetrators thereof' (ICTY Statute Art. 7(3), ICTR Statute Art. 6(3)). According to the ICTY, this does not mean that the commander shares in responsibility for the actions of his subordinates, but rather that he bears individual responsibility for failing to carry out his duty to prevent and punish international crimes (*Halilović*, ICTY Case IT-01-48 T, Judgement, 16 Nov 2005, para. 54).

Partly owing to the rise of the 'joint criminal enterprise', the tribunals have in practice confined the application of command responsibility to a limited number of military commanders (Bonafé, 2007).

The notion of collective responsibility should be distinguished from that of organizational responsibility. From a criminological point of view, state crimes are, by definition, organizational crimes, in the sense that they are either carried out in pursuit of the operative goals of a state agency, or tolerated by the agency because tolerating them serves such goals (Green and Ward, 2004; Mullins et al., 2004). Exactly what are the operative goals of an organization and how they influence individual decisions are complex questions in some cases. 'State crime' in the criminological sense is not a legal or moral category, but denotes a category of actions which can be adequately understood only if organizational dynamics as well as individual motivation are taken into account. The complexity of those dynamics is not easily captured in legal terms:

> It is commonplace in the social sciences ... that members of a modern organization often do not uniformly share its avowed objectives, but rather employ it to their own ends – frequently at odds with official ones. To view their sundry activities – their assorted comings and goings – as reflecting a single, shared purpose, plan, or agreement, is to miss all that is tragic and comic in the social life of organizations. (Osiel, 2005: 1794)

In *Bosnia and Herzegovina* v *Serbia and Montenegro* (2007) the International Court of Justice held that a state could, in principle, be held responsible for the crime of genocide, but that the former Federal Republic of Yugoslavia could not be held responsible for the acts of the Bosnian Serb Army or various paramilitary groups implicated in the genocidal massacre at Srebrenica, because they lacked sufficient 'effective control'. The Court's scrupulous analysis of state responsibility is in marked contrast to the free-wheeling use of notions of 'joint criminal enterprise' in the prosecution of Yugoslavia's former president Milošević, which seemingly aimed to lend credence to a tendentious reading of recent Balkan history, in which all blame was heaped on the political leadership, with Milošević as arch-villain (Cohen, 2002).

A fair trial?

The Milošević trial also illustrates the extreme difficulty of telling a multi-faceted historical story through the medium of an adversarial criminal trial. In the documentary *Milosevic on Trial* (part 1, BBC4, 12 Feb 2007), the prosecutor, Geoffrey Nice QC, muses:

> If you've got 80,000 people being deported, how many witnesses do you need? The judges, it may be, only want or need enough evidence to enable them to make a conclusion that they're happy with. The victims want the story to be told.

The prosecution's insistence on 'telling the story' at interminable length proved a tactical disaster. The tribunal felt obliged to set time limits on the parade of witnesses, and Milošević (representing himself for enhanced theatrical effect: Steinitz, 2005) took advantage of this by dragging out his cross-examination of each witness, as well as doing his best to reveal the identities of those protected by anonymity (Stover, 2007: 48–9). The length of the trial reflected the prosecution's insistence (supported by the Appeals Chamber) on trying all the allegations arising from the Kosovo, Bosnian and Croatian conflicts in a single indictment (Boas, 2007). Apparently the prosecutors were worried that if events in Kosovo were dealt with first, the Security Council, under pressure from the US to bring the ICTY's proceedings to an end (Hagan et al., 2006), would press for a discontinuance of the other cases (Moghalu, 2006: 74). In March 2006, more than four years after the first witness gave evidence, Milošević's death brought the proceedings to a close.

The problem of combining the production of a historical account with the determination of an individual's guilt for specific actions bedevils all major war crimes trials. The Nuremberg Trials at the end of World War II are, in many respects, deservedly remembered as a paragon of fairness to a defeated enemy, but their greatest contribution to shaping post-war perceptions of the Nazi regime was achieved through the showing of a film about concentration camps (not those used in the extermination of the Jews) which 'was classically prejudicial: it hardened attitudes against the defendants because of things that were not shown to be their doing and concerning which many of them were not charged' (Landsman, 2005: 28). 'The didactic purposes' of Adolf Eichmann's trial in Jerusalem in 1961 'required the presentation of great masses of evidence that had nothing to do with Eichmann ... At least 40 of the 121 witnesses had nothing to say about Eichmann' (ibid.: 94). At the trial of Antony Sawoniuk, a retired railway ticket inspector charged in England in 1999 with two murders committed in Belorus in 1942, evidence was admitted implicating him in several murders other than the two specific killings of Jews with which he was charged (*Sawoniuk* [2000] 2 Cr App R 220; see also Hirsh, 2003). It is hard to imagine anything more prejudicial; the jury could hardly be blamed for thinking that whether or not he was proved guilty of the two specific murders, he was certainly a murderer and deserved to be convicted.

The criminal law is often accused of ignoring the political context of individual crimes. The same complaint is made of transitional and international trials (Minow, 1998; Dembour and Haslam, 2004; Stover, 2007), but so is the opposite complaint: that the individual's alleged guilt is *not* decontextualized in the way the liberal model of criminal justice demands. The demand for decontextualization arises, at least in part, from the linkage of punishment to guilt for specific actions. Proceedings which do not aim at punishment have more scope to contextualize individual actions without being seen as unfair, but they generally remain centred on individual responsibility and are often limited by time constraints and political pressures (Hayner, 2002; Stanley, 2008).

Stealing conflicts?

In a famous article, Nils Christie (1977) accused the criminal justice system of 'stealing' conflicts from their participants. Christie saw conflicts as valuable resources. He had relatively minor disputes in mind but the same can be said of the opportunity for perpetrators and survivors of atrocities to confront one another. Painful as such encounters must be, they could provide opportunities for clarifying norms and rebuilding divided societies. When conflicts are characterized by searing hatred, renewed confrontations between the parties may be dangerous. Thousands of French collaborators and Italian fascists, for example, were murdered towards the end of World War II (Drumbl, 2007). But while conflicts between individuals need to be carefully regulated to prevent violent retaliation (Borneman, 1997), this does not necessarily entail that they have to be removed to distant international tribunals, or even formal courts within the state concerned. McEvoy (2007: 413) reports that grass-roots groups in Northern Ireland, that bring together former Loyalist and Republican paramilitaries, see 'transitional justice' as something that 'belongs' to remote legal officials, though it is, in a sense, precisely what they are engaged in. He calls for a 'ceding of ownership' of conflicts to community-based restorative justice projects (ibid.: 429).

In defence of international trials, it can be argued that those who commit crimes against humanity are (to use the phrase traditionally applied to pirates) 'enemies of all mankind':

> ... crimes against humanity assault one particular aspect of human being, namely our character as political animals. We are creatures whose nature compels us to live socially, but who cannot do so without artificial political organization that inevitably poses threats to our well-being, and, at the limit, to our very survival ... Precisely because we cannot live without politics, we exist under the permanent threat that politics will turn cancerous and the indispensable institutions of organized political life will destroy us. That is why all humankind shares an interest in repressing these crimes. (Luban, 2004: 90–1)

Luban's point that states are a particularly dangerous form of organization is undoubtedly valid (Rummel, 1994) but it is less clear that the best way for humankind to control states is by the trial of individual leaders. States, as Wilkins (2001) argues, are made up of individuals but those individuals are bound together by a set of rules, traditions, or principles and it is those, rather than the leaders, that need to be changed in order to change the state's behaviour. Criminal prosecutions are certainly one way of institutionalizing new rules and principles but Wilkins argues that they are most likely to have that effect when their verdicts are 'internalized' by the state and by its citizens. The state, in other words, should 'own' the tribunal and the citizens should accept the moral rightness of its verdicts (ibid.: 95).

Even under the most propitious conditions – where the character of the regime has radically changed, but the new regime is not seen by a large part of the society as being bent on revenge – trials may not be an ideal means to foster normative change. By singling out a small subset of wrong-doers they may too easily let the majority of those who colluded with or benefitted from the criminal regime, as well as active perpetrators, off the hook (Osiel, 2005; Roche, 2005; Drumbl, 2007). Truth commissions appear to be one way in which states can retain their 'ownership' over internal conflicts without all the divisive consequences of trials (Roche, 2005).

One of the sharpest contests over the 'ownership' of a violent conflict has occurred recently in Northern Uganda. The Ugandan state has fought a prolonged war against the Lord's Resistance Army (LRA), which has been backed by neighbouring Sudan. There have been many acts of brutality on both sides, but the LRA has gained particular notoriety for the killing, mutilation and rape of civilians and for the abduction of children who are forced to join its forces and participate in extreme violence (Allen, 2006; Baines, 2007). In 1999 the Government, in response to lobbying from local leaders, granted an amnesty to former rebels who agreed to denounce the rebellion. President Museveni took this step reluctantly and was opposed to any amnesty for senior LRA leaders, while the LRA itself inflicted brutal reprisals on some of those who took advantage of the offer (Allen, 2006: 75–7). In 2004, Uganda referred its own internal conflict to the newly-established International Criminal Court and stated that the amnesty would not stand in the way of prosecuting LRA leaders. Such self-referrals have been encouraged by the ICC Prosecutor as a relatively uncontroversial way of generating cases for the new court (Happold, 2007). The self-referral, however, proved extremely controversial in Uganda, where many saw it as a political manoeuvre by President Museveni and an obstacle to peace. The Acholi Religious Leaders' Peace Movement, whose members have made courageous efforts to end the conflict, argued that the war could not be stopped by branding LRA leaders as criminals.

Many prominent figures in Uganda maintain that the conflict would be better dealt with by a traditional process called *mato oput* (drinking the bitter root), which involves a combination of mediation, compensation, communication with the dead through spirit mediums, and a ceremony of reconciliation (Baines, 2007). It is unclear how widely this view is shared (Allen, 2006). Many of the 'cultural leaders' recognized under a 1995 constitutional reform in Uganda appear to be weak and corrupt, and *mato oput* would not be easy to apply to such extreme and widespread crimes (Baines, 2007). Despite fears of the ICC's stymieing the peace process, talks between the government and LRA resumed and an accord signed in June 2007 provides for a new division of the Ugandan High Court to be set up to try charges arising out of the conflict. It also provides for a truth commission and stipulates that traditional justice should play a central role in accountability. Human Rights Watch (2008: 12), in contrast to the views of its local leader, claims that the Court 'is widely credited with helping to move the parties to the negotiating table and with contributing to a focus on accountability at the peace talks'. At the time of writing, President Museveni is seeking 'to persuade the ICC that [LRA leader Joseph] Kony should face traditional justice at home' (Burgis, 2008). Kony is refusing to sign a peace accord until the warrants are withdrawn, but Silvana Arbia, the Registrar of the ICC, has been quoted as saying that the Court would not withdraw the warrants even if Uganda promised to hold a domestic trial (Ford, 2008).

This does not seem to be so much a case of the ICC 'stealing' a conflict as of the Ugandan government giving it away to gain a political advantage, and then trying to snatch it back again. The argument that international justice represents all humanity's interest in combating 'politics gone cancerous' seems easier to apply to the acts of the government forces than to those of the LRA. It is in the government's IDP (Internally Displaced Persons) camps that the 'indispensable institutions of organized political life', in Luban's phrase, turn against their own citizens in acts of torture and rape (Allen, 2006). The Prosecutor has not investigated crimes on the government side on the grounds that the gravest violations have been committed by the LRA (Happold, 2007). Although the government's crimes are almost certainly less *numerous* than those of the LRA, it is questionable whether they are less *grave*. In prosecuting only the latter, the ICC prosecutor risks being seen as a tool of the Ugandan state. Yet the claims of local elders to 'own' the conflict seem no less debatable and self-interested than those of the ICC. It is possible that the need to persuade the Prosecutor and the Pre-Trial Chamber that it is 'in the interests of justice' to discontinue their investigations will help to ensure that processes within Uganda provide some genuine accountability for perpetrators on both sides.

Empire?

The danger inherent in the idea of 'enemies of all humankind' – as Luban recognizes – is that they may be seen as enemies who are less than human and whom any state with the power and the will is justified in fighting. The apparently benign growth of international criminal law can also be viewed as a manifestation of what Hardt and Negri (2000) call 'Empire': a form of power which resides in a network of transnational institutions, including not only formal institutions but non-governmental organizations (NGOs) and the media. Hardt and Negri see the transformation of international law, from a system 'defined by contracts and treaties, to the definition and constitution of a new sovereign, supranational world power' (2000: 10) as symptomatic of the more general transformation of world power they describe. Drawing on two very different legal theorists of the Weimar era, Hans Kelsen and Carl Schmitt (see Dyzenhaus, 1997), they argue that international law is becoming 'sovereign' in the sense advocated by Kelsen, as a single world legal order from which national legal systems derive their authority; and that the amorphous network of 'imperial' power is also sovereign in Schmitt's sense that it 'decides the state of exception', that is, it has the power to suspend normal legal rules and institute a state of war or emergency. As both Kelsen and Schmitt maintained, sovereignty depends ultimately on force. The universal, consensual norms embodied in international law (such as human rights) serve to legitimize war as 'a police action ... in the service of right and peace' (Hardt and Negri, 2000: 10, 12). In Schmitt's view, the language of 'humanity' was a ruse used by particular groups to demonize their enemies: 'To confiscate the word humanity, to invoke and monopolize such a term probably has certain incalculable effects, such as denying the enemy the quality of being human' (quoted by Luban, 2004: 86, n.2). In consulting experts on Iraq in the build-up to war, Tony Blair seemed only to want confirmation that Saddam Hussein and his regime were 'evil' (Tripp, 2007).

Although Hardt and Negri do not specifically discuss international criminal law, in some respects their analysis fits the development of international justice well. As we have seen, the crucial difference between international crimes and ordinary violent crimes as defined in virtually every legal system is that international crimes can be committed only in connection with some systematic pattern of organized violence. The fundamental reason for this feature of international criminal law appears to be that its aim is not simply to punish individuals, but to set limits to the sovereignty of states. As Broomhall (2003: 42–3) puts it:

> The imposition of individual responsibility [at the Nuremberg trials] would, it was hoped, provide moral vindication and practical support for the maintenance of international order. By marking the point at which sovereignty gives way to the prerogatives of the international community, international criminal law's affirmation of the underlying interests of that community confirmed respect for these interests as a minimum condition of membership in international society.

What the definitions of crimes against humanity, war crimes and genocide all require is the existence of a state of exception: a situation in which the organized use of violence is unbounded by the ordinary rules of domestic law. By defining crimes in this way, international justice asserts its own right to fill the legal vacuum created by states of exception, and to judge the legitimacy of state conduct by its own criteria. International criminal law thereby exercises precisely the two aspects of sovereignty that Hardt and Negri ascribe to 'Empire', asserting a superior authority over national laws and the right to determine the existence and legitimacy of states of exception.

During the Cold War, neither side was willing to accept such limitations of sovereignty, with the result that the lofty aspirations of the Nuremberg trials came to very little. As Kuper argued in his path-breaking study of genocide, the exclusion of mass political killing from the Genocide Convention (1948) indicated the wish of many governments 'to retain an unrestricted freedom to suppress political opposition' (Kuper, 2002 [1981]: 60). The so-called Cold War was in many places a very hot war, with states engaging in ruthless counter-insurgency warfare and repressive terror (Green and Ward, 2004: Ch. 7). After 1989, 'the tacit acceptance of human rights violations on both sides of the Cold War divide became simultaneously more visible and less tolerable' (Hagan, 2003: 29), largely due to the activities of broadcasters and humanitarian NGOs. In Hardt and Negri's view (2000: 36), NGOs like Amnesty and Human Rights Watch 'are in effect (even if this runs counter to the intentions of the participants) some of the most powerful pacific weapons of the new world order'. They certainly played a key role in lobbying for the creation of the ICTY, ICTR and ICC.

The sovereignty-limiting rationale of international criminal justice is also apparent in the fact that both the ICTY and ICTR were established under the UN's powers to deal with threats to 'international peace and security' (Kerr, 2004). The establishment of the tribunals was very far, however, from a determined attempt to establish a new world order. The ICTY was, as Bass (2000: 207) puts it, 'built to flounder', with inadequate resources and, at best, luke-warm support from the US and its allies. The Tribunal had no arrest powers, and the American-led peacekeeping forces who arrived after the 1995 Dayton agreement initially showed no enthusiasm for arresting war criminals. As a Pentagon official explained, 'There's a resistance to mission creep. There's a resistance to policing' (quoted by Bass, 2000: 248).

The drive towards the establishment of a new form of sovereignty came not from the 'international community' but rather from the tribunals' own staff, particularly in the case of the ICTY have emerged as political actors with their own cosmopolitan agenda (Roach, 2006). In a series of detailed empirical studies of the ICTY, John Hagan and his colleagues depict the Prosecutor's Office, in particular, as a determined group of moral entrepreneurs committed to the ideals of liberal legalism: the promotion of the rule of law at an international level (Hagan, 2003; Hagan and Levy, 2004; Hagan et al., 2006; Kutnjak Ivkovic and Hagan, 2006). The Canadian judge Louise Arbour, during her term as the ICTY's Chief Prosecutor, engaged in what Hagan (2003: 112) calls a 'symbolic framing contest', promoting the value of universal jurisdiction as opposed to national sovereignty, and associating the image of the ICTY with 'the armed and uniformed look of criminal law enforcement' in contrast to what Arbour referred to as 'the world of limousines and striped-pants diplomats' (ibid.: 113).

The 'framing contest' between international justice and conventional notions of sovereignty reached its height during the 1999 Kosovo war. Arbour's high-profile investigation of Serbian atrocities, and subsequent indictment of Slobodan Milošević, is seen by Hagan as a publicity coup which advanced the ICTY's role in delivering 'real time' rather than merely 'historical' justice (ibid.: 113–7). Others see it as the ICTY becoming a 'propaganda arm of NATO', especially in view of its failure to investigate or prosecute legally questionable NATO air strikes on Serbia (Mandel, 2001: 96). The truth is probably more complex: prosecutors wanted to show impartiality, and did undertake some limited investigation, but given the tribunal's dependence on NATO and US power, it ultimately 'could not bite the finger that fed it' (Moghalu, 2006: 61).

International criminal law has, however, come into sharp conflict with US power, culminating in the Bush administration's decision in 2002 to 'unsign' the treaty establishing the ICC and to sign the American Servicemen's Protection Act prohibiting co-operation with the Court. As Ralph (2007) argues, both the USA's interests as a superpower and its self-image as an autonomous democratic community encourage it to favour a traditional view of international society as made up of formally equal sovereign states. Moreover, the Bush administration's tactics in the 'war on terror' depended on its ability to place its own, often highly contentious, interpretations on international norms such as the prohibition of torture (Greenberg and Dratel, 2005). The US's 'legal exceptionalism' conflicts with the 'legal liberalism' of the ICC and the ad hoc tribunals, causing the tribunals to come under pressure to wind down their activities (Hagan et al., 2006).

Although Hardt and Negri (2000) differentiate the emerging global Empire from simple US imperialism, they failed to foresee the extent of conflict between the two. Without wishing to idealize the 'new world order' with its transnational networks of lawyers, NGOs, bureaucrats and business people (Slaughter, 2005), it is hard to deny that an 'Empire' based on the rule of law is preferable to one based on raw power, or to an 'anarchical society' in which states are licensed to do what they like subject only to the power of rival states and to their own people's capacity for resistance.

Conclusion

The critiques of international and transitional criminal justice examined in this chapter overlap in many respects with those of domestic criminal law considered in earlier chapters. Thus we can identify:

- A 'libertarian' critique, which in this context is concerned to protect the freedom and formal equality of states as well as individuals. Much as the libertarian critique of domestic criminal law complains that moralistic or paternalistic legislation infringes the sovereignty of the individual over her own body, the enforcement of an international morality infringes the sovereignty of states, particularly small nations, over their territories (Laughland, 2007a). At the same time, the international legal regime violates individual rights through its vague rules and post-hoc judicial legislation (Laughland, 2007b).
- A 'scientific' critique. International criminal law is based on a faith in punishment that has little or no empirical support. Perhaps even more than in domestic criminal justice, it ignores the processes that cause violent actions, in which rationality and free will seem to have little part to play. Even if, at some level, state crimes are a product of rational choice, there is little reason to suppose that rational leaders will be deterred by the prospect of punishment. On the contrary, the prospect of punishment is an incentive to stay in power at all costs.
- A socio-political critique. International and transitional criminal justice, and related non-criminal processes such as truth commissions, individualize state crimes and conceal their deeper structural causes. Even the South African Truth and Reconciliation

Commission, so often seen as an exemplary instance of non-punitive transitional justice, was unable to challenge effectively the structural inequalities that were a legacy of Apartheid (Stanley, 2001). International criminal justice serves to legitimize a new global elite while scapegoating a few political leaders from weak states and rebel movements.

- *A restorative justice critique.* Criminal law 'steals' conflicts from their participants. Reconciliation can be achieved only by face-to-face processes at the grass roots, or 'on the grass' as in the neo-traditional *gacaca* courts in Rwanda. International law and legalistic forms of transitional justice adopt Western-imposed standards of procedural fairness which may stifle their effectiveness (Drumbl, 2007).

Our response to those critiques is to maintain that processes of calling individuals to account, of seeking the truth about grave crimes and publicly recognizing their victims, are intrinsically valuable whether or not they are demonstrably effective in preventing future crimes, and whether or not they involve punishment. It is quite conceivable that the development of international and transitional criminal justice will have significant effects on the incidence of state violence, but as in the case of ordinary criminal law this would most likely occur over a long historical timescale and be very difficult to demonstrate empirically, let alone to predict. Advocates of cosmopolitan criminal law should, we suggest, rely less on speculation about its effects than on the values it embodies: its commitment to rational moral discourse, to the search for truth (elusive though it may be), and to human rights.

The 'libertarian' critique is valid in so far as it alerts us to the potential unfairness of punitive proceedings, but the idea that states are 'unimpeachable' by any laws except their own (Laughland, 2007a) is harder to swallow. The 'scientific' critique rightly questions inflated claims for the effectiveness of international justice, but leaves what we see as its core values unscathed. The socio-political critique points up grave flaws in international and transitional justice and alerts us to its political dangers, but again it does not detract from its central values. The restorative justice critique is one with which we have considerable sympathy, but we agree with Roche (2005) that international criminal law and non-criminal forms of justice need not conflict. On the contrary, the threat of prosecution for unco-operative suspected perpetrators may be necessary to make truth commissions credible, and may help to ensure that amnesties are granted only as part of a genuine search for truth and reconciliation.

In the terms we used in Chapter 8, we could perhaps class our position as combining weak retributivism with a kind of 'strong quasi-retributivism'. We agree with strong retributivists that some process of calling wrong-doers to account is intrinsically and not just instrumentally valuable. We are not, however, persuaded that the infliction of suffering, even on the worst criminals, has such intrinsic value. If it has value only as a means to an end, then it should not be pursued at the expense of peace and reconciliation.

Summary

This chapter has discussed three types of law: international criminal law; criminal law as a form of transitional justice; and the exercise of universal or extra-territorial jurisdiction. The rise of these forms of justice amounts to a significant change in the way the law seeks to regulate state violence, but brings with it a host of problems. We have suggested, however, that holding the perpetrators of state crime to account can be defended as an intrinsically valuable exercise, even if it has no demonstrable effects in repressing state crime.

STUDY QUESTIONS

1. Have we been unduly pessimistic about the benefits of international and transitional criminal justice? If law is not the answer to state crime, what is?

2. To what extent does the search for justice conflict with the search for peace?

3. Are state crime and international justice suitable subjects for criminological research? If not, why not? If so, how do you account for the relative lack of such research?

4. What are the relative merits of trying alleged torturers, war criminals etc. in their own states or before an international tribunal?

5. What are the advantages or disadvantages of truth commissions compared to criminal trials?

6. How has the situation in Northern Uganda developed since we finished this chapter in April 2009? How would you assess the ICC's role in this process?

FURTHER READING

In marked contrast to their neglect in criminology, international criminal law and transitional justice are distinctly 'trendy' subjects in the world of legal scholarship, and the relevant literature is immense. We especially recommend Mark Drumbl's *Atrocity, Punishment and International Law* (2007). Though we disagree with Drumbl on certain points, he asks all the right questions and brings a wealth of research and insight to bear in answering them. The distinguished criminologist John Hagan has written a pioneering sociological study of the ICTY, *Justice in the Balkans* (2003), to which his article with Ron Levy and Gabrielle Ferales (Hagan et al., 2006) provides an important update. The leading work on truth commissions is Priscilla Hayner's *Unspeakable Truths* (2001). Tim Allen's *Trial Justice: The International Criminal Court and the Lord's Resistance Army* (2006) is an excellent case study of the dilemmas associated with international and transitional justice.

Conclusion

The main aim of this book has been to encourage criminologists and students of criminology and other social sciences to think critically about the relationship between their disciplines and the institution and doctrines of criminal law. To understand criminal law as a social institution, we have argued, requires a long-term historical perspective. Such a perspective can also help us to think critically and imaginatively about the gains and losses that have flowed from the emergence of criminal justice in its modern form. Such critical thinking also requires us to engage with difficult issues about choice, responsibility and blame which are central topics of moral and legal philosophy.

Since our aim has to been to provoke discussion rather than to reach any firm conclusions, this conclusion, such as it is, will be brief and inconclusive. We have seen that criminal law fulfils two main functions. First, it provides the legal framework for a set of institutions that are the most visible manifestation in peacetime of the state's monopoly of coercive force within its own territory. These institutions aim to discourage certain forms of conduct and, although their effects are notoriously difficult to measure, they almost certainly do achieve that aim to some extent. The publicity given to the rules of criminal law enables citizens to understand what the forms of conduct are that the law aims to discourage. It also, particularly in liberal democracies, imposes limits on state coercion and renders it somewhat predictable. It thereby protects freedom: an aspect of criminal law particularly emphasized by 'liberal realists' like H.L.A. Hart (2008).

A second function of criminal law, in some but not all cases, is to give formal expression to moral censure on behalf of a community or polity that the courts are in some sense understood to represent. The 'liberal idealists', as we have called them, take this to be *the* central function of the criminal law. There is an overlap between this function and the first, because the conventionally accepted means of expressing censure in criminal justice typically involve coercion, and because such censure may be one way of discouraging the censured conduct. Nevertheless, the two functions are distinct. The process of calling people to account for grave wrong-doing may well be thought to have intrinsic value even if there is no evidence that it makes people behave any better – and particularly in the field of international criminal justice, the latter claim is speculative at best. Conversely, the imposition of coercive sanctions may be useful for regulatory purposes even where no moral fault is attributed to their targets.

In some respects, indeed, yoking these two functions together in one institution seems distinctly unsatisfactory. If responsibility, blame and punishment are manifestations of 'reactive attitudes' of resentment towards harm-doers, are they appropriately expressed through an impersonal, formally rational, bureaucratic system of coercive sanctions? And is that very rationality in delivering what is deemed to be socially necessary coercion undermined when it is used as a channel for collective emotions, or the synthetic surrogates for such emotions purveyed by the media and politicians? The restorative justice critique we identified in Chapter 1 would acknowledge the importance of censure and the reactive attitudes while seeking to divorce them as far as possible from state-monopolized coercion. By contrast, both the 'libertarian' and 'scientific' critiques, in their different ways, evoke a vision of a rational system of coercion divorced as far as possible from messy emotions. All three are challenged by the social justice critique which questions whether either coercion or censure can be justly administered in an unjust society.

In leaving the reader to ponder these critiques, we should not overlook the fact that the real threats to criminal law today come not from the musings of left-leaning criminologists, but from a quite different direction. In a recent article entitled 'Defending Criminal Law', two of Britain's leading criminal justice scholars (Ashworth and Zedner, 2008) identify seven threats to the conventional model of criminal justice: the increasing use of (1) diversion; (2) fixed penalties imposed without a trial; (3) summary trials; (4) hybrid civil–criminal procedures such as ASBOs; (5) strict liability; (6) incentives to plead guilty; and (7) preventive orders such as exclusion from certain occupations or restrictions on travel. While the first of these includes some limited moves towards restorative justice, the unifying theme behind all seven trends is that they increase the freedom of the managerialist state bureaucracy to coerce citizens while dispensing with some or all of the cumbersome, time-consuming and expensive constraints of conventional criminal process. Faced with the 'logic of our times', in the words of the poet C. Day-Lewis (1973), even those 'who lived by honest dreams' may feel called upon to 'defend the bad against the worse'.

Glossary

Actus reus (guilty act). The element of a criminal offence that comprises an act or omission, or the causing of a result, as opposed to a mental state.

Adversarial procedure. A form of criminal or civil procedure in which the parties to litigation are chiefly responsible for the collection and presentation of evidence and for defining the legal issues to be resolved by the court. Cf. **inquisitorial procedure**.

Automatism. A condition in which a person's bodily movements are not under conscious control. Some forms of automatism give rise to a defence of **insanity** (e.g. bodily movements during an epileptic seizure); others to a defence of non-insane automatism. Automatism is a complete defence because it negates the requirement for a **voluntary act**, an essential element of the *actus reus* of almost every offence.

Compensation. Somebody who suffers loss or injury as a result of another person's wrongful act can seek a monetary payment (compensation) – usually from the wrong-doer – to make up for their loss or suffering. The legal remedy of compensation can be sought through private law, although there are also schemes whereby victims of crime can seek compensation and whereby offenders can be ordered to pay compensation to their victims.

Confession. An out-of-court statement by a defendant, not necessarily admitting guilt, but in some way incriminating.

Corporate criminal liability. The area of criminal law which is concerned with liability of corporate bodies (such as companies) for offences committed as a result of their activities.

Crime against humanity. A crime such as murder, enslavement or rape committed as part of a widespread or systematic attack against a civilian population.

Determinism. As applied to human action, determinism is the idea that human actions are necessitated by some preceding event or condition. For some, this raises questions of whether human action is willed and over whether humans have **free will**. The issues are very complex.

Diminished responsibility. A **partial defence** to murder based upon a mental disorder not amounting to **insanity**.

Duress. A defence, generally regarded as an **excuse** rather than a **justification**, which asserts that the defendant was compelled by threats to act as they did.

Excuse. A form of moral exculpation or legal defence that does not deny the doing of a wrongful act but denies that the actor was blameworthy.

Free will. As applied to human action, the doctrine of free will holds that human actions can result from a decision by a human being exercising a capacity to select a course of action from amongst various alternatives. Debates about the nature and existence of free will are very complicated. Compare with **determinism**.

Genocide. A crime aimed at the complete or partial destruction of an ethnic, national or religious group. The legal definition of genocide is not limited to mass killing but includes, for example, the forcible removal of children from the group. It does not include the mass killing of people on the ground of their political beliefs or economic status.

Habitual offenders. One of a variety of terms used to refer to people who regularly break the criminal law, despite being frequently convicted and punished. As explained in this book, the 'habitual offender' is a nineteenth century discovery or even creation. Various theories have been developed in efforts to understand whether habitual offenders differ in other ways from non-habitual offenders and a great deal of penal policy debate since the nineteenth century has been about how to deal with 'habituals'.

Hearsay. Any out-of-court statement which is used in court as evidence of the truth of what was stated. Evidence of, for example, threats or lies uttered outside court is not hearsay because it is used to prove that the words were said, not that what was said was true.

Infanticide. A form of homicide which can be committed only by a woman and only against her own baby aged under one year.

Inquisitorial procedure. A form of criminal or civil procedure in which the selection and presentation of evidence is controlled chiefly by the court rather than by the parties to litigation. Cf. **adversarial procedure**.

Insanity. A mental condition, resulting from some form of 'disease', that exempts the person affected from criminal responsibility for a particular offence. It does not necessarily involve anything that would be medically classified as a mental illness or disorder. For example, a person who caused injury while sleepwalking would have a defence of insanity.

Instrumentalism. Instrumentalists think of the purpose of social policies and practices as being to achieve certain ends – some desirable state of affairs – and judge them primarily in terms of their effectiveness and efficiency in achieving those ends. An instrumentalist conception of criminal justice interventions would discuss them as if their primary, if not only, purpose is to achieve something desirable in the future, such as the prevention of re-offending or crime reduction.

Intention. The exact legal meaning of this term has been subject to varying interpretations, discussed in Chapter 4. In essence, the current position is that anyone who does a **voluntary act** is taken to intend not only the consequences they want to ensue, but also those that they foresee as virtually certain.

International criminal law. A body of international law under which individuals (not states) can be tried and punished before international tribunals such as the International Criminal Court or the International Criminal Tribunal for Rwanda.

Justification. A form of moral exculpation or legal defence that admits doing the act in question but asserts that doing it was right or at least permissible. **Necessity** and self-defence are the main legal forms of justification.

Libertarianism. A libertarian is concerned to protect human freedom, where freedom is understood largely as the ability to live one's life and go about one's business without unnecessary constraint. Libertarianism identifies several major threats to such freedom, but today libertarianism is particularly concerned with the threat represented by an intrusive government through the apparatus of criminal justice.

Loss of control. A partial defence to murder which replaces what was formerly known as provocation, and applies to certain killings committed as a result of fear or justifiable anger.

Manslaughter. The main form of homicide other than **murder**. It can be divided into (a) *involuntary manslaughter,* where death results from an act that was (i) reckless, (ii) grossly negligent, or (iii) unlawful and dangerous; and (b) *voluntary manslaughter,* where the defendant intended to kill or cause serious harm but had a **partial defence** of (i) **diminished responsibility**; (ii) provocation or **loss of control**; or (iii) participation in a suicide pact.

Mens rea (guilty mind). The state of mind that has to be proved in order to convict a person of a criminal offence.

Murder. The *actus reus* of murder is an act that unlawfully causes the death of another person. The *mens rea* is the **intention** of causing either death or serious harm to the victim or to another person.

Necessity. A defence which asserts that the defendant's act was justified as a means to avoid some greater evil.

Negligence. A failure to take such care as one is under a legal duty to take. *Gross negligence*, the **mens rea** of one type of **manslaughter**, is negligence that the jury finds to be so serious that it amounts to a crime.

Partial defence. A defence which, if accepted, results not in acquittal but in conviction for a lesser offence, e.g. **manslaughter** rather than **murder**. **Diminished responsibility**, **infanticide** and **loss of control** are partial defences to murder.

Plea bargaining. A process of negotiation in which the defendant is encouraged to plead guilty in order to receive a lesser sentence than would otherwise be imposed following conviction. There are three main forms in the English system: *charge bargaining* (the defendant pleads guilty to one or more charges in exchange for other or more serious charges being dropped); *fact bargaining* (the defendant pleads guilty on the basis of an agreed account of the 'facts', making the offence appear less serious than it otherwise might); and *sentence bargaining* (the judge indicates the sentence that will be imposed if the defendant pleads guilty – but should not explicitly state how much heavier the sentenced will be if a not guilty plea leads to conviction).

Policing. Although historically the term had different referents, since the nineteenth century 'policing' has largely come to mean the criminal law enforcement activities of the institution of 'the police'. There are important questions about whether police work goes well beyond law enforcement into other types of social control. It is also important to recognize that a lot of law enforcement is done by agencies other than the police, and indeed the boundaries between the police and other agencies are often blurred. In the context of this book, the professionalization of policing which occurred in the nineteenth century was highly significant in expanding the reach of criminal law into society and altering radically the nature of criminal law enforcement.

Punishment. The voluntary infliction of something unpleasant upon a person as a response to some deed by that person which is disapproved of by authority.

Radical evil. In Kant's philosophy, the propensity of human beings in general to follow their inclinations rather than the moral law; it is 'radical' in the sense of being the 'root' of human evil. For Hannah Arendt, truly 'radical evil' could not be explained in this way; it was 'the unpunishable, unforgivable, absolute evil which could no longer be understood or explained by the evil motives of self-interest, greed, covetousness, resentment, lust for power and cowardice' (Arendt, 1968: 459).

Recklessness. The state of mind of someone who is aware of a risk and unreasonably decides to take it.

Responsibility. To be *criminally responsible* is to be liable to criminal prosecution and punishment, either generally or in respect of a particular act. (Thus children under ten are not criminally responsible for anything, while psychotic persons may be exempt from responsibility for specific acts committed as a result of their delusions.) To be *morally responsible* is, roughly speaking, to be a person who can properly be called to account for one's actions in general, or for a particular act.

Restorative justice. A way of responding to crime and other wrong-doing in which (i) the central goal is to get wrong-doers to recognize, acknowledge and endeavour to repair the harm emanating from their misconduct, and (ii) those directly and indirectly affected by a wrongful act participate in discussing and deciding what happened, what harm has resulted and what should be done to repair that harm. Restorative justice has been much mooted and discussed in recent years as an alternative to judicial punishment.

Retributivism. A complex way of thinking about the ethics of punishment, which can be compared and contrasted with **instrumentalism**. Perhaps the best way to explain the idea in a few words is to say that, for the retributivist, the primary question to ask about an act (or proposed act) of punishment is not 'what will it achieve?' but 'is it just?' or 'is it deserved?' A lot of retributivist discourse is about explaining why some people deserve to be punished – but a retributivist inquiry into punishment could conceivably arrive at the conclusion that punishment can only be justified – if at all – under conditions which are lacking in our society.

Self-help theory. A theory of the origins of law and the state developed by scholars in reaction to **social contract theory**. Self-help theory assumes that, prior to the emergence of the state, there was a state of nature which was characterized by high levels of inter-personal and inter-group violence. In self-help theory, this violence was organized around fairly sophisticated principles of **vengeance**. Early states tended to supervise and institutionalize vengeance. Later, states began to take over the administration of 'punishment' and later still they reserved a monopoly of the legitimate use of punitive violence.

Sin. A morally bad act, thought or state of being. Throughout the Judeo-Christian tradition, the question 'what is sin?' has been intensely discussed and debated. Throughout history, the concepts of crime and sin have been intricately connected.

Modern criminal law seeks to define crime in purely secular terms, but understandings of crime arguably continue to be influenced by notions of sin.

Social contract theory. A general theory about the nature of political obligation particularly associated with sixteenth to eighteenth century theorists such as Hobbes, Locke and Rousseau. Since the eighteenth century, social contract theory has had an important influence on thinking about criminal law.

Strict liability. An offence of strict liability is an offence for which it is not necessary to prove (for one or more of the *actus reus* elements) that the defendant had a particular state of mind or *mens rea*. Strict liability in criminal law is highly controversial but is much more prevalent than sometimes recognized.

Summary trial. Trial before a magistrates' court. *Summary offences* can be tried only in this way; *triable-either-way* offences can be tried either summarily or in the Crown Court.

Transitional justice. A process by which officials of a former regime, and sometimes people engaged in resistance against the former regime, are investigated by some form of judicial or quasi-judicial tribunal – not necessarily a criminal court – for actions alleged to have violated domestic or international law in force at the time, or that have been made illegal retrospectively.

Universal jurisdiction. The power claimed by courts in some countries to try serious crimes, particularly those against **international criminal law**, irrespective of where they were committed or the nationality or the accused.

Vengeance/private vengeance. Actions whereby those who suffer by (what they perceive to be) a misdeed retaliate against the perpetrator of the injury and/or that person's kin or companions. Such retaliation can often take a violent form: the perpetrator and their kin/companions might be killed or mutilated, property might be seized or destroyed, and so on.

Voluntary act. An act that is under the conscious control of the person doing it; an essential element of the *actus reus* for nearly all criminal offences.

War crime. A breach of the laws and customs of war that is sufficiently grave to amount to a criminal act. War crimes include **crimes against humanity** and crimes against peace, i.e. the waging of aggressive war contrary to international law. Individual soldiers are held responsible for their own acts and, in some circumstances, those of their subordinates, but not for the possible illegality of the war itself.

A Note on Cases

This book refers to a number of law reports which are cited in the conventional manner used in legal writing. Two types of citation are used for English cases. Recent decisions have a neutral citation number such as [2007] EWCA Crim 3, meaning judgement number 3 of the Court of Appeal (Criminal Division) for 2007. Older cases are cited according to the series of law reports in which they appear. The date comes first, either in round or square brackets. Square brackets mean that a volume is identified by its date: e.g. [1999] 2 All ER 1 means the All England Reports for 1999, volume 2, page 1. The date of the report may be a year or more later than the case was decided. Round brackets denote the year of the decision when it appears in a series of reports that does not have dated volumes. For example *Tolson* (1889) 23 Q.B.D. 168 means the case of the Queen against Tolson, decided in 1889 and reported in volume 23 of the Queen's Bench Division Reports starting at page 168. (The name of the case can also be written *R v Tolson,* but in writing about criminal law where most cases start with '*R v*', this is often omitted.)

Readers working or studying in a university with a law department will probably have access to the legal databases LexisNexis and Westlaw, which are the easiest ways to find cases, statutes, and articles in legal journals. Westlaw is the more useful for English criminal law as it includes the Criminal Appeal Reports (Cr. App. R.) and *Criminal Law Review* (Crim. LR). If you don't have these, a very good free alternative is the BAILII (British and Irish Legal Information Institute) database, www.bailii.org.

Other frequently used abbreviations are:

AC – Appeal Cases
Cox C.C. – Cox's Criminal Cases
JP – Justice of the Peace Reports
QB – Queen's Bench Division reports
UKHC – High Court
UKHL – House of Lords

We also refer to a number of decisions of the International Criminal Tribunals for the Former Yugoslavia (ICTY) and for Rwanda. These are in the database of the Netherlands Institute of Human Rights, http://sim.law.uu.nl/sim/caselaw/tribunalen.nsf.

References

African Rights (1994) *Rwanda: Death Despair and Defiance*. London: African Rights.

Alberini, A. and Austin, D. (1999) 'Strict Liability as a Deterrent in Toxic Waste Management: Empirical Evidence from Accident and Spill Data', *Journal of Environmental Economics and Management*, 38(1): 20–48.

Alexander, F. and Staub, H. (1956) [1931] *The Criminal, the Judge and the Public* (2nd ed.). Glencoe: Free Press.

Alexy, R. (2001) 'A Defence of Radbruch's Formula' in M.D.A. Freeman (ed.) *Lloyd's Introduction to Jurisprudence* (7th ed.). London: Sweet & Maxwell.

Alexy, R. (2002) *The Argument from Injustice: A Reply to Legal Positivism*. Tr. B.L. Paulson and S.L. Paulson. Oxford: Clarendon Press.

Allen, C. (1997) *The Law of Evidence in Victorian England*. Cambridge: Cambridge University Press.

Allen, R. (2007) 'From Punishment to Problem Solving: A New Approach to Children in in Trouble', in Z. Davies and W. McMahon (eds.) *Debating Youth Justice: From Punishment to Problem Solving?* London: Centre for Crime and Justice Studies.

Allen, T. (2006) *Trial Justice: The International Criminal Court and the Lord's Resistance Army*. London: Zed.

Alvarez, A. (2001) *Governments, Citizens and Genocide*. Bloomington: Indiana University Press.

Anderson, T., Schum, D. and Twining, W. (2005) *Analysis of Evidence* (2nd ed.). Cambridge: Cambridge University Press.

Archer, D. and Gartner, R. (1984) *Violence and Crime in Cross-National Perspective, 1900–1974*. New Haven: Yale University Press.

Arendt, H. (1968) [1951] *The Origins of Totalitarianism*. San Deigo: Harcourt Brace Jovanovich.

Arendt, H. (1977) *Eichmann in Jerusalem: A Report on the Banality of Evil*. Harmondsworth: Penguin.

Ashworth, A. (2006) *Principles of Criminal Law* (5th ed.). Oxford: Oxford University Press.

Ashworth, A. and Blake, M. (1996) 'The Presumption of Innocence in English Criminal Law', *Criminal Law Review*, (May): 306–17.

Ashworth, A. and Redmayne, M. (2005) *The Criminal Process* (3rd ed.). Oxford: Oxford University Press.

Ashworth, A. and Zedner, L. (2008) 'Defending the Criminal Law: Reflections on the Changing Character of Crime, Procedure and Sanctions', *Criminal Law and Philosophy*, 2: 21–51.

Athens, L.H. (1989) *The Creation of Dangerous Violent Criminals*. London: Routledge.

Auld, R. (2001) *Criminal Courts Review*. Available online at http://www.criminal-courts-review.org.uk/auldconts.htm (accessed 29 May 2008).

Baines, E.K. (2007) 'The Haunting of Alice: Local Approaches to Justice and Reconciliation in Northern Uganda', *International Journal of Transitional Justice*, 1: 91–114.

Baker, J.H. (2002) *An Introduction to English Legal History* (4th ed.). London: Butterworths LexisNexis.

Ballinger, A. (2005) '"Reasonable" Women Who Kill: Re-interpreting and Re-defining Women's Responses to Domestic Violence in England and Wales 1900–1965' *Outlines: Critical Social Studies*, 7(2): 65–82. Available online at www.outlines.dk/contents.

Bandalli, S. (2000) 'Children, Responsibility and the New Youth Justice', in B. Goldson (ed.) *The New Youth Justice*. Lyme Regis: Russell House.

Barclay, G.C. and Tavares, C. (1999) *Digest 4: Information on the Criminal Justice System in England and Wales*. London: Home Office.

Bartlett, R. (1986) *Trial by Fire and Water: The Medieval Judicial Ordeal*. Oxford: Clarendon Press.

Bass, G.J. (2000) *Stay the Hand of Vengeance: The Politics of War Crimes Tribunals*. Princeton: Princeton University Press.

Beattie, J.M. (1986) *Crime and the Courts in England, 1660–1800*. Oxford: Clarendon Press.

Beckmann, A. (2001) 'Deconstructing Myths: the Social Construction of "Sadomasochism" versus "Subjugated Knowledges" of Practitioners of Consensual "SM"', *Journal of Criminal Justice and Popular Culture*, 8(2): 66–95.

Bellamy, J.G. (1998) *The Criminal Trial in Later Medieval England*. Stroud: Sutton.

Berman, H.J. (1983) *Law and Revolution: The Formation of the Western Legal Tradition*. Cambridge, MA: Harvard University Press.

Beyleveld, D. and Wiles, P. (1975) 'Man and Method in Matza's *Becoming Deviant*', *British Journal of Criminology*, 15: 111–27.

Beyleveld, D. and Wiles, P. (1979) 'How to Retain Your Soul and Be a Political Deviant', in D. Downes and P. Rock (eds.) *Deviant Interpretations: Problems in Criminological Theory*. Oxford: Martin Robertson.

Bianchi, H. (1994) *Justice as Sanctuary: Toward a New System of Crime Control*. Bloomington: Indiana University Press.

Blackstone, W. ([1768] 1979) *Commentaries on the Laws of England: A Facsimile of the First Edition of 1765–1769*. Chicago: University of Chicago Press.

Boas, G. (2007) *The Milošević Trial: Lessons for the Conduct of Complex International Criminal Proceedings*. Cambridge: Cambridge University Press.

Bodkin, A. (1922) Letter to Sir Claude Schuster, National Archive, LCO 2/476.

Bolton, D. (2008) *What is Mental Disorder?* Oxford: Oxford University Press.

Bonafé, B. (2007) 'Finding a Proper Role for Command Responsibility', *Journal of International Criminal Justice*, 5(3): 599–618.

Borneman, J. (1997) *Settling Accounts: Violence, Justice, and Accountability in Postsocialist Europe*. Princeton, N.J.: Princeton University Press.

Bourgois, P. (1995) *In Search of Respect: Selling Crack in El Barrio*. Cambridge: Cambridge University Press.

Braithwaite, J. (1989) *Crime, Shame and Reintegration*. Cambridge: Cambridge University Press.

Braithwaite, J. (2002) *Restorative Justice and Responsive Regulation*. Oxford: Oxford University Press.

Braithwaite, J. (2006) 'Doing Justice Intelligently in Civil Society', *Journal of Social Issues*, 62(2): 393–409.

Braithwaite, J. and Pettit, P. (1990) *Not Just Deserts: A Republican Theory of Criminal Justice*. Oxford: Clarendon.

Brett, R. and Specht, I. (2004) *Young Soldiers: Why they Choose to Fight*. Boulder: Lynne Rienner.

Broomhall, B. (2003) *International Justice and the International Criminal Court: Between Sovereignty and the Rule of Law*. Oxford: Oxford University Press.

Briscoe, S. and Aldersey-Williams, H. (2007) *Panicology*. London: Viking.

Bull, H. (2002) *The Anarchical Society: A Study of Order in World Politics* (3rd ed.). Basingstoke: Palgrave.

Burgis, T. (2008) 'Uganda Disputes ICC Charges Against Kony', *Financial Times*, 11 March.

Burns, R.P. (1999) *A Theory of the Trial*. Princeton: Princeton University Press.

Cairns, D.J.A. (1998) *Advocacy and the Making of the Adversarial Trial, 1800–1865*. Oxford: Clarendon.

Carson, W.G. (1970) 'Some Sociological Aspects of Strict Liability and the Enforcement of Factory Legislation', *Modern Law Review*, 33(4): 396–412.

Cayley, D. (1998) *The Expanding Prison: The Crisis in Crime and Punishment and the Search for Alternatives*. Cleveland, OH: Pilgrim Press.

CEPT (Commission on English Prisons Today) (2007) *The Principles and Limits of the Penal System: Initiating a Conversation*. The Howard League. Available online at http://www.prisoncommission.org.uk/fileadmin/howard_league/user/pdf/Commission/HL_Commission_Seminar_1_Report.pdf.

Christie, N. (1977) 'Conflicts as Property', *British Journal of Criminology*, 17: 1–15.

Christie, N. (1982) *Limits to Pain*. Oxford: Martin Robertson. Available online at http://www.prisonpolicy.org/scans/limits_to_pain/

Christie, N. (2004) *A Suitable Amount of Crime*. London: Routledge.

Christoph, J.B. (1962) *Capital Punishment in British Politics*. London: Allen & Unwin.

Clarkson, C. (1998) 'Corporate Culpability', *Web Journal of Current Legal Issues 2*. Available online at http://webjcli.ncl.ac.uk/1998/issue2/clarkson2.html.

Clarkson, C.M.V. (2005) *Understanding Criminal Law* (4th ed.). London: Sweet & Maxwell.

Cockburn, J.S. (1972) *A History of English Assizes, 1558–1714*. Cambridge: Cambridge University Press.

Cohen, L.J. (2002) *Serpent in the Bosom: The Rise and Fall of Slobodan Milošević* (revised ed.). Boulder: Westview.

Cohen, S. (1979) 'Guilt, Justice and Tolerance: Some Old Concepts for a New Criminology', in D. Downes and P. Rock (eds.) *Deviant Interpretations*. Oxford: Robertson.

Cohen, S. (2001) *States of Denial: Knowing about Atrocities and Suffering*. Cambridge: Polity.

Consedine, J. (1999) *Restorative Justice: Healing the Effects of Crime* (revised ed.). Lyttelton, New Zealand: Ploughshares.

Convention on the Prevention and Punishment of the Crime of Genocide (1948) http://www.preventgenocide.org/law/convention/text.htm

Cornish, W.R. (1968) *The Jury*. London: Allen Lane.

Cornish, W.R. and Clark, G. (1989) *Law and Society in England 1750–1950*. London: Sweet & Maxwell.

Coyle, A. (2007) 'The Limits of the Penal System', in CEPT (2007).

CPS (2006) *Annual Report and Resource Accounts 2005–6* (HC 1203). London: The Stationery Office.

Cressey, D. (1971) 'Role Theory, Differential Association and Compulsive Crimes', in A.M. Rose (ed.) *Human Behavior and Social Processes: An Interactionist Approach*. London: Routledge.

Critchley, T.A. (1967) *A History of the Police in England and Wales*. London: Constable.

Damaska, M. (1986) *The Faces of Justice and State Authority*. New Haven: Yale University Press.

Darbyshire, P. (1997) 'Previous Misconduct and Magistrates' Courts – Some Tales From the Real World', *Criminal Law Review*, (Feb): 105–15.

Davie, N. (2005) *Tracing the Criminal: The Rise of Scientific Criminology in Britain*, 1860–1918. Oxford: Bardwell.

Day-Lewis, C. (1973) 'Where are the War Poets?', in P. Larkin (ed.) *The Oxford Book of Twentieth Century English Verse*. Oxford: Oxford University Press.

D'Cruze, S., Walklate, S. and Pegg, S. (2006) *Murder: Social and Historical Approaches to Understanding Murder and Murderers*. Cullompton: Willan.

de Swaan, A. (2001) 'Dyscivilization, Mass Extermination and the State', *Theory, Culture & Society*, 18(2–3): 265–76.

Dell, S. (1971) *Silent in Court: The Legal Representation of Women who Went to Prison*. London: Bell.

Delmas-Marty, M. and Spencer, J.R. (eds.) (2002) *European Criminal Procedures*. Cambridge: Cambridge University Press.

Dembour, M.-B. and Haslam, E. (2004) 'Silencing Hearings? Victim-witnesses at War Crimes Trials', *European Journal of International Law*, 15(1): 151–77

Dennis, I. (2007) *The Law of Evidence* (3rd ed.). London: Sweet & Maxwell.

des Forges, A. (1999) *Leave None to Tell the Story*. Washington DC: Human Rights Watch.

Devlin, P. (1965) *The Enforcement of Morals*. Oxford: Oxford University Press.

Doran, S., Jackson, J.D. and Seigel, M.L. (1995) 'Rethinking Adversariness in Nonjury Criminal Trials', *American Journal of Criminal Law*, 23: 1–59.

Dorling, D. (2004) 'Prime Suspect: Murder in Britain', in P. Hillyard, C. Pantazis, S. Tombs and P. Gordon (eds.) *Beyond Criminology: Taking Harm Seriously*. London: Pluto.

Downes, D. and Rock, P. (1988) *Understanding Deviance* (2nd ed.). Oxford: Clarendon Press.

Downs, D.A. (1996) *More than Victims: Battered Women, the Syndrome Society and the Law*. Chicago: University of Chicago Press.

Drumbl, M.A. (2005) 'Collective Violence and Individual Punishment: The Criminality of Mass Atrocity', *Northwestern University Law Review*, 99: 539–609.

Drumbl, M.A. (2007) *Atrocity, Punishment and International Law*. Cambridge: Cambridge University Press.

Dubber, M. (2004) 'The Criminal Trial and the Legitimation of Punishment', in A. Duff, L. Farmer, S. Marshall and V. Tadros (eds.) *The Trial on Trial: Volume 1, Truth and Due Process*. Oxford: Hart.

Dubber, M. and Farmer, L. (eds.) (2007) *Modern Histories of Crime and Punishment*. Stanford, CA: Stanford University Press.

Duff, R.A. (1986) *Trials and Punishments*. Cambridge: Cambridge University Press.

Duff, R.A. (1990) *Intention, Agency and Criminal Liability*. Oxford: Blackwell.

Duff, R.A. (2001) *Punishment, Communication and Community*. Oxford: Oxford University Press.

Duff, R.A. (2002a) 'Theories of Criminal Law', *Stanford Encyclopedia of Philosophy*. Available online at http://plato.standford.edu/ ~ seop/entries/criminal-law/.

Duff, R.A. (2002b) 'Punishing the Young', in I. Weijers and A. Duff (eds.) *Punishing Juveniles*. Oxford: Hart.

Duff, R.A. (2007) *Answering for Crime: Responsibility and Liability in Criminal Law*. Oxford: Hart.

Duff, R.A., Farmer, L., Marshall, S. and Tadros, V. (eds.) (2004) *The Trial on Trial: Volume 1, Truth and Due Process*. Oxford: Hart.

Duff, R.A., Farmer, L., Marshall, S. and Tadros, V. (eds.) (2006) *The Trial on Trial: Volume 2, Judgment and Calling to Account*. Oxford: Hart.

Duff, R.A., Farmer, L., Marshall, S. and Tadros, V. (2008) *The Trial on Trial: Volume 3, Towards a Normative Theory of the Criminal Trial*. Oxford: Hart.

Dunbar, I. and Langdon, A. (1998) *Tough Justice: Sentencing and Penal Policies in the 1990s.* Oxford: OUP.

Durkheim, E. (1960) *The Division of Labor in Society.* Tr. George Simpson. Glencoe, Ill: The Free Press.

Dyzenhaus, D. (1997) *Legality and Legitimacy: Carl Schmitt, Hans Kelsen, and Hermann Heller in Weimar.* Oxford: Clarendon Press.

Eisner, M. (2001) 'Modernization, Self-Control and Lethal Violence: The Long-term Dynamics of European Homicide Rates in Theoretical Perspective', *British Journal of Criminology,* 41(4): 618–38.

Elias, N. (2000) [1939] *The Civilizing Process.* Tr. E. Jephcott (revised ed.). Oxford: Blackwell.

Ellis, H. (1890) *The Criminal* (1st ed.). London: Walter Scott.

Elster, J. (2004) *Closing the Books: Transitional Justice in Historical Perspective.* Cambridge: Cambridge University Press.

Erikson, K. (1966) *Wayward Puritans: A Study in the Sociology of Deviance.* New York: Wiley.

Evans, E. (1987) [1906] *The Criminal Prosecution and Capital Punishment of Animals.* London: Faber & Faber.

Farmer, L. (1997) *Criminal Law, Tradition, and Legal Order: Crime and the Genius of Scots Law: 1747 to the Present.* Cambridge: Cambridge University Press.

Farrington, D.P. (2007) 'Childhood Risk Factors and Risk-focussed Prevention', in M. Maguire, R. Morgan and R. Reiner (eds.) *The Oxford Handbook of Criminology* (4th ed.). Oxford: OUP.

Farrington, D.P. and Welsh, B.C. (2007) *Saving Children from a Life of Crime: Early Risk Factors and Effective Interventions.* Oxford: Oxford University Press.

Faulkner, D. (2007) 'The Political Art of Penal Moderation' discussion paper. Available online at http://www.prisoncommission.org.uk/fileadmin/howard_league/user/pdf/Commission/Penal_moderation_-_David_Faulkner.pdf.

Feeley, M. and Simon, J. (1992) 'The New Penology: Notes on the Emerging Strategy of Corrections and its Implications', *Criminology,* 30: 449–74.

Feeley, M. and Simon, J. (1994) 'Actuarial Justice: The Emerging New Criminal Law', in D. Nelken (ed.) *The Futures of Criminology.* London: Sage.

Feinberg, J. (1994) [1970] 'The Expressive Function of Punishment', in A. Duff and D. Garland (eds.) *A Reader on Punishment.* Oxford: Oxford University Press.

Fennell, P., Harding, C., Jörg, N. and Swart, B. (eds.) (1995) *Criminal Justice in Europe: A Comparative Study.* Oxford: Clarendon Press.

Ferri, E. (1913) *The Positive School of Criminology.* Tr. E. Untermann. Chicago: Charles H Kerr and Co.

Fichtelberg, A. (2005) 'Crimes Beyond Justice? Retributivism and War Crimes', *Criminal Justice Ethics,* (Winter/Spring): 31–47.

Fine, R. (2000) 'Crimes Against Humanity', *European Journal of Social Theory,* 3: 293–312.

Fingarette, H. (1988) *Heavy Drinking: The Myth of Alcoholism as a Disease.* Berkeley, CA: University of California Press.

Fischer, J.M. and Ravizza, M. (1998) *Responsibility and Control: A Theory of Moral Responsibility.* Cambridge: Cambridge University Press.

Fisse, B. and Braithwaite, J. (1993) *The Impact of Publicity on Corporate Offenders.* Albany, NY: SUNY Press.

Fletcher, G.P. (1978) *Rethinking Criminal Law.* Boston: Little Brown.

Fletcher, G.P. (1998) *Basic Concepts of Criminal Law.* Oxford: Oxford University Press.

Fletcher, G.P. (2002) 'Liberals and Romantics at War: The Problem of Collective Guilt', *Yale Law Journal*, 111: 1499–573.

Ford, E. (2008) 'Africa News Round-up – 30.5.08'. Available online at http://www.guardian.co.uk/katine/2008/may/30/katineamref.news (accessed 23 June 2008).

Foucault, M. (1977) *Discipline and Punish: The Birth of the Prison*. Harmondsworth: Penguin.

Freud, S. (1961) [1925] 'Moral Responsibility for the Content of Dreams', in *The Standard Edition of the Complete Psychological Works of Sigmund Freud*, Vol. XIX. London: Hogarth Press.

Gardner, A. (1928) 'Science Approaches the Lawbreaker', *Howard Journal*, 2(3): 203–7.

Gardner, J. (2007) *Offences and Defences: Selected Essays in the Philosophy of Criminal Law*. Oxford: Oxford University Press.

Gardner, J. (2008) 'Introduction' to H.L.A. Hart, *Punishment and Responsibility* (2nd ed.). Oxford: Oxford University Press.

Garland, D. (1990) *Punishment and Modern Society*. Oxford: Clarendon.

Garland, D. (2001) *The Culture of Control: Crime and Social Order in Contemporary Society*. Oxford: Oxford University Press.

Garland, D. and Sparks, R. (2000) 'Criminology, Social Theory and the Challenge of Our Times', in D. Garland and R. Sparks (eds.) *Criminology and Social Theory*. Oxford: OUP.

Garland, D. and Young, P. (1983) 'Towards a Social Analysis of Penality', in D. Garland and P. Young (eds.) *The Power to Punish*. London: Heinemann.

Gattrell, V.A.C. (1994) *The Hanging Tree: Execution and the English People 1770–1865*. Oxford: Oxford University Press.

Geis, G. (1960) 'Jeremy Bentham', in H. Mannheim (ed.) *Pioneers in Criminology*. London: Stevens & Sons.

Geis, G. and DiMento, J.F.C. (2002) 'Empirical Evidence and the Legal Doctrine of Corporate Criminal Liability', *American Journal of Criminal Law*, 29: 341–75, reprinted in S. Simpson and C. Gibbs (eds.) *Corporate Crime*. Aldershot: Ashgate, 2007.

Gillingham, J. (2002) 'From *Civilitas* to Civility: Codes of Manners in Medieval and Early Modern England', *Transactions of the Royal Historical Society*, 12: 267–89.

Gobert, J. and Punch, M. (2003) *Rethinking Corporate Crime*. London: Butterworths LexisNexis.

Godfrey, B. and Lawrence, P. (2005) *Crime and Justice 1750–1950*. Cullompton: Willan.

Goldson, B. and Muncie, J. (2006) 'Rethinking Youth Justice: Comparative Analysis, International Human Rights and Research Evidence', *Youth Justice*, 6(2): 91–106.

Goldson, B. and Muncie, J. (2007) 'Youth Justice with Integrity. Beyond Allen's "New Approach"', in Z. Davies and W. McMahon (eds.) *Debating Youth Justice: From Punishment to Problem Solving?* London: Centre for Crime and Justice Studies.

Goodman, L.E. (1987) 'Determinism and Freedom in Spinoza, Maimonides and Aristotle: A Retrospective Study', in F. Schoeman (ed.) *Responsibility, Character and the Emotions*. Cambridge: Cambridge University Press.

Goring, C. (1918) 'The Aetiology of Crime', *Journal of Mental Science*, 64: 129–46.

Gorringe, T. (1996) *God's Just Vengeance*. Cambridge: Cambridge University Press.

Gottfredson, M.R. and Hirschi, T. (1990) *A General Theory of Crime*. Stanford: Stanford University Press.

Gourevitch, P. (1999) *We Wish to Inform You That Tomorrow We Will be Killed With Our Families*. London: Picador.

Green, P. and Ward, T. (2004) *State Crime: Governments, Violence and Corruption*. London: Pluto.

Green, P. and Ward, T. (2009) 'Violence and the State', in R. Coleman, J. Sim, S. Tombs and D. Whyte (eds.) *State, Power, Crime*. London: Sage.

Green, T.A. (1985) *Verdict According to Conscience: Perspectives on the English Trial Jury, 1200–1800*. Chicago: University of Chicago Press.

Greenberg, K.J. and Dratel, J.L. (eds.) (2005) *The Torture Papers: The Road to Abu Ghraib*. Cambridge: Cambridge University Press.

Groot, R.D. (1988) 'The Early-Thirteenth-Century Criminal Jury', in J.S. Cockburn and T.A. Green (eds.) *Twelve Good Men and True*. Princeton: Princeton University Press.

Habermas, J. (2000) 'Bestiality and Humanity: A War on the Border between Law and Morality', in W.J. Buckley (ed.) *Kosovo: Contending Voices on Balkan Interventions*. Michigan: Eerdmans Publishing.

Hagan, J. (2003) *Justice in the Balkans: Prosecuting War Crimes in the Hague Tribunal*. Chicago: University of Chicago Press.

Hagan, J. and Levy, R. (2004) 'Social Skill, the Milosevic Indictment, and the Rebirth of International Criminal Justice', *European Journal of Criminology*, 1(4): 115–75.

Hagan, J., Levy, R. and Ferrales, G. (2006) 'Swaying the Hand of Justice: The Internal and External Dynamics of Regime Change at the International Criminal Tribunal for the Former Yugoslavia', *Law & Social Inquiry*, 31: 585–615.

Haldar, P. (1998) 'Words with the Shaman: On the Sacrifice in Criminal Evidence', in P. Rush, S. McVeigh and A. Young (eds.) *Criminal Legal Doctrine*. Aldershot: Ashgate.

Hallsworth, S. (2000) 'Rethinking the Punitive Turn: Economies of Excess and the Criminology of the Other', *Punishment and Society*, 2(2): 145–60.

Hamber, D. (2002) '"Ere their Story Die": Truth, Justice and Reconciliation in South Africa', *Race & Class*, 44: 61–79.

Hans, V. (2000) *Business on Trial: The Civil Jury and Corporate Responsibility*. New Haven: Yale University Press.

Happold, M. (2007) 'The International Criminal Court and the Lord's Resistance Army', *Melbourne Journal of International Law*, 8(1): 160.

Harding, A. (1966) *A Social History of English Law*. Harmondsworth: Penguin.

Hardt, M. and Negri, A. (2000) *Empire*. Cambridge, MA: Harvard University Press.

Harrington, V. and Mayhew, P. (2001) *Mobile Phone Theft. Home Office Research Study 235*. London: Home Office.

Hart, H.L.A. (1958) 'Positivism and the Separation of Law and Morals', *Harvard Law Review*, 71: 593–629.

Hart, H.L.A. (1963) *Law, Liberty, and Morality*. Oxford: Oxford University Press.

Hart, H.L.A. (2008) [1968] *Punishment and Responsibility* (2nd ed.). Oxford: Oxford University Press.

Hastie, R. and Pennington, N. (1996) 'The O.J. Simpson Stories: Behavioral Scientists' Reflections on The People of the State of California v. Orenthal James Simpson', *University of Colorado Law Review*, 67: 957–76.

Hawles, J. (1785) [1680] *The Englishman's Right: A Dialogue between a Barrister at Law and a Juryman*. Shrewsbury: T. Wood.

Hay, D. (1975) 'Property, Authority and the Criminal Law', in D. Hay, P. Linebaugh, J. Rule, E. Thompson and C. Winslow (1975) *Albion's Fatal Tree*. Harmondsworth: Allen Lane.

Hay, D. (1988) 'The Class Composition of the Palladium of Liberty: Trial Jurors in the Eighteenth Century', in J. Cockburn and T.A. Green (eds.) *Twelve Good Men and True*. Princeton: Princeton University Press.

Hay, D., Linebaugh, P., Rule, J., Thompson, E. and Winslow, C. (1975) *Albion's Fatal Tree: Crime and Society in Eighteenth Century England*. Harmondsworth: Allen Lane.

Hayner, P.B. (2001) *Unspeakable Truths: Confronting State Terror and Atrocity*. London: Routledge.

Heath, J. (1963) *Eighteenth Century Penal Theory*. Oxford: Oxford University Press.

Held, D. (1995) *Democracy and the Global Order*. Cambridge: Polity.

Herring, J. (2008) *Criminal Law: Text, Cases and Materials* (3rd ed.). Oxford: Oxford University Press.

Hildebrandt, M. (2006) 'Trial and "Fair Trial": from Peer to Subject to Citizen', in R.A. Duff, L. Farmer, S. Marshall and V. Tadros (eds.) *The Trial on Trial: Volume 2, Judgment and Calling to Acccount*. Oxford: Hart.

Hillyard, P. and Tombs, S. (2004) 'Beyond Criminology', in P. Hillyard, C. Pantazis, S. Tombs and P. Gordon (eds.) *Beyond Criminology: Taking Harm Seriously*. London: Pluto.

Hillyard, P. and Tombs, S. (2007) 'From "Crime" to Social Harm', *Crime, Law and Social Change*, 48(1–2): 9–25.

Hirsh, D. (2003) *Law against Genocide: Cosmopolitan Trials*. London: Glasshouse Press.

Ho, H.L. (2004) 'The Legitimacy of Mediaeval Proof', *Journal of Law and Religion*, 19: 259–98.

Hobbes, T. (1914) *Leviathan*. London: J M Dent.

Hodgson, J. (2005) *French Criminal Justice*. Oxford: Hart.

Home Office (1997) *No More Excuses: A New Approach to Tackling Youth Crime in England and Wales*. Available online at http://www.homeoffice.gov.uk/documents/jou-no-more-excuses?view=Html#named8 (accessed 30 May 2008).

Horder, J. (1992) *Provocation and Responsibility*. Oxford: Clarendon.

Horder, J. (2001) 'Killing the Passive Abuser: A Theoretical Defence', in S. Shute and A.P. Simester (eds.) *Criminal Law Theory: Doctrines of the General Part*. Oxford: Oxford University Press.

Horder, J. (2007) 'The Criminal Liability of Organisations for Manslaughter and Other Serious Offences', in S. Hetherington (ed.) *Halsbury's Laws of England: Centenary Essays 2007*. London: Butterworths.

Hörnle, T. (2006) 'Democratic Accountability and Lay Participation in Criminal Trials', in A. Duff, L. Farmer, S. Marshall and V. Tadros (eds.) *The Trial on Trial: Volume 2, Judgment and Calling to Acccount*. Oxford: Hart.

Hornsby, J. (1993) 'On What's Intentionally Done', in S. Shute, J. Gardner and J. Horder (eds.) *Action and Value in the Criminal Law*. Oxford: Clarendon.

Horovitz, S. (2006) 'Transitional Justice in Sierra Leone', in N. Roht-Arriaza and J. Mariezcurrena (eds.) *Transitional Justice in the Twenty-first Century*. Cambridge: Cambridge University Press.

House of Commons (2002) *Home Affairs – Second Report*. Available online at http://www.publications.parliament.uk/pa/cm200203/cmselect/cmhaff/83/8310.htm (accessed 9 June 2007).

Hoyle, C. (2007) 'Restorative Justice: the potential for penal reform', in CEPT (2007).

Hudson, B. (1996) *Understanding Justice*. Buckingham: Open University Press.

Hudson, B. (2003) *Justice in the Risk Society*. London: Sage.

Hughes, G. (1958) 'Criminal Omissions', *Yale Law Journal*, 67(4): 590–637.

Hulsman, L. (1981–2) 'Penal Reform in the Netherlands', *Howard Journal*, 20: 150–9 and 21: 35–47.

Human Rights Watch (2008) 'Uganda: New Accord Provides for War Crimes Trials'. Available online at http://www.hrw.org/en/news/2008/02/19/uganda-new-accord-provides-war-crimes-trials (accessed 2 April 2009).

Hyde, W. (1916) 'The Prosecution and Punishment of Animals and Lifeless Things in the Middle Ages and Modern Times', *University of Pennsylvania Law Review*, 64(7): 696–730.

Ishay, M.R. (2004) *The History of Human Rights*. Berkeley: University of California Press.

Jackson, C. (1990) 'Irish Political Opposition to the Passage of Criminal Evidence Reform at Westminster, 1883–98', in J.F. McEldowney and P. O'Higgins (eds.) *The Common Law Tradition: Essays in Irish Legal History*. Dublin: Irish Academic Press.

Jareborg, N. (1995) 'What Kind of Criminal Law do We Want?', in A. Snare (ed.) *Beware of Punishment*. Oslo: Pax Forlag.

Jefferson, M. (2000) 'Corporate Criminal Liability in the 1990s', *Journal of Criminal Law*, 64: 106.

Johnstone, G. (1996) *Medical Concepts and Penal Policy*. London: Cavendish.

Johnstone, G. (2000) 'Penal Policy Making: Elitist, Populist or Participatory?', *Punishment and Society*, 2(2): 161–80.

Johnstone. G. (2002) *Restorative Justice: Ideas, Values, Debates*. Cullompton: Willan.

Johnstone, G. and Van Ness, D. (eds.) (2007) *Handbook of Restorative Justice*. Cullumpton: Willan.

Jones, T.H. (1995) 'Insanity, Automatism and the Burden of Proof on the Accused', *Law Quarterly Review*, 111: 475–516.

Jorgensen, N.H.B. (2000) *The Responsibility of States for International Crimes*. Oxford: Oxford University Press.

Kahan, D.M. and Nussbaum, M.C. (1996) 'Two Conceptions of Emotion in Criminal Law', *Columbia Law Review*, 96: 269–374.

Karstedt, S. (2002) 'Emotions and Criminal Justice', *Theoretical Criminology*, 6(3): 299–317.

Katz, J. (1988) *Seductions of Crime*. New York: Basic Books.

Keating, H. (2007) 'Reckless Children', *Criminal Law Review*, (Jul.): 546–58.

Kelsen, H. (1961) *General Theory of Law and the State*. New York: Russell & Russell.

Kerr, R. (2004) *The International Criminal Tribunal for the Former Yugoslavia: An Exercise in Law, Politics, and Diplomacy*. Oxford: Oxford University Press.

King, P. (1988) '"Illiterate Plebeians, Easily Misled": Jury Composition, Experience and Behavior in Essex, 1735–1815', in J. Cockburn and T.A. Green (eds.) *Twelve Good Men and True*. Princeton: Princeton University Press.

King, P. (2000) *Crime, Justice, and Discretion in England, 1740–1820*. Oxford: Oxford University Press.

Kittrie, N. (1971) *The Right to be Different: Deviance and Enforced Therapy*. Baltimore, MD: Penguin.

Klerman, D. (2003) 'Was the Jury Ever Self-Informing?', *Southern California Law Review*, 77(1): 123–49.

Kuper, L. (2002) 'Genocide: its Political Use in the Twentieth Century' (excerpt from book of same title, 1981), in A.L. Hinton (ed.) *Genocide: An Anthropological Reader*. Oxford: Blackwell.

Kutnjak Ivkovic, S. and Hagan, J. (2006) 'The Politics of Punishment and the Siege of Sarajevo: Toward a Conflict Theory of Perceived International (In)Justice', *Law & Society Review*, 40: 369–409.

Lacey, N. (1988) *State Punishment*. London: Routledge.

Lacey, N. (2001) 'In Search of the Responsible Subject: History, Philosophy and Social Sciences in Criminal Law Theory', *Modern Law Review*, 64: 350–71.

Lacey, N. (2007) 'Legal Constructions of Crime', in M. Maguire, R. Morgan and R. Reiner (eds.) *The Oxford Handbook of Criminology* (4th ed.). Oxford: Oxford University Press.

Lacey, N., Wells, C. and Quick, O. (2003) *Reconstructing Criminal Law: Text and Materials* (3rd ed.). London: LexisNexis Butterworths.

Lamb, S. (1996) *The Trouble with Blame: Victims, Perpetrators and Responsibility*. Cambridge, MA & London: Harvard University Press.

Landsman, S. (1990) 'The Rise of the Contentious Spirit: Adversary Procedure in Eighteenth Century England', *Cornell Law Review*, 75: 497–607.

Landsman, S. (2005) *Crimes of the Holocaust*. Philadelphia: University of Pennsylvania Press.

Langbein, J.H. (1974) *Prosecuting Crime in the Renaissance*. Cambridge: Harvard University Press.

Langbein, J.H. (1977) *Torture and the Law of Proof*. Chicago: University of Chicago Press.

Langbein, J.H. (2003) *The Origins of Adversary Criminal Trial*. Oxford: Oxford University Press.

Laughland, J. (2007a) 'The Crooked Timber of Reality: Sovereignty, Jurisdiction and the Confusions of Human Rights', *The Monist*, 90(1): 3–25.

Laughland, J. (2007b) *Travesty: The Trial of Slobodan Milošević and the Corruption of International Justice*. London: Pluto.

Law Commission (1996) *Evidence in Criminal Proceedings: Hearsay and Related Topics*. Available online at http://www.lawcom.gov.uk/docs/lc245.pdf (accessed 29 May 2008).

Law Commission (2001) *Evidence of Bad Character in Criminal Proceedings*. Available online at http://www.lawcom.gov.uk/docs/lc273(1).pdf (accessed 29 May 2008).

Law Commission (2004) *Partial Defences to Murder*. Available online at http://www.lawcom.gov.uk/docs/lc290(2).pdf (accessed 31 May 2008).

Law Commission (2006) *Murder, Manslaughter and Infanticide*. London: TSO.

Lea, J. and Young, J. (1984) *What is to be Done about Law and Order?* Harmondsworth: Penguin.

Leigh, L.H. (1982) *Strict and Vicarious Liability: A Study in Administrative Criminal Law*. London: Sweet & Maxwell.

Lenman, B. and Parker, G. (1980) 'The State, the Community, and the Criminal Law in Early Modern Europe', in V. Gatrell, B. Lenman and G. Parker (eds.) *Crime and the Law: The Social History of Crime in Western Europe since 1500*. London: Europa.

Lifton, R.J. (1986) *The Nazi Doctors: Medical Killing and the Psychology of Genocide*. London: Macmillan.

Lloyd-Bostock, S. (2000) 'The Effects on Juries of Hearing about the Defendant's Previous Criminal Record: A Simulation Study', *Criminal Law Review*, (Sep.): 734–55.

Lloyd-Bostock, S. (2006) 'The Effects on Lay Magistrates of Hearing That the Defendant is of "Good Character", Being Left to Speculate, or Hearing That He Has a Previous Conviction', *Criminal Law Review*, (Mar.): 189–212.

Loader, I. (2007) 'Why Penal Moderation?' discussion paper. Available online at http://www.prisoncommission.org.uk/fileadmin/howard_league/user/pdf/Commission/Why_penal_moderation.pdf.

Luban, D. (2004) 'A Theory of Crimes Against Humanity', *Yale Journal of International Law,* 29: 85–167.

MacCormick, N. (2005) *Rhetoric and the Rule of Law.* Oxford: Oxford University Press.

Mackay, R.D. (1993) 'The Consequences of Killing Very Young Children', *Criminal Law Review,* (Jan.): 21–30.

Mackay, R.D. (1995) *Mental Condition Defences in the Criminal Law.* Oxford: Oxford University Press.

Mackay, R.D. (2004) 'The Diminished Responsibility Plea in Operation – An Empirical Study', in Law Commission, *Partial Defences to Murder,* Appendix B. London: The Stationery Office.

Mamdani, M. (2001) *When Victims Become Killers: Colonialism, Nativism and Genocide in Rwanda.* Princeton: Princeton University Press.

Mandel, M. (2001) 'Politics and Human Rights in International Criminal Law: Our Case against NATO and the Lessons to be Learned from it', *Fordham International Law Journal,* 25: 95.

Matravers, M. (2004) 'More than Just Illogical: Truth and Jury Nullification', in R.A. Duff, L. Farmer, S. Marshall and V. Tadros (eds.) *The Trial on Trial: Volume 1, Truth and Due Process.* Oxford: Hart.

Matravers, M. (2007) *Responsibility and Justice.* Cambridge: Polity.

Matthews, R., Hancock, L. and Briggs, R. (2004) *Jurors' Perceptions, Understanding, Confidence and Satisfaction in the Jury System: A Study in Six Courts.* Home Office Online Report 05/04. Available online at http://www.homeoffice.gov.uk/rds/pdfs2/rdsolr 0504.pdf (accessed 28 June 2008).

Matza, D. (1964) *Delinquency and Drift.* New York: Wiley.

Matza, D. (1969) *Becoming Deviant.* Englewood Cliffs, NJ: Prentice-Hall.

Maudsley, H. (1874) *Responsibility in Mental Disease.* London: J. & A. Churchill.

McAra, L. and McVie, S. (2007) 'Youth Justice? The Impact of System Contact on Patterns of Desistance from Offending', *European Journal of Criminology,* 4(3): 315–45.

McAuley, F. (2006) 'Canon Law and the End of the Ordeal', *Oxford Journal of Legal Studies,* 26(3): 473–513.

McAuley, F. and McCutcheon, J. (2000) *Criminal Liability.* Dublin: Round Hall Sweet & Maxwell.

McBarnet, D.J. (1981) *Conviction: Law, the State and the Construction of Justice.* London: Macmillan.

McClelland, J.S. (1996) *A History of Western Political Thought.* London: Routledge.

McConville, M., Bridges, L. and Pavlovic, A. (1994) *Standing Accused: The Organization and Practices of Criminal Defence Lawyers in Britain.* Oxford: Clarendon Press.

McConville, M., Sanders, A. and Leng, R. (1991) *The Case for the Prosecution: Police Suspects and the Construction of Criminality.* London: Routledge.

McEvoy, K. (2007) 'Beyond Legalism: Towards a Thicker Understanding of Transitional Justice', *Journal of Law & Society,* 34(4): 410–40.

McEwan, J. (1998) *Evidence and the Adversarial Process: The Modern Law* (2nd ed.). Oxford: Hart.

Merton, R.K. (1957) *Social Theory and Social Structure.* New York: Free Press.

Mettraux, G. (2005) *International Trials and Ad Hoc Tribunals.* Oxford: Oxford University Press.

Milgram, S. (1974) *Obedience to Authority.* New York: Harper & Row.

Miller, W.I. (2006) *Eye for an Eye*. Cambridge: Cambridge University Press.

Minow, M. (1998) *Between Vengeance and Forgiveness*. Boston: Beacon.

Moberly, W. (1968) *The Ethics of Punishment*. London: Faber and Faber.

Moghalu, K.C. (2006) *Global Justice: The Politics of War Crimes Trials*. Westport: Praeger.

Monachesi, E. (1960) 'Cesare Beccaria', in H. Mannheim (ed.) *Pioneers in Criminology*. London: Stevens & Sons.

Moore, M.S. (1985) 'Causation and the Excuses', *California Law Review*, 73: 1091.

Moore, M.S. (1997) *Placing Blame: A Theory of Criminal Law*. Oxford: Clarendon Press.

Moran, L. (1997) 'Eloquence and Imagery: Corporate Criminal Capacity and Law's Anthropomorphic Imagination', in P. Rush, S. McVeigh and A. Young (eds.) *Criminal Legal Doctrine*. Aldershot: Ashgate.

Morgan, R. and Russell, N. (2000) *The Judiciary in Magistrates' Courts*. Available online at http://www.homeoffice.gov.uk/rds/pdfs/occ-judiciary.pdf (accessed 29 May 2008).

Morris, N. (1982) *Madness and the Criminal Law*. Chicago: University of Chicago Press.

Morrison, W. (1995) *Theoretical Criminology: From Modernity to Postmodernism*. London: Cavendish.

Morrissey, B. (2003) *Women Who Kill: Questions of Agency and Subjectivity*. London: Routledge.

Morse, S.J. (1998) 'Excusing and the New Excuse Defenses: A Legal and Conceptual Review', *Crime and Justice*, 23: 329–405.

Moston, S. and Stephenson, G.M. (1993) *The Questioning and Interviewing of Suspects Outside the Police Station*. London: HMSO.

Mullins, C.W., Kauzlarich, D. and Rothe, D. (2004) 'The International Criminal Court and the Control of State Crime: Prospects and Problems', *Critical Criminology*, 12: 285–308.

Munday, R. (1993) 'Jury Trial, Continental Style', *Legal Studies*, 13(2): 204–24.

Munday, R. (2005) 'Round Up the Usual Suspects! Or What we have to Fear from Part 11 of the Criminal Justice Act 2003', *Justice of the Peace*, 169(18): 328–35.

Murphy, J. (1973) 'Marxism and Retribution', *Philosophy and Public Affairs*, 2: 217–43.

Musson, A. (1996) *Public Order and Law Enforcement: The Local Administration of Criminal Justice, 1294–1350*. Woodbridge: Boydell Press.

Newburn, T. (2007) *Criminology*. Cullompton: Willan.

Nicolson, D. (1995) 'Telling Tales: Gender Discrimination, Gender Construction and Battered Women Who Kill', *Feminist Legal Studies*, 3: 185–206.

Nino, C.S. (1996) *Radical Evil on Trial*. New Haven: Yale University Press.

Nobles, R. and Schiff, D. (2000) *Understanding Miscarriages of Justice*. Oxford: Oxford University Press.

Norrie, A. (1991) *Law, Ideology and Punishment: Retrieval and Critique of the Liberal Ideal of Criminal Justice*. Dordrecht: Kluwer.

Norrie, A. (1999) 'After Woollin', *Criminal Law Review*, 552.

Norrie, A. (2000) *Punishment, Responsibility and Justice: A Relational Critique*. Oxford: Oxford University Press.

Norrie, A. (2001) *Crime, Reason and History: A Critical Introduction to Criminal Law* (2nd ed.). Cambridge: Cambridge University Press.

Norrie, A. (2005) *Law and the Beautiful Soul*. London: Glasshouse.

Norton-Taylor, R. (2007) 'Protestors Acquitted of Sabotaging US Bomber', *Guardian*, 23 May.

O'Hagan, A. (2007) 'Short Cuts', *London Review of Books*, 29(24): 20.

Olson, T. (2000) 'Of Enchantment: The Passing of the Ordeals and the Rise of Jury Trial', *Syracuse Law Review*, 50: 109–96.

Ormerod, D. (2005) *Smith & Hogan: Criminal Law* (11th ed.). Oxford: Oxford University Press.

Osiel, M. (2001) *Mass Atrocity, Ordinary Evil, and Hannah Arendt: Criminal Consciousness in Argentina's Dirty War*. New Haven: Yale University Press.

Osiel, M. (2005) 'The Banality of Good: Aligning Incentives Against Mass Atrocity', *Columbia Law Review,* 105(1): 751–862.

Pavlich, G. (2005) *Governing Paradoxes of Restorative Justice*. London: Glasshouse Press.

Pearce, F. (1976) *Crimes of the Powerful*. London: Pluto.

Pemberton, S. (2007) 'Social Harm Futures: Exploring the Potential of the Social Harm Approach', *Crime, Law and Social Change,* 48(1–2): 27–41.

Perkin, H. (1969) *The Origins of Modern English Society 1780–1880*. London: Routledge & Kegan Paul.

Phelps, T.G. (2004) *Shattered Voices: Language, Violence and the Work of Truth Commissions*. Philadelphia: University of Pennsylvania Press.

Philips, D. (1983) '"A Just Measure of Crime, Authority, Hunters and Blue Locusts": The "Revisionist" Social History of Crime and the Law in Britain, 1780–1850', in S. Cohen and A. Scull (eds.) *Social Control and the State: Historical and Comparative Essays*. Oxford: Martin Robertson.

Poland, H.B. (1901) 'Changes in Criminal Law and Procedure since 1800', in Council of Legal Education, *A Century of Law Reform: Twelve Lectures on the Changes in the Law of England During the Nineteenth Century*. London: Macmillan (reprinted in 1972 by Rothman Reprints Inc., South Hackensack, NJ).

Polk, K. (1995) *When Men Kill: Scenarios of Masculine Violence*. Cambridge: Cambridge University Press.

Pollock, F. and Maitland, F. (1898) *The History of English Law before the Time of Edward I, Volume 2* (2nd ed.). Cambridge: Cambridge University Press.

Povey, D. (ed.) (2004) *Crime in England and Wales 2002/3, Supp. Vol. 1: Homicide and Gun Crime*. London: Home Office.

Povey, D. (ed.) (2008) *Homicide, Firearms Offences and Intimate Violence 2006/7* (2nd ed.). London: Home Office.

Pratt, J. (2000) 'Emotive and Ostentatious Punishment: Its Decline and Resurgence in Modern Society', *Punishment and Society,* 2(4): 417–39.

Pratt, J. (2002) *Punishment and Civilization: Penal Tolerance and Intolerance in Modern Society*. London: Sage.

Pratt, J. (2007) *Penal Populism*. Oxford: Routledge.

Pratt, T. (2009) *Addicted to Incarceration*. Thousand Oaks, CA: Sage.

Prunier, G. (1995) *The Rwanda Crisis 1959–94: History of a Genocide*. London: Hurst & Co.

Quick, O. and Wells, C. (2006) 'Getting Tough with Defences', *Criminal Law Review,* (Jun.): 514–25.

Quint, P.E. (2000) 'The Border Guard Trials and the East German Past – Seven Arguments', *American Journal of Comparative Law,* 48: 541–72.

Radzinowicz, L. (1966) *Ideology and Crime*. London: Heinemann.

Radzinowicz, L. and Hood, R. (1990) *The Emergence of Penal Policy in Victorian and Edwardian England*. Oxford: Oxford University Press.

Ralph, J. (2007) *Defending the Society of States: Why America Opposes the International Criminal Court and its Vision of World Society*. Oxford: Oxford University Press.

Redmayne, M. (2002a) 'The Law Commission's Character Convictions', *International Journal of Evidence & Proof,* 6: 71–93.

Redmayne, M. (2002b) 'The Relevance of Bad Character', *Cambridge Law Journal*, 61(3): 684–714.

Redmayne, M. (2005) 'Theorising Jury Reform', in R.A. Duff, L. Farmer, S. Marshall and V. Tadros (eds.) *The Trial on Trial: Volume 2, Judgment and Calling to Account*. Oxford: Hart.

Reiger, C. (2006) 'Hybrid Attempts at Accountability for Serious Crimes in Timor Leste', in N. Roht-Arriza and J. Mariezcurrena (eds.) *Transitional Justice in the Twenty-first Century*. Cambridge: Cambridge University Press.

Reiman, J. (2006) 'Book Review: Beyond Criminology', *British Journal of Criminology*, 46(2): 362–4.

Reiman, J. (2007) *The Rich Get Richer and the Poor Get Prison: Ideology, Class and Criminal Justice* (8th ed.). New York: Wiley.

Reiner, R. (2000) *The Politics of the Police* (3rd ed.). Oxford: Oxford University Press.

Reith, C. (1948) *A Short History of the British Police*. Oxford: Oxford University Press.

Reydams, L. (2003) *Universal Jurisdiction*. Oxford: Oxford University Press.

Richardson, G. (1987) 'Strict Liability for Regulatory Crime: the Empirical Evidence', *Criminal Law Review*, 295–306.

Risse, T., Ropp, S.C. and Sikkink, K. (1999) *The Power of Human Rights: International Norms and Domestic Change*. Cambridge: Cambridge University Press.

Roach, S.C. (2006) *Politicizing the International Criminal Court: The Convergence of Politics, Ethics and Law*. Lanham, MD: Rowman & Littlefield.

Roberts, P. and Zuckerman, A. (2004) *Criminal Evidence*. Oxford: Oxford University Press.

Roberts, S. (1979) *Order and Dispute: An Introduction to Legal Anthropology*. Harmondsworth: Penguin.

Robertson, G. (2000) *Crimes Against Humanity: The Struggle for Global Justice*. London: Penguin.

Roche, D. (2005) 'Truth Commission Amnesties and the International Criminal Court', *British Journal of Criminology*, 45: 565–81.

Rock, P. (1993) *The Social World of an English Crown Court*. Oxford: Clarendon Press.

Rothman, D. (1971) *The Discovery of the Asylum*. Boston, MA: Little Brown & Co.

Rotman, E. (1990) *Beyond Punishment*. New York: Greenwood Press.

Rowan-Robinson, J., Watchman, P. and Barker, C. (1990) *Crime and Regulation: A Study of the Enforcement of Regulatory Codes*. Edinburgh: T. & T. Clark.

Rumgay, J. (1998) *Crime, Punishment and the Drinking Offender*. Basingstoke: Macmillan.

Rummel, R.J. (1994) *Death by Government*. New Brunswick, N.J.: Transaction.

Sadat, N.L. (2002) *The International Criminal Court and the Transformation of International Law*. Ardsley, NY: Transnational Publishers.

Saleilles, R. (1911) *The Individualization of Punishment*. Tr. R.S. Jastrow. London: William Heinemann.

Sanders, A. (2002) 'Core Values, the Magistracy, and the Auld Report', *Journal of Law and Society*, 29(2): 324–41.

Sanders, A. and Young, R. (2006) *Criminal Justice* (3rd ed.). Oxford: Oxford University Press.

Schabas, W.A. (2003) 'National Courts Finally Begin to Prosecute Genocide, the "Crime of Crimes"', *Journal of International Criminal Justice*, 1: 39–63.

Schabas, W.A. (2005) 'Genocide Trials and *Gacaca* Courts', *Journal of International Criminal Justice*, 3: 879–95.

Schauer, F. (2006) 'On the Supposed Jury-Dependence of Evidence Law', *University of Pennsylvania Law Review*, 155: 165–202.

Scott, E.S. and Grisso, T. (2005) 'Developmental Incompetence, Due Process, and Juvenile Justice Policy', *North Carolina Law Review*, 83: 793–845.

Sentencing Guidelines Council (2004) *Reduction in Sentence for a Guilty Plea.* Available online at http://www.sentencing-guidelines.gov.uk/docs/Guilty_plea_guideline.pdf (accessed 29 May 2008).

Sereny, G. (1995) *Albert Speer: His Battle with Truth.* New York: Random House.

Shapiro, B.J. (1991) *Beyond Reasonable Doubt and Probable Cause: Historical Perspectives on the Anglo-American Law of Evidence.* Berkeley: University of California Press.

Shapiro, B.J. (2000) *A Culture of Fact: England, 1550–1720.* Ithaca: Cornell University Press.

Shapiro, B.J. (2001) 'Classical Rhetoric and the English Law of Evidence', in L. Hutson and V. Kahn (eds.) *Rhetoric and Law in Early Modern Europe.* New Haven, CT: Yale University Press.

Sharpe, J.A. (1984) *Crime in Early Modern England 1550–1750.* London: Longman.

Sharpe, J.A. (1990) *Judicial Punishment in England.* London: Faber & Faber.

Simpson, A.W.B. (1984) *Cannibalism and the Common Law.* Chicago: Unviersity of Chicago Press.

Simpson, A.W.B. (1988) *Invitation to Law.* Oxford: Blackwell.

Slapper, G. and Tombs, S. (1999) *Corporate Crime.* Harlow: Longman.

Slaughter, A.M. (2005) *A New World Order.* Princeton: Princeton University Press.

Slobogin, C. (2005) 'The Civilization of Criminal Law', *Vanderbilt Law Review*, 58: 121–67.

Smart, J.J.C. (1961) 'Free-will, Praise and Blame', *Mind*, 70: 19–34.

Smith, B.P. (2007a) 'English Criminal Justice Administration, 1650–1850: A Historiographic Essay', *Law and History Review*, 25(3): 593–634.

Smith, B.P. (2007b) 'The Myth of Private Prosecution in England, 1750–1850', in M. Dubber and L. Farmer (eds.) *Modern Histories of Crime and Punishment.* Stanford, CA: Stanford University Press.

Smith, D.J. (2007) 'Crime and the Life Course', in M. Maguire, R. Morgan and R. Reiner (eds.) *The Oxford Handbook of Criminology* (4th ed.). Oxford: Oxford University Press.

Smith, K.J.M. (1998) *Lawyers, Legislators and Theorists: Developments in English Criminal Jurisprudence 1800–1957.* Oxford: Clarendon Press.

Smith, M.H. (1922) *The Psychology of the Criminal.* London: Methuen.

Spencer, J.R. (2002) 'Evidence', in M. Delmas-Marty and J.R. Spencer (eds.) *European Criminal Procedures.* Cambridge: Cambridge University Press.

Spierenburg, P. (2008) *A History of Murder.* Cambridge: Polity.

Spinoza, B. (1997) [1677] *Ethics.* Tr. RHM Elwes, MTSU Philosophy WebWorks hypertext ed. Available online at http://www.mtsu.edu/~rbombard/RB/Spinoza/ethica4.html (accessed 12 May 2008).

Stanley, E. (2001) 'Evaluating the Truth and Reconciliation Commission', *Journal of Modern African Studies*, 39(3): 525–45.

Stanley, E. (2005) 'Truth Commissions and the Recognition of State Crime', *British Journal of Criminology*, 45(4): 582–97.

Stanley, E. (2008) 'The Political Economy of Transitional Justice in Timor-Leste', in C. McEvoy and L. McGregor (eds.) *Transitional Justice from Below: Grassroots Activism and the Struggle for Change.* Oxford: Hart.

Stein, A. (2005) *Foundations of Evidence Law.* Oxford: Oxford University Press.

Steinitz, M. (2005) 'The Milosevic Trial – Live!', *Journal of International Criminal Justice*, 3: 103–23.

Stenton, D. (1964) *English Justice Between the Norman Conquest and the Great Charter, 1066–1215*. London: Allen & Unwin.

Stephen, J.F. (1860) 'On Trial by Jury, and the Evidence of Experts', *Papers Read before the Juridical Society*, 2: 236.

Stephen, J.F. (1863) *A General View of the Criminal Law of England*. London: Macmillan.

Stephen, J.F. (1883, undated facsimile reprint) *History of the Criminal Law of England*. New York: Burt Franklin.

Storch, R. (1976) 'The Policeman as Domestic Missionary: Urban Discipline and Popular Culture in Northern England, 1850–1880', *Journal of Social History*, 9(4): 481–509.

Stover, E. (2007) *The Witnesses: War Crimes and the Promise of Justice in the Hague*. Philadelphia: University of Pennsylvania Press.

Strawson, P.F. (2001) [1962] 'Freedom and Resentment', in L.P. Pojman (ed.) *Classics of Philosophy, vol. III: The Twentieth Century*. Oxford: Oxford University Press.

Stuart, B. (1996) 'Circle Sentencing: Turning Swords into Ploughshares', in B. Galaway, and J. Hudson (eds.) *Restorative Justice: International Perspectives*. Monsey, NY: Criminal Justice Press.

Stuntz, W. (1997) 'The Uneasy Relationship Between Criminal Procedure and Criminal Justice', *Yale Law Journal*, 107(1): 1–76.

Sullivan, G. (1996) 'The Attribution of Culpability to Limited Companies', *Cambridge Law Journal*, 55(3): 515–46.

Sumner, C. (1990) 'Rethinking Deviance', in C. Sumner (ed.) *Censure, Politics and Criminal Justice*. Buckingham: Open University Press.

Sutherland, J. (1998) 'Introduction' to W. Collins, *The Woman in White*. Oxford: Oxford University Press.

Sykes, G. and Matza, D. (1957) 'Techniques of Neutralization: A Theory of Delinquency', *American Sociological Review*, 22: 664–70.

Tadros, V. (2005) *Criminal Responsibility*. Oxford: Oxford University Press.

Tallgren, I. (2002) 'The Sensibility and Sense of International Criminal Law', *European Journal of International Law*, 13: 561–95.

Tapper, C. (2004) 'Criminal Justice Act 2003, Part III: Evidence of Bad Character', *Criminal Law Review*, (Jul.): 553–55.

Taylor, L. (1976) 'The Significance and Interpretation of Replies to Motivational Questions: the Case of Sex Offenders', in P. Wiles (ed.) *The Sociology of Crime and Delinquency in Britain*. London: Martin Robertson.

Thayer, J.B. (1898) *A Preliminary Treatise on Evidence at Common Law*. Boston: Little, Brown.

Thompson, E.P. (1977) *Whigs and Hunters*. Harmondsworth: Penguin.

Thompson, E.P. (1991) *Customs in Common*. London: Merlin Press.

Tifft, L. and Sullivan, D. (1980) *The Struggle to be Human: Crime, Criminology and Anarchism*. Orkney: Cienfuegos Press.

Tilly, C. (1992) *Coercion, Capital and European States 990–1990*. Oxford: Blackwell.

Tombs, S. (1995) 'Law, Resistance and Reform: "Regulating" Safety Crimes in the UK', *Social & Legal Studies*, 4(3): 343–66.

Tombs, S. (2007) 'Violence, Safety Crimes and Criminology', *British Journal of Criminology*, 47(4): 531–50.

Tombs, S. and Hillyard, P. (2004) 'Towards a Political Economy of Harm: States, Corporations and the Production of Inequality', in P. Hillyard, C. Pantazis, S. Tombs and P. Gordon (eds.) *Beyond Criminology: Taking Harm Seriously*. London: Pluto.

Tripp, C. (2007) 'Militias, Vigilantes, Death Squads', *London Review of Books*, 25 Jan.

Turner, B. (1995) *Medical Power and Social Knowledge* (2nd ed.). London: Sage.

Turner, J.W.C. (1962) *Kenny's Outlines of Criminal Law* (18th ed.). Cambridge: Cambridge University Press.

Tutu, D. (1999) *No Future Without Forgiveness*. London: Rider.

UN (1985) *United Nations Standard Minimum Rules for the Administration of Juvenile Justice*. Available online at http://www.unhchr.ch/html/menu3/b/h_comp48.htm (accessed 30 May 2008).

Uniacke, S. (2007) 'Emotional Excuses', *Law and Philosophy*, 26: 95–117.

Vaughan, B. (2008) 'Review of John Pratt: *Penal Populism*', *Theoretical Criminology*, 12(1):121–3.

Vogler, R.K. (2005) *A World View of Criminal Procedure*. Aldershot, Ashgate.

von Hirsch, A. (1976) *Doing Justice*. New York, Hill & Wang.

Wallace, R.J. (1994) *Responsibility and the Moral Sentiments*. Cambridge, MA: Harvard University Press.

Ward, C. (2006) 'Punishing Children in the Criminal Law', *Notre Dame Law Review*, 82: 429–79.

Ward, T. (1986) 'Symbols and Noble Lies: Abolitionism, Just Deserts and Crimes of the Powerful', in H. Bianchi and R. van Swaaningen (eds.) *Abolitionism: Towards a Non-Repressive Approach to Crime*. Amsterdam: Free University Press.

Ward, T. (1999) 'The Sad Subject of Infanticide: Law, Medicine and Child Murder, 1860–1938', *Social & Legal Studies*, 8: 163–80.

Ward, T. (2002) 'Legislating for Human Nature: Legal Responses to Infanticide, 1860–1938', in M. Johnson (ed.) *Infanticide: Historical Essays on Child Murder and Concealment, 1550–2000*. Aldershot: Ashgate.

Ward, T. (2004) 'Experts, Juries and Witch-hunts: From Fitzjames Stephen to Angela Cannings', *Journal of Law and Society*, 31(3): 369–86.

Ward, T. (2006a) 'English Law's Epistemology of Expert Testimony', *Journal of Law and Society*, 33(4): 572–95.

Ward, T. (2006b) 'Two Schools of Legal Idealism: A Positivist Introduction', *Ratio Juris*, 19(2): 127–40.

Waterman, A. and Dempster, T. (2006) 'Bad Character: Feeling our Way One Year On', *Criminal Law Review*, (Jul.): 614–28.

Watson, G. (2004) *Agency and Answerability*. Oxford: Clarendon.

Weijers, I. (2002) 'The Moral Dialogue: a Pedagogical Perspective on Juvenile Justice', in I. Weijers and A. Duff (eds.) *Punishing Juveniles*. Oxford: Hart.

Weitekamp, E. (2003) 'The History of Restorative Justice', in G. Johnstone (ed.) *A Restorative Justice Reader*. Cullompton: Willan.

Wells, C. (2001) *Corporations and Criminal Responsibility* (2nd ed.). Oxford: Oxford University Press.

Wheelwright, J. (2002) '"Nothing In Between": Modern Cases of Infanticide', in M. Jackson (ed.) *Infanticide: Historical Perspectives on Child Murder and Concealment, 1550–2000*. Aldershot: Ashgate.

Whitelock, D. (1952) *The Beginnings of English Society*. Harmondsworth: Penguin.

Whitman, J.Q. (1995) 'At the Origins of Law and the State: Supervision of Violence, Mutilation of Bodies, or Setting of Prices?', *Chicago Kent Law Review,* 71(1): 41–84.

Whitman, J. (2003) *Harsh Justice.* Oxford: Oxford University Press.

WHO (2002) *World Report on Violence and Health.* Geneva: World Health Organization.

Wiener, M. (1990) *Reconstructing the Criminal: Culture, Law and Policy in England, 1830–1914.* Cambridge: Cambridge University Press.

Wiener, M. (2006) *Men of Blood: Violence, Manliness and Criminal Justice in Victorian England.* Cambridge: Cambridge University Press.

Wilkins, B.T. (2001) 'Whose Trials? Whose Reconciliation?', in A. Jokic (ed.) *War Crimes and Collective Wrongdoing: A Reader.* Oxford: Blackwell.

Williams, G. (1953) *Criminal Law: the General Part.* London: Stevens & Sons.

Wilson, W. (2002) *Central Issues in Criminal Theory.* Oxford: Hart.

Wilson, W., Ebrahim, I., Fenwick, P. and Marks, R. (2005) 'Violence, Sleepwalking and the Criminal Law Part 2: The Legal Aspects', *Criminal Law Review,* (Aug.): 613–23.

Wippman, D. (1999) 'Atrocities, Deterrence, and the Limits of International Justice', *Fordham International Law Journal,* 23: 473–88.

Wootton, B. (1963) *Crime and the Criminal Law: Reflections of a Magistrate and Social Scientist.* London: Stevens.

Woozley, A.D. (1968) 'What is Wrong with Retrospective Law?', *Philosophical Quarterly,* 18(70): 40–53.

Wright, R., Brookman, F. and Bennett, T. (2006) 'The Foreground Dynamics of Street Robbery in Britain', *British Journal of Criminology,* 46: 1–15.

Yazzie, R. and Zion, J. (1996) 'Navajo Restorative Justice: The Law of Equality and Justice', in B. Galaway and J. Hudson (eds.) *Restorative Justice: International Perspectives.* Monsey, NY: Criminal Justice Press.

Young, J. (1999) *The Exclusive Society.* London: Sage.

Young, P.J. (1987) 'Punishment, Money and Legal Order', PhD thesis, University of Edinburgh.

Zander, M. and Henderson, P. (1993) *Crown Court Study.* London: HMSO.

Zedner, L. (2002) 'Dangers of Dystopias in Penal Theory', *Oxford Journal of Legal Studies,* 22(2): 341–66.

Zedner, L. (2005) *Criminal Justice.* Oxford: Oxford University Press.

Zehr, H. (1990) *Changing Lenses: A New Focus for Crime and Justice.* Scottdale, PA: Herald Press.

Zimring, F.E. (2000) 'Penal Proportionality and the Young Offender: Notes on Immaturity, Capacity and Diminished Responsibility', in T. Grisso and R.G. Schwartz (eds.) *Youth on Trial: A Developmental Perspective on Juvenile Justice.* Chicago: University of Chicago Press.

Index of Cases

Index